A Thousand and One
Egyptian Nights

11/2009

To Elizabeth
with love
from,
Sarah

A Thousand and One Egyptian Nights

An American Christian's Life Among Muslims

Jennifer Drago

Herald Press

Scottdale, Pennsylvania
Waterloo, Ontario

Library of Congress Cataloging-in-Publication Data

Drago, Jennifer, 1962-
A thousand and one Egyptian nights : an American Christian's
life among Muslims / Jennifer Drago.
    p. cm.
    ISBN-13: 978-0-8361-9365-7 (pbk. : alk. paper)
    1. Drago, Jennifer, 1962- 2. Missionaries—United States—
Biography. 3. Missionaries—Egypt—Biography. 4. Missions to
Muslims—Egypt. I. Title.
    BV2626.D73A3 2007
    266.0092—dc22
    [B]
                            2006036467

Bible text is from the *Contemporary English Version*, Copyright
© American Bible Society, 1995. Used by permission.

All photos provided by the author.

16 15 14 13 12 11 10 09 08 07   10 9 8 7 6 5 4 3 2 1

To order or request information, please call 1-800-245-7894,
or visit www.heraldpress.com.

To Brad, Nicholas, Rebecca, and Emily,
who have cooked, cleaned, and schooled themselves
so this book could be written.
You now have your wife and mother back.
Or was it really the computer you wanted?

To my mom and dad, wonderful parents and people.

Contents

Key Characters

All Egyptian characters have an assumed name to protect their true identity. Characters that are repeated throughout the book are listed below:

Suad—our housekeeper, Muslim, uneducated village woman
Fatma—our neighbor, Muslim, lower class
Sister Heba—director of St. Anthony's Language School
Sister Maria—director of girl's orphanage
Um Abdullah—middle-class Muslim woman, housewife
Doctor Negwa—middle-class Muslim woman, gynecologist
Sandy—Christian, middle-class, TV news reporter
Um Amzat—fruit and vegetable seller, Christian, uneducated village woman
Suzanne—visually impaired, middle-class Christian
James and Linda Herr-Wheeler—Mennonite Central Committee (MCC) country representatives

The author is referred to in the book as Jennifer, Gigi, and Um Nicholas.

1

God Will Make a Way

"Suad, what would you do if you could not work, if you were really sick for several months. How would you get money to live?"

"I would pray to God to heal me, to make me strong. I would pray for people to come and help me. I know God wants me to be stronger and healthier. He would send people to help me."

"So you would pray to God to heal you? And God would tell other people like me that I should help you with food or money, right?"

"*La'a.* [No.] Not should help me but you wish to help me because you know that God loves you and you want to help other people."

Familiar Christian theology? Probably, but Suad is Muslim, a very devout and prayerful one. Today we are sitting at my kitchen table, drinking tea; she has finished the cleaning, for she is also our housekeeper. Housekeeper? Maid? Those words sound so elite and so unlike me. But a year after our arrival, when we moved out of our cramped apartment to more comfortable arrangements, the pressure was on to hire a housekeeper.

"Surely, you will get someone to help you keep the apartment clean," said our landlord, who wanted us to maintain a decent place. "Everything gets dusty very quickly here. The desert is just right out there, you know." We did have a great view of the desert mountains from our window. My Egyptian friends had also brought up the need for us to have a housekeeper: "It's not just to help you out in the house. You give some work to a poor woman who needs money. It's like a social obligation."

Suad was recommended to me by my friend, Doctor Negwa, who pays Suad to clean her house and medical clinic. "Suad is a

Suad and the author prepare dinner.

poor and simple woman," she said. "You will need to explain everything to her and show her how to work your appliances, like a vacuum cleaner." No problem there—we don't have one. "This is important: You or the children must be in the house with her all the time. She cannot be alone with your husband. It's not that we don't trust Mr. Brad. No. But she is a village woman and is not used to being with men who are not related to her."

With these instructions, we were ready to begin working together.

I look at Suad sitting next to me in her peasant attire: long pants and long-sleeve shirt covered by a long, loose, flowery blue dress, plus another plain brown dress over that one, making three layers on this miserably hot, August day. Additionally she wears three layers of scarves. One wraps around her head and ties on top, the second goes over that one and ties in front, covering her neck, and the third is draped over those two and flows down her back. It's a combination of both peasant and Muslim dress. "How does she manage in this heat?" I wondered, as I readjusted the fan to give her some air.

Whack! Slap!

The sounds coming through my neighbor's open windows bring me back to the present. Suad and I stop talking, and listen to the crying and shouting from the apartment next door.

"He's beating her again. What can I do?" I ask.

"Nothing. Don't you go over there. *Malkeesh dowa.* It's not your business."

"What about the guards downstairs? I should go get them to do something."

Suad shakes her head. "They are here to protect you and your family. It's not their business either what he does to her. You can't do anything for her; God will make a way."

"In your religion, is it okay for a husband to beat his wife?" I already know the official answer was no, but it's always interesting to toss out the same question and see how many different answers I can get.

"Yes, if she is not a 'clean' person, he can beat her." I am not exactly sure what that means and make a mental note to ask the women that I will sit with tonight as we watch our daughters play basketball.

I let Suad's comments sink in as I think about Fatma and the pain she is experiencing, not just from the beating but from her everyday life. Her apartment is an empty shell with a few pieces of broken furniture. The refrigerator door only stays closed with a piece of rope tied around it; but it doesn't matter, as there is no food in it. The kitchen is filthy with years of grease stains caked on the stove and walls. The sink is stacked with pots, dirty dishes, and spoons; the cold water won't turn off, so a small stream flows constantly. The walls, once white, are now dingy, smeared with handprints, stains, and smudges. The apartment so symbolizes her life—neglected, worn out, and abused.

Fatma has no real options. Her husband refuses to let her work but will not give her any money. She cannot live on her own, as that is not acceptable in this traditional, conservative society. Her parents live nearby in a small apartment and are not willing to let her and the boys live with them. I can understand that they might be poor and uneducated, but haven't they heard her screams? Haven't they seen her beaten, battered body? Surely putting up with cramped living quarters is better than sending a daughter back to her abusive husband.

"What would you do if your daughter was married to a man that beat her?" I ask.

Suad straightens up in her chair and shakes her head so that her orange earrings swing about. She has a piece of apple in her hand and begins to shake it emphatically at me. "Simple. I would take her from him. One of my sisters left her husband because he beat her. She left her daughter with him and went back to our father's house. My father married her again to another man, and now she has two children with him. He's a good man."

Slam! Thud!

I hear Mumtez, the seven-year-old, cry out. Then Medo, three, wails and hollers. They are two precious boys who get their share of beatings from both father and mother. It is now their turn. We sit in silence for a few minutes; Suad sips her tea and I peel the apple since she doesn't like to eat the skin. We hear the *muezzin*, the man who gives the call to prayer, over the loudspeaker, reminding all faithful Muslims that it is time for the noon prayer.

"How about you, Suad? What would you do in her place?"

"I would leave him. Divorce him. Go to my mother's house. For my sake and the sake of my children. On the life of our God, I would divorce him."

Fatma herself was in my kitchen just this morning as I washed the dishes, showing me the bruises on her legs, the rips in her blouse, the flapping sole of her shoe that is falling apart. This has happened so often I now callously refer to it as her "body-tour"—bruises, belt marks, scratches, cuts, carpet burns, scrapes.

"Why don't you leave him? Divorce him?"

"I can't. You know our saying, a house without a man is like a body without a soul." She lowered her voice and told me that they had no money; they hadn't eaten anything the day before. I glimpsed at the boys devouring the bananas on my table and knew her words were true.

All of this is so frustrating for me. "Am I responsible for her?" I had asked myself as I wrapped up some food in a plastic bag for them.

"Suad, *busi* [look]. The husband never gives Fatma any money for food or for the kids, but he buys nice clothes for himself. He smokes foreign cigarettes, not the cheap local kind. She's always telling me that she has nothing, and it's true. But what am I supposed to do? I don't want to give her money, although I have sometimes."

"Madam Gigi, don't give her money. You are a foreigner and she knows you have money. She will always ask you for more," Suad advises me. "God will help her."

"I know that, Suad, but it's hard for me to do nothing. I told Fatma last week that she can clean the building stairs, from top to bottom, all four flights and I would pay her for this. You know what she told me? She can't do this, because her husband's brother owns the apartment downstairs and he might see her. I told her to tell her brother-in-law that she has no food and no money from his brother and that's why she's cleaning the stairs."

Suad takes a bite of melon, shakes her head, and gives a little laugh that says "you silly, naïve girl."

"If the brother sees her working, he will tell her husband and he will beat her." Snap! She whips her fingers about and snaps them loud and hard, the common hand signal when Egyptians refer to beatings. Fatma is wise too in that respect; she ignores the foolish advice that I somehow feel compelled to give her; my advice is hardly suitable for her culture.

I sip some more of my tea, almost cold by now, for I have spent more time talking than drinking. I gesture with my hand to Fatma's window and continue the conversation. "Suad, who is responsible for her?"

"Her husband is. And if not him, then her parents."

"You know, Fatma married when she was eighteen years old, and her parents did not approve of her husband."

"That's a stupid girl who gets married without her parents' permission. Now they are not responsible for her. And her husband, seeing that they aren't responsible for her, can now do anything he wants to her because her parents will not do anything. God forbid, he is not afraid of them. I tell you, she is stupid. Why did she marry him?"

"She says she loves him."

Suad just smiles and shakes her head in disbelief. A silly reason to marry. In Suad's world, marriage isn't about two individuals falling in love, but about two families—the bride's and the groom's —joining together. The purpose of marriage isn't love, happiness, and fulfillment but the procreation of children, the continuation of life. Love might, or might not, be a result of this.

"When your husband was alive, did he beat you?"

"No."

"Why? Because he was a good man?"

"Because he was old and sick."

Suad pushes herself away from the table and picks up a towel from among the folded clothes on the table. She walks to a corner of our small kitchen, lays down the towel, now transformed into a prayer rug, and faces east, the direction of Mecca, the direction all Muslims face when praying. I gather the teacups, plates, and fruit peelings on a tray and take them into the kitchen. Suad is on her knees, her face to the floor, undisturbed by my presence.

I pick up Fatma's cold, untouched tea from earlier this morning and toss it down the drain. She had complained of intense stomach pains, so I had made her some *yansoon* (anise seed tea). We were laughing and joking as she watched me make three-bean salad, something she had never seen before. "You can't put sugar with oil and vinegar. You can't put sugar with beans," she insisted.

These were rare moments, and I enjoy the times that distract us from her daily troubles. But her husband's voice had called out to her, so she gathered the boys and quickly left. She would come over later that night and tell me how he held her by her ponytail, dragged her down the stairs, and kicked her in her already pained stomach.

The prayer is finished, the towel refolded, and Suad, taking pride in her appearance, stands in front of the mirror, making sure her scarves are just right and her hair covered. She gathers her belongings, pauses by the door, and asks, "Is your house beautiful now?"

"Our house looks so much better now! We can breathe the clean air, not all the dust. Thank you. I am very happy." I discretely slip her money, as she is always embarrassed to take it. While the pay is important, for Suad it isn't enough. She needs to hear that her work is appreciated and valued.

This morning she had brought with her a huge bag full of

round, flat Egyptian bread, freshly bought from the bakery down the street. The bread is for her neighbor, who uses it to make and sell *fuul* (bean sandwiches) to support herself and her nine children. Suad easily lifts the bag, which probably weighs thirty pounds, balances it perfectly on her head, and gracefully descends three flights of stairs without ever using her hand to steady her load.

"I'll see you next Tuesday, *in sha'allah* [God willing]," I call out.

"In sha'allah," she responds.

૮

As an American, a Christian, and a social worker, I had a very hard time "doing nothing" about my neighbor Fatma's situation. It's not my nature or my culture to passively listen to someone's screams. I had been taught to pick up the phone and call the police, who would put the husband in handcuffs and jail. I could flip through the Yellow Pages and find social services to help her. I knew churches that could put together a bag of food for her family. I had been raised with a can-do approach—form a committee, start a new program, do some fundraising, publicize the issue. "We've got a problem in our community, folks, and what are we going to do about it?"

But that's at home, in the United States. I was not in familiar territory anymore. This was a foreign country with a whole different set of cultural and traditional values, a whole different set of rules and norms. I could not play by my own rules, and I hardly understood the new ones there in Egypt.

The books I had read about women in the Middle East uncovered remarkable diversity in their lives. There were veiled women, highly educated women, oppressed women, divorced women, liberated women, circumcised women, stay-at-home women, financially successful women, and working-just-trying-to-survive women. I knew all these types of women through books and stories, but it was a whole different story when the woman was in the flesh, in my living room, and in my life. Fatma wasn't a beggar I could just walk past on the street, feel sorry for, and forget about a few hours later. She wasn't a character in a story whose life I could forget about after I finished the last chapter. Fatma was personal, living only five feet away from me; I couldn't just close the door and pretend she didn't exist.

Spousal abuse, child abuse, arranged and unarranged marriages. Violence as discipline. Helpless kids. A passive and depressed mother. A cruel husband. Parents who can't or won't help. My head was dizzy with the thought of it all. What had I gotten myself into? For a short while, I had even entertained the fantasy of opening a house for abused women, battling the forces of fathers and husbands and other powers-that-be. I had read of many well-intentioned but naïve foreigners who set up programs to cure the social ills of a particular country—programs that often went against the culture. I suspected they did more harm than good, and so I quickly abandoned my fantasy.

This was Egypt's problem, and I knew there were enough progressive, intelligent women to tackle these issues. Several times I had read in the English language newspaper, *Al Ahram*, about women's organizations, some working under the guidance of the president's wife, Suzanne Mubarak, and some working independently. These women in the newspaper could cite all sorts of laws in flowery, legalistic language, but for women like Fatma, such laws were useless. Many of these laws appeared wonderful and impressive on paper, but people were often ignorant of them. They weren't enforced, or more often, cultural traditions were stronger than the laws.

One of our reasons for moving out of our first "cubby-hole" apartment was so we could have neighbors. I wanted someone to sit and drink tea with and borrow eggs from. I wanted the kids to have built-in playmates. I knew many wonderful Egyptians with whom I wanted to be neighbors. Instead I got to experience a different side of Egyptian life, a life that, judging from the looks of surprise and horror I sometimes received when I shared these stories, was also unfamiliar to many Egyptians.

As for my part, I would do what I could: listen, bandage wounds, share food, provide a doctor. Sometimes that is all you can do and it is enough. Fatma was not what I was expecting for a neighbor, but she was what I got. And I could only surmise that God saw some reason for us to be together.

2

Once Upon a Time

"Come in the living room. Daddy wants to tell you a story."

My husband, Brad, settled on the sofa in Comer, Georgia, with our daughter Emily curled up beside him. Our son, Nick, was stretched out in his favorite chair while daughter Rebecca took to a pillow on the floor. Brad had always enthralled them with his story-telling skills, so they sat with eager, wide eyes.

"Once upon a time, there was a family that decided to go to the Middle East to live. They would have adventures and challenges, buy fruits and vegetables from the market, maybe carry them home on their heads, go to school and learn a new language, meet other kids and play their games, eat food with their fingers, ride camels at the pyramids. So Mom and I are thinking that we want our family to do something like that after the summer."

Ten-year-old Rebecca, who had intuited the ending before her dad revealed it, had tears streaming down her cheeks and wailed, "What about my friends? Do I have to leave them?"

Nick, twelve years old, always calm and steady, replied enthusiastically, "Cool! I can learn Arabic!"

Eight-year-old Emily didn't know which emotion to exhibit. She'd look at Rebecca and moan with her, then look at Nick's face and share his joy.

It was January 2003, and the kids would have six months to adjust to the idea of leaving that summer. In preparation for our three-year stay, we read lots of books on Arab culture, attended a local mosque, saw some tourist videos on Egypt, got some tapes from the library on Arabic language, and prepared ourselves as best as we could for the adventures and challenges ahead. It wasn't long before Rebecca rallied and said she'd go "if Maria can visit me." Saying her best friend could visit was an easy promise to give.

I had always had the desire to live abroad with my family. I wanted not just to expose but to immerse my kids in another culture, another language, another way of life. I wanted them to experience how others dress, eat, worship God, solve their problems, and have fun. I wanted them to know that they belong to a whole world of people with needs and wants just as valid as their own. I wanted my children to know what it's like to be a volunteer service worker in a foreign country so that this could be an option in their future. I did not want us to go to Egypt to live as Americans but to live the Egyptian life and experience as much as we could.

Lofty goals, to be sure. But those were just the ones for our kids; Brad and I had our own desires. This was a year and a half after the September 11, 2001, terrorist attacks, and there were ongoing wars in Afghanistan and Iraq. The United States was making mass arrests, imprisonments, and deportations of Arabs and Muslims to Guantanamo Bay and other prisons. President Bush was asking, "Why do they hate us?" and people were asking us, "Why do you want to go to Egypt? Don't you know they are all terrorists who want to kill Americans? Don't you watch CNN?" And the ringer that really racked up the "mother guilt": "It's fine for you to go, but how can you put your kids in that situation, that danger?"

Actually we didn't watch CNN, or any other television for that matter. But Brad and I had traveled separately in 2002 to Jerusalem and Jordan, and instead of meeting hostile people, we met very friendly, welcoming Arabs—Muslims and Christians—who were delighted that we were there. Many gave us this message to bring back to the United States: *Please tell your people that we like Americans. It's the policies of your president that we disagree with. But we know Americans are good, kind people.* A very generous statement I thought, since it was those "good, kind people" who had elected President George Bush and supported his policies in Israel and Iraq.

Brad and I had wondered and discussed and prayed. Could we live in Egypt, the most populous and poorest Arab country, and convey our experiences of everyday life to Americans? Could we give an alternative to news about bombings and terrorism by focusing on ordinary men and women going about their daily lives? Could we put a human face on the people who seem so mysterious behind the veils and turbans? Could our family in a small way bridge the gap of misunderstanding between Americans and Arabs, between Muslims and Christians?

Yes, the list of lofty goals grew. And why not? Dreams never come true without ideals that sound impossible. What I did know for sure was that our kids were the right age for going abroad and that all four of our parents were still healthy and independent. The opportunity was available, and we needed to seize it. Yet it was still a hard decision to make; we had been feeling very satisfied and contented with our lives.

Since 1996, we had been living in rural Georgia in an intentional Christian community called Jubilee Partners. Brad was responsible for maintenance and had a never-ending to-do list. I was responsible for the refugee program that brought us in contact with hundreds of Bosnians, Afghanis, and Sudanese. In fact, it was through these refugees that I always said, "I can travel the world without leaving home." But I wasn't satisfied with being an "armchair" traveler. Our community, while only consisting of six families, gave us a lot of support and encouragement in our plans to go.

Once we had decided we wanted to go, the next question was how to get there? As we were committed Christians, it was important for us to go through a church-based organization. We also wanted a program that would support a family and underwrite the expenses. We had heard many positive things about Mennonite Central Committee (MCC). The organization had volunteers in numerous countries and, while they had projects, their focus was mainly on relationships with people. Their philosophy was not to create another project but to team up with local churches or organizations and partner with them.

We also embraced their commitment to peacemaking and non-violence. And fortunately they embraced us and helped us find a placement that would be satisfactory for a family. Though we are not Mennonites, when we were offered a three-year position in Egypt, we immediately took to the idea.

The pictures I had seen of pyramids, mosques, and old city markets always looked exotic. I had also heard that Egypt was a friendly and welcoming place for families, because much of Egyptian life centers around kids and marriage. We would soon learn the benefits and drawbacks of a culture that values family over individualism.

But for the moment, we were basking in the glory of going to Egypt, a country that calls itself *Masr*.

After learning of our assignment in the town of Beni Suef, we went to a bookstore and read from *The Rough Guide to Egypt*, "Beni Suef is one of Egypt's poorest governates, with high unemployment due to a shortage of arable land. There's no reason to visit the ramshackle capital of Beni Suef, 140 km south of Cairo."

"Sounds like our kind of place," Brad concluded. "No tourists, poor, probably an interesting place to live for three years." We bought the book.

Thus began a flurry of activities in the summer: passports, doctors' visits, eye checkups, shots for hepatitis and typhoid fever, packing up the house, packing and repacking our own bags—limit two each—and farewell parties with friends. While listening to Arabic language tapes and trying at least to learn the numbers, we drove to Alabama and Louisiana to say goodbye to our families.

At the Atlanta airport, we bid farewell to our Jubilee community. Our life with them was very rich and fulfilling and even though we made commitments to return, our faces were streaming with tears. It was September 2003. Only two years before, President Bush had remarked, "This day has changed our way of life." Yes, it changed our life, but not in a way he implied. He had called on Americans to support war and to go shopping; we were learning Arabic greetings and about to set foot in the Arab world.

Cairo, a city of eighteen million, was described to us as "chaos of the senses"—crowds of people shuffling about, exhaust fumes from cars and buses, horns honking incessantly, vendors yelling out names of wares for sale, the call to prayer emanating from centuries-old mosques. After a whirlwind week of orientation, we were disoriented and overwhelmed.

We soon boarded a train to Beni Suef, the home of Suad and Fatma, and settled into reasonably comfortable, second-class seats. Through the dirty windows, we absorbed life along the Nile River. Irrigation canals that parallel the river serve the same purpose today that they have for millennia: providing water for people, animals, and crops. Regardless of the environmental state of the canals, women and girls were squatting on the steep, trash-covered bank with their dishes and huge metal pots submersed in the water, scrubbing them clean. A few feet away a man was bathing his horse. A few naked boys were jumping and splashing about. A small, colorful fishing boat floated by with one man rowing and the other tossing a huge net with the hopes of pulling it back in full of fish.

The green and fertile Nile valley is dotted with tiny fields where millions of farmers and villagers try to survive amid overcrowding, poverty, and filth. Though obviously weary from their hard work, the *fellaheen* (farmers) walked with a certain dignity and pride, as if they saw themselves as responsible for keeping millions of Egyptians well fed. They rode to their fields, perched atop piles of fresh green alfalfa stacked on their donkeys. Women, wearing black peasant dresses with long, black, netted veils that swept down to the dirt path, followed behind huge, bony-flanked water buffaloes. Children, who should have been in school at that time of day, were playing along, swatting at the goats and sheep straying from the paths. The men all wore their peasant "uniforms"—a *galabaya*, a long, loose, cotton robe over underclothes, and an *emma*, a turban wound tightly around the head to protect them from the sun. (Their clothing is a puzzle that I have never understood. Why do the men wear cotton, light-colored clothes and the women have hot, sticky, black polyester?)

As the train rambled through the picturesque countryside, I reminisced about all the Christmas plays in which the birth of Jesus is reenacted. How often have mothers rummaged through the house to find dishtowels and bathrobes to costume their little shepherds and wise men? In Egypt, I felt like I had just left the twenty-first century and entered the New Testament era. It looked just like the pictures in the kids' Bible storybook. "Look at the stables and animals and people!" I exclaimed. "It must be so easy to do a Christmas pageant here." But when Christmas came in Egypt, the mangers were always stocked with plastic figurines made in China.

The farmland yielded to villages with mud-walled houses, buildings with the plaster crumbling off, and garbage littering the rutted, dirt streets. Women passed by with huge water jugs gracefully balanced on their heads, animals scurried about on top of sand piles, and an occasional camel loped along in a field, loaded down with a pile of wheat.

All of the country south of Cairo is called Upper Egypt. The people are called *Saidi* and are the butt of jokes, portrayed as ignorant, stubborn, stupid, and lazy. But information we read about the area was more depressing than racial jokes: few government services, high illiteracy, few jobs, and a fertile ground for recruiting militant Islamists.

As the brakes brought the train to a screeching halt, we woke the kids, gathered our belongings, and tried to squeeze past the pushing and shoving people waiting on the platform, who would not yield to let us disembark first. Did anyone mention that the *Saidi* are an impatient lot?

ت

Our family stood in front of St. Anthony's Language School. This is where our kids would attend school, where I would work, where Brad would teach evening English classes for adults, and most important of all, where we would live. Before we left the United States, Linda, our MCC country representative, had sent us a postcard showing a six-story school framed by bright, green trees. She had scribbled a note on the back: "Don't be fooled by the trees; you're going to live in a hot, dusty little town." Finally actually standing in front of the school, I could see that she was right. The trees had been painted onto the postcard for scenic effect.

We walked up the six flights of stairs—105 steps to be exact— into a small, gray room with long cracks in the concrete walls. The living room, to its credit, had a nice sofa, two chairs, and a small TV mounted to the wall. The kids went into the room that they would share and found three beds and one bookcase to hold all their clothes, books, and everything. There was neither a closet nor room for a dresser. Our small bedroom had a double bed, a wardrobe, and a dorm-size fridge. The kitchen was a one-person, standing-room-only affair—a small sink, an old-fashioned drum washing machine, and a stove that would arrive the next day, *in sha'allah*—God willing. The bathroom looked to be the best feature, that is, until we wanted to take showers.

It was obvious that we needed a lot of infrastructure for living: furniture, bookshelves, sheets, cookware, automatic washing machine, water pump. The school had agreed to provide housing for us but no one thought through how to make the apartment comfortable and livable for a family of five. We did not so much mind the fridge in our bedroom; there was clearly no room in the kitchen for it. But we definitely needed something that could hold more than a few water bottles. Though I disliked the notion of being the "ugly American abroad" by demanding stuff that seemed so obvious, I asked for a larger refrigerator, and after some prodding, one was moved in from the teachers lounge downstairs.

Nicholas had a look of disbelief on his face. "This is where we are going to live for three years? No way."

I was willing to be a bit more optimistic and put up with inconveniences. "There's a lot of overcrowding in Egypt," I said. "If this is how the Egyptians live, then we can manage it too." Linda ticked off a list of stuff that we would eventually be getting, and said, "That will make the place sustainable, but I think you need to look at it as camping out for a while."

Functional plumbing is perhaps the most common convenience lacking in developing countries. Our apartment had all the right fixtures; they were just completely incapable of giving us water when we wanted it. I would often wistfully think of the women doing dishes and laundry in the canals. We only had reliable water for a few hours daily, which frustrated every water-related thing: washing clothes and dishes, cooking, using the toilet, showering. So much energy was put into getting water that I didn't dare ask for the water heater to be repaired; it was easier to heat water on the stove for twice-weekly baths. "Well," I thought, "the girls have read a lot of *Little House on the Prairie* stories, and now they get to actually live it." Fortunately they were in good spirits through it all.

For unknown reasons, we could not have water in the kitchen and the bathroom at the same time. The washing "machine," which was moved into the bathroom when the stove arrived, needed to be filled with water by hand. When there was none in the bathroom, we made numerous trips to the kitchen, pitcher in hand, to shuttle water back to the machine. Manually rinsing and wringing the clothes was equally cumbersome and time consuming. I quickly realized that I'd teach in the school or do laundry, but clearly couldn't do both. It was a happy day when, after two months, our automatic washing machine arrived. I didn't even mind that it took two hours to do one load!

We met with the school director and produced passports and paperwork that were immediately taken to the local office of state security. The next day, an armed police guard was placed at the school. This has been standard operating procedure for any foreigners living in Upper Egypt since Islamist militants killed fifty-eight foreigners and four Egyptians in a 1997 massacre in Luxor, six hundred miles to the south of us. Our guards, three elderly men neatly dressed in khaki uniforms, would provide us with twenty-four-hour protection by sitting in plastic chairs and dozing off and on. I began to care for them as I would any grandpa, giving them ample supplies of hot, sweet tea and peanuts.

Soon enough, we found out that the guards were mainly concerned about where we were going and what time we would return; they rarely accompanied us when we went out. Since our Arabic was still very primitive, I just handed them our train tickets to Cairo so they could see our departure time and date. Looking over the guard's shoulder, I could tell that, while he was studying them intently, he was holding the tickets upside down. "*Shukran* [Thanks]," he said, returning them with a smile. I suppose literacy isn't a necessity for being a guard.

Our second day was spent meeting new people, shopping, unpacking, and figuring out how to make this five-hundred-square-foot concrete cubby hole our home. We needed a break, so when the evening had cooled off, we went out to explore our neighborhood. Beni Suef has around 250,000 inhabitants but with the feel of a sprawling village. The streets were teeming with people shopping, doing errands, working, and visiting.

Right next to the school was a collection of mud-brick houses connected by small alleyways. A tethered goat scratched around for scraps to eat; a poultry vendor with several metal cages holding about twenty chickens closed up for the day. I wondered if I would ever have the courage to buy a live chicken from a street stall. We ducked under a clothesline tied to the street's only tree, which would eventually be cut down to renovate the sidewalk in a "beautification project."

We turned onto a busy street and were overwhelmed by the noise and traffic. Men strolled arm in arm; women pushed babies in strollers; taxis, microbuses, and bicycles wove in and out of traffic; beggars sat on the curb with hands quietly outstretched. A horse and buggy galloped along; a donkey cart carrying fancy furniture brushed past us. A mother pushed her wheelchair-bound son while a boy walked by with a tray of hot tea held high in the air. Fearing a collision, I grabbed hold of my girls' hands, and we attempted to cross the street. "Let's duck in there," Brad said, eyeing a sweet shop, whose scrumptious display beckoned us to enter.

The kids oohed and aahed as they pointed to the many treats they wanted to try. I looked at the young woman behind the counter and studied her Muslim dress: a white cape fit snugly around her chubby face and flowed all the way down to her hips. Underneath was her long, gray dress sweeping the floor as she came around the counter, grabbed Emily by the shoulders, and began smothering her in kisses: "How are you, my dear? *Inti asal.* [You are honey.]" I waited with bated breath to see how Emily would react. She was surprised by kisses from a stranger but smiled shyly and came to stand behind me. Then the barrage of questions from the other workers began: "Where are you from? What's your name? Why are you here?" We chatted as best we could while they wrapped our selected goodies in glossy paper and tied it up with ribbon.

Our country representatives had warned us ahead of time that we needed to answer the "where are you from" question with careful consideration. Admitting to being Americans carries implications in this part of the world. We needed to be aware of current developments and their impact. For example, what about the bloody images of U.S. actions in Iraq that were being shown on TV? Had there been Israeli military excursions in the Occupied Territories? Had the United Nations condemned some Israeli action, and was the United States the only country to veto the condemnation?

It was not enough to just be aware of the actions of the United States, but those of Israel as well, considering that in the Middle East, Israel is often viewed as an appendage of America. Further, we also had to consider who was asking us the question. Was it a man with a bushy beard, a supposed sign of Islamic fundamentalists? If we had any reservations about stating our American roots, maybe we could rely on the good, clean politics of our northern neighbor and reply, "We're from Canada."

But that is a lot to think about when you are standing in what appears to be a charming little shop with innocent and curious shopkeepers. "We're from America," I answered. *"Ahlan wa sahlan,"* they replied. Welcome. Relief! And that would always be the only response we ever heard.

We headed toward the door. "Ya, madam," said a young male clerk addressing me, "one more question. Are you Muslim or Christian?"

"Christian," I answered.

"*Ahlan wa sahlan.*"

We took our package, waved goodbye, and walked home amid a steady stream of greetings. "Welcome in Egypt," "What's your name?" and "Alloo. How are youuu?"

Similar regards would follow us every time we left the privacy of the schoolyard. We were no longer individual, private people but belonged to the masses who seemed not to understand our boundaries. This was a hard lot for Americans who value privacy and space between one person and the next.

We would all have our stories: Rebecca sitting on a café stool in an outdoor restaurant when a young man walked by and ran his palm over her hair; Emily at the beach with a hand full of suntan lotion when an unknown young man dipped his fingers in and started rubbing her shoulders; Nicholas napping on a bus when the bus hostess started tickling him. Women I had never met would often approach me so closely I could feel their breath on my face and would kiss me when we parted. Even Brad would get used to holding hands with men. We no longer had an invisible aura of sacred space around us; in a country as densely populated as Egypt, there is no "personal space."

One more stop before heading home. We spied a juice bar with net bags of oranges and mangoes hanging from the ceiling and colorful wood shavings on the floor. We pointed to the fruit, used a few rudimentary words and hand gestures, and were served delicious, fresh-squeezed orange juice. The owner kindly rounded up some plastic stools for us to sit on. Rebecca had been dutifully carrying around a piece of trash, fruitlessly searching for a place to dispose of it. The American dictum "no littering" was still uppermost in her mind. Finally! She spotted a trash can across the street, nailed onto a tree, walked over to it, and jumped up to throw the trash in, as the can was much higher than she could reach.

"What's this?" the fruit stand owner asked, gesturing at Rebecca's actions. He shook his head, walked across the street and

Delicious fruits and vegetables are available year-round.

took out the trash, walked back across the street, and threw the trash onto the curb to join all the other rubbish, gesturing with his hands that this is where the trash belongs. We just sat there in surprised silence, not knowing what to make of it.

We finished our juices and paid, or at least tried to. "*Khalli! Khalli!*" said the storeowner. Brad and I looked at each other, puzzled, as that didn't sound like any of the Arabic numbers we had learned. So how much is it? We had no idea, so Brad shoved some money toward the man. He threw his hands up in the air. "*Khalli,*" he said again, and we stood there in uncertainty. Maybe it wasn't enough money, so Brad offered him more. The storeowner just laughed at us, shook his head, and refused the extra amount.

So he didn't want more money. Hmm. It was all quite comical and confusing at that point. We shrugged, gathered our packages, and began to walk away, leaving the initial offer of money still sitting on the counter. We were further confounded when, a few seconds later, his assistant, a young boy in an imitation Nike baseball cap, caught up with us and gave us a wad of small bills as change.

We turned the corner toward the school, dodging the little kids playing soccer in the street, and met up with the school's *bowab*—the gatekeeper and, by extension, controller of our comings and goings. It is a time-honored occupation throughout the Middle East, somewhere between babysitter and security guard, to keep an eye on a building and the people within it. The bowab is also the one to turn to when you need directions or to buy something or just to find out the latest gossip.

We had heard from another MCCer that if you're not careful, the bowab can make your life miserable, so I was determined to start off on the right foot. I tore open the package of sweets and offered it forward. He smiled and took a handful. I did the same with our police guard. Yesss! I felt successful; refusing an offer of food would have been an insult in this culture.

We said goodnight, knowing they would both sleep there in the schoolyard, the bowab in his small room with a bed and one-pot burner for making tea, and the guard on a makeshift bed of two benches pushed together and padded with a heavy, fuzzy wool blanket.

Sometime later, I looked out the window of our sixth-floor apartment to check out the nighttime view. The traffic, both people and cars, was still going strong at midnight; Beni Suef is no sleepy little town. Several men were sitting in chairs around a TV, watching a soccer game, occasionally letting out a whoop of approval. But I was most fascinated by the family near us, who had a small, flat roof. Mother and young sons were sitting while father was rolling out a plastic mat. They lay down on it while he ducked back downstairs and emerged with a small, black-and-white TV. Sleeping on the roof looked like an idyllic way to beat the heat.

I lay in bed thinking about all we had seen and learned that day. I continued wondering why someone would take trash *out* of a trashcan and throw it on the street. I had done my homework and wasn't completely ignorant about life in the Middle East. But I wasn't quite prepared for all the noise, trash, and chaos of the streets of Beni Suef. I knew many Muslim women wear head coverings, but I was startled by the sheer numbers of them in the streets.

I was puzzled over the question from the shop clerk: Muslim or Christian? There was no third option. I had never been asked that question before, so it caught me off guard. It was obvious that the female employees were Muslims, but the males, dressed in jeans and T-shirts, were more difficult to label. Was my simple answer enough, or should I have added that I respect the Muslim faith? But if the clerk was a Christian, would he consider that a betrayal to our faith? It really didn't matter, as I wasn't linguistically capable of saying anything beyond "Christian." In the future, we would get a lot more practice as this question would be frequently asked.

I also thought about the juice bar owner and that curious word *khalli*. We would find out that it means "keep your money, it's on the house." We would hear it repeatedly in Beni Suef. It is a typical gesture of Egyptian courtesy, and customers politely respond by again offering the money, which the shopkeeper finally accepts. The juice bar man could have kept all the money we offered, but he had sent it back, giving us almost everything we had given him. I was touched by his honesty and kindness and was reminded of another fact I knew about Egypt: Arab hospitality is world renowned, and rightly so. We would soon have many experiences in discovering for ourselves the richness of Egyptian generosity.

3

The Sandstorms
of Settling In

"When can we start school? There are a lot of kids down there who want us to come." It was 7:30 a.m., and the bright sun and loud street noise had awakened us two hours earlier. From our balcony, we could see the small schoolyard below filling up with kids. I was hoping we could settle in a little more before getting started school, but the kids were all eager for it. We had met the day before with the principal, Sister Heba, who was also responsible for seeing to our needs, and she was just as eager for the kids to start.

St. Anthony's Language School is a private school run by the Coptic Orthodox Church. A "language school" means English is not merely taught as a subject, but science and math are also taught in English. It appealed to us, of course, that our kids could have their main subjects taught in a language they knew. French and German are added to the curriculum after third grade. Such private language schools are very popular throughout Egypt, as they are seen as the key to giving a child a good future. The student body is roughly half Christian and half Muslim and, being the elite private school in Beni Suef, these students were the sons and daughters of doctors, engineers, judges, and businessmen. I had attended private Catholic schools for some of my education, so I knew that any school run by the church would have high-quality education and discipline. But that assumption was wrong.

Much to our surprise, no one at the school, other than the principal, had been informed of our coming. No one was prepared for us. We were handed a schedule, in Arabic, that I tried to decipher. Let's see—start at the right side of the page and read to the left. The first day of the school week is Saturday, skip Sunday for

31

the Christian Sabbath, then Monday through Thursday, skip Friday for the Muslim prayer day. Goodbye to two-day weekends! Each day had different subjects with no two days alike; some days had ten periods, other days nine. Just looking at the schedule made me dizzy with confusion. I glanced over at little Emily, a mere third-grader who now had eleven different subjects, and I wondered how she would keep up.

My three kids were immediately plunged into instant, albeit unwanted, "stardom." The school had never had foreigners before, and the students, who knew no boundaries, could not get enough of them. One day, observing from our sixth-floor view, I could see blonde Rebecca surrounded by a mass of dark, long-haired girls until she completely shrunk underneath them. Girls were tickling her, playing with her hair, pinching her cheeks, rubbing her arms, and kissing her face. In the classroom they would surround her desk, all of them repeating the same annoying questions, none of them able to pronounce her name, no matter how slowly she repeated it. One girl picked up her half-eaten sandwich and shoved it in Rebecca's face, trying to feed her! By the end of the period, Rebecca, on the verge of tears, fled to the sanctuary of our cubby-hole apartment.

After a month of unrelenting "welcoming," I complained to one of the English teachers who had befriended us and was surprised by his smiling face. "You know why the children do this?" she asked. "They want her to be happy. They love Rebecca so much and so do I." I was expecting the teacher to be sympathetic to our frustrations and perhaps even to talk to the students about ways they could help Rebecca feel more comfortable in class. What the students and teachers called "hospitality" felt to us like harassment. The result of her classmates' "hospitality" was that the more the children pursued her, the more she sought refuge away from them.

I comforted Rebecca with the thoughts that this was only because she was new and it would die down soon. Wrong again. She would spend all school year coping with varying degrees of "hospitality" and would eventually develop her own coping skills. Running away and yelling "stop" usually seemed to work, except for one large girl who for months had been repeatedly pinching her and grabbing her clothes. I had spoken to this girl several times about how to be friends with Rebecca, but she persisted in interacting this way. One day during recess, I saw Rebecca smack the girl hard on her arm. I had always taught my kids not to resort to violence, but this time I held my tongue, as I thought the girl got what she deserved. Unfortunately it made more of an impression on me than on her.

Little Emily received the same warm welcome and attention but tolerated it better. Once when I was in her class, observing, her English teacher asked, "Emily, is it right to say *I am* or *you are* happy?"

"I am," came Emily's correct reply.

"Yea!" cried Rheem, the little green-eyed girl sitting next to her. She swung her scarf-covered head around and planted four kisses on Emily's cheeks. You would have thought Emily had just answered a million-dollar question.

Surprisingly it would be her French class that brought her to tears. Emily, who naturally could not tell the difference between spoken Arabic and French, had no idea when one language ended and the next began as the teacher spoke to the class. The first exam was coming up soon, and picking up on her classmates' fear of failure, she was in a constant state of panic. I talked with her French teacher, Mona, who I immediately liked.

"You know, I was not trained to teach students," she explained. "I used to be a French translator with a tour company in Luxor. Then came the terrorist attacks in 1997 and all the tourists left, so I lost my job. What could I do then? My husband's family is from Beni Suef, so we moved here, but I really don't like it and I don't like teaching."

Many Egyptians had been personally affected by this attack, which wrecked the tourist industry that so many depended on to make a living. Even the terrorist group responsible for the killings realized the negative impact this action had on their fellow Egyptians, causing many of the terrorists to renounce violence. But the impact had already been made on Mona. By the end of the school year, she and her family would emigrate to Australia.

Nicholas took note of the dusty dirt schoolyard and immediately joined whatever class was playing soccer, probably getting in about five games on his first day of school. Groups of boys were always hanging on him, arms flung over his shoulders, others holding his hand. For a twelve-year-old boy from a culture where this amount of affection means something entirely different, he handled it gracefully.

Our initial goals were to have the kids attend all their subjects, since we wanted them to learn Arabic. It was a noble goal, but we didn't take into serious account how difficult it is for English speakers to learn Arabic. The U.S. State Department rates it as the third most difficult language. Also, the school wanted our kids to speak English so the others could learn from them.

After a few days observing the kids at school, it was as clear that they would not be able to tolerate the learning environment, or lack of it, all day long. So we worked out a compromise with the principal to have the kids attend only the English-speaking classes, plus classes on computers and physical education.

Registering for school wasn't as complicated as we had anticipated, but it did mean Nicholas would undergo another name change. While we were in the Atlanta airport on our way to Cairo, we had to tell him that *nick* is an Arabic curse word, and thus in Egypt we should only use his full name, Nicholas. I was surprised how well he took that news, not even asking what the "bad word" meant. As it turned out, our fears were unwarranted. After about a year, we realized we had never actually heard any Egyptian use *nick*. Thanks to uncensored American movies, the English version was more common.

During the school registration process, the most important question was, "What is your father's name?" Nicholas underwent yet another name change as he lost "Smith" and became Nicholas Brad Donald—*Brad* being his father's name and *Donald* his grandfather's. In the Arab world, a person's "last name" is actually his grandfather's first name. To complete the registration, all official documents needed to be stamped—literally. So I went to the post office and bought postage stamps, which I then affixed onto the school enrollment forms. We also needed a document notarized by the U.S. Embassy, giving our children permission to attend school. This actually necessitated two train trips to Cairo, because the first time Brad went the embassy was closed for Columbus Day. When you are thousands of miles from home, American holidays slip into insignificance.

My job was defined as "teacher resource to improve the level of English." To start out, I thought I should sit in a few classes and observe. I sat in the back of Nicholas's science class, fully expecting an atmosphere in which everyone would be on their best behavior for the foreign guest in the room. But a soccer game with a paper-wad ball was still going on long after the bell rang. The teacher entered and immediately went to the blackboard and wrote for the next fifteen minutes. Gradually the boys stopped playing and sat in their desks, taking out their notebooks to copy what was on the board.

I used the time to check out the environment. The room had just been painted a dark, dull gray. Paint was splattered on the floor and desks, a silent testament to painters who hadn't used drop cloths. The long chalkboard was hardly readable from the second row. The big, wooden, clunky desks were reminiscent of American schools in the early twentieth century. The school was only nine years old, but with no maintenance it looked about fifty. An empty bookshelf, a daily class schedule, and a picture of President Mubarak graced a wall. The teacher had a chair and a small, rickety, wooden table. The only bright spots were the aging posters, made years earlier by former students and tacked on the back wall. No clock, no calendar, no bright pictures, no maps, not a book in the room. I had heard of these type of classrooms from the refugees I worked with, but it was a whole different feeling to put your own child in one.

The teacher had finished writing and was walking around the room. She stopped in front of Nicholas's desk. "Why are you not writing this information?" she asked. Nicholas flipped open his textbook and pointed, "Because it is all right here in the textbook. I can just read it from the book." Wrong answer. She pulled him by his ear with one hand and flung his notebook to the floor with her other hand. She moved on to the next boy, whose work didn't meet her standards, and ripped out the pages he had just written, crumpled them, and threw them to the floor. Another boy got a whack on the head, another had his arm twisted behind his back, another got slapped on the back, and yet another was sent to stand up in the back of the room, arms high in the air for the remaining class time. The girls got off easy by just being yelled at.

I sat completely horrified by what I had witnessed. But a glance around the room showed that no one else was bothered. It was a regular class with nothing special for the foreign guest. The kids did not sit quietly in fear of getting hit next. Instead they were jumping up and down, switching desks, playing cards, chatting in groups, calling out to their friends, and eating sandwiches. The teacher, constantly yelling, went from one crisis to the next without ever gaining control of the class.

I could not have managed a minute longer when I was literally saved by the bell. *Teacher resource* seemed an overwhelming and impossible job. How could I make any changes in the way to teach when the method was quite simple: write from the textbook onto the board, have students write and memorize what was on the board and then recite what they'd written back to teacher? Is this what they learned at teachers college?

I knew I couldn't save the Egyptian kids from their dysfunctional educational system, but I was concerned about my own kids. How could I have taken them from their lovely, small-town schools with brightly painted walls displaying endless educational materials and their soft-spoken teachers asking them to sit and use their "inside voices"? What in the world had I walked into?

Thus ended our first week in school. Thursday night, which is the weekend night, brought several invitations from just-met school friends. We were just sitting down to eat lunch when one mother came up to our apartment. "You must come to Noha's birthday party tonight," she said. "She wants you so bad."

"Thank you. I am not sure what we are doing this evening. But thank you anyway," I replied, wondering who she was and if Rebecca even knew her daughter. So many kids in such a short time were just a blur of dark hair and dark skin.

But the woman insisted. "You must come for my daughter's sake. For my daughter's happiness."

"Well, I really don't know. My husband is in Cairo, and we are tired from school."

"We will come to the school at eight. You must do this for my daughter. She loves your daughter so much."

I closed the door and looked questioningly at Rebecca, who responded, "I have no idea who that is, Mama."

I had always considered myself an assertive person in a polite way, but I was completely taken back by the persistent actions of this parent. I thought there was a universal understanding among parents that we support each other and respect each other's no. But that was in our other country. Here, it seemed the unspoken rule was to keep pushing until you got what you wanted.

Brad was still in Cairo, getting the precious school documents from the embassy, so I was left to sort out the evening plans. Nicholas was invited to go with some boys whose names he did not remember to a church that he did not know the name of to play soccer at eight. Rebecca wanted to go to the girl's birthday party, even though she did not know her name or where the party would be. I had no names for anyone, no addresses, no phone numbers. We didn't even have a phone yet, so what if there was an accident or an emergency? How would I know about it? Parenting is always a tough job, but for new arrivals in a foreign country, these decisions were agony. Yet in Nicholas's case, since these were his first friends, I thought it would be worse not to let him go.

Three boys showed up on two bicycles, none wearing helmets. My only comforting thought was that they go to a private church school, so they must be good people—a correct assumption as I would happily discover. Off Nicholas went, straddling the back of a bicycle with his friend steering and dodging people, cars, playing children, donkey carts, horse-drawn carriages, street vendors, and screeching microbuses with the requisite four men hanging out the door. "Lord, what have I done?" I uttered to myself.

Just as I was fretting and regretting my decision, a teacher from the school pulled up *on* the family car, which was a motorcycle driven by her husband. Their two-year-old daughter was in front of him while the mother sat behind, sidesaddle, with her two-month-old baby in her arms. All without helmets, of course. I figured this was my sign that there would be no security and all was in God's hands. If I wanted helmets and seatbelts, I had no business being in the developing world.

ئ

Noha's family's driver picked up Rebecca, Emily, and me in front of the school promptly at eight. We still had not met the daughter but were greeted by her younger brother and were seated in the reception room of their home. A quick glance at the religious pictures hanging on the wall told me we were in the home of a Muslim family. In the center was a framed picture of the *Kaaba*, a huge black cube that is the figurative house of God, the pilgrimage site in Mecca, Islam's holiest city. Bright lights flashed around the picture frame. The thousands of pilgrims surrounding the Kaaba were glimmering with the shiny color of abalone shell, while a fake waterfall glowed and flowed in illuminated splendor. I had seen photos of the Kaaba and observed that its beauty was in its simplicity —black and immense. I knew that Muslims, like Jews, prohibited physical representations of God, prophets, and saints. But I had to wonder, why wasn't there a prohibition against religious kitsch?

We had plenty of time to observe the reception room. I had incorrectly assumed that a party for fifth-graders would begin at eight and end by ten. Emily was in my lap, whining to go home, when the other girls began to arrive at ten. Not only were we way too early, but we were way underdressed. The other girls all had on fancy party dresses with their hair "done up."

But we were never made to feel out of place. People welcomed us, spoke to me in halting English, and filled my plate with more food than I could ever eat. It was to be one of my first lessons: Egyptians are a very forgiving people who overlook a lot of our cultural mistakes. Finally the party got underway in earnest; the music was cranked up, and the girls danced among themselves.

We arrived back at the school at midnight, only to be met with the anger of Taha, the bowab on duty: "You said you would be back at ten; it's now midnight!" I wanted to say, "You know how late parties start in Egypt. You know the hosts won't bring us back when I said we needed to go home. You know your culture better than I do." But, alas, all the words I could manage were apologies accompanied by shrugs of my shoulders; the goodwill generated by the sweets I had previously shared with him had obviously worn off.

Brad was home from Cairo, having successfully accomplished his errands. Nicholas returned home safely with all body parts intact. We fell into bed, exhausted.

ﻉ

"Mom, my head itches." Nicholas complained the next morning. I checked his head and sure enough, it was covered with lice. "Great, just what we need now," I thought, recalling the time when the girls had had head lice back in the States and what an ordeal it was. I looked up the Arabic word for lice in the little pocket dictionary and went with Nicholas to a barber conveniently located near the school. I pointed to his hair and proudly used my new vocabulary word. The barber went to the pharmacy next door and came back with dandruff shampoo. I shook my head, then went with the barber to the pharmacy and found lice shampoo. The barber smiled triumphantly, put Nicholas in a chair, and began shampooing his hair.

It was a small barbershop, two chairs only, and cluttered with scissors, hair gels, and brushes. When I glanced at the four men waiting on benches, leafing through newspapers or reading the Qur'an, I realized I had stepped into "the men's world," a place where Egyptian women don't go. This was the man's job; Brad, who was organizing books for his English classes, should have taken Nicholas. Yet the men in the shop did not seem put out by my presence; one guy even went next door to borrow a chair so I could sit. This was another truth we were to discovered: So often people go out of their way to make us feel welcome and comfortable, whether offering a seat, a cup of hot tea, or a soft drink.

After putting in the oily lice shampoo, the barber cut Nicholas's hair, blow-dried it, and styled it ever so lovely. He put the lice-exposed hairbrush back in with all his other hairbrushes and wiped Nicholas's neck with paper tissues that he then threw out onto the street to join other litter at the curb. I was instructed to wash his hair after eight hours, paid the barber, and left, flabbergasted about lice treatment. Now ahead of me was the task of washing all of Nicholas's bed linens and clothes in cold water in a barely functioning washing machine that merely swirled the clothes around in water. But the greater worry was that I knew lice and nits were still lurking in my son's hair.

It was more than I could handle. We found our friend, Magdy, who had been assigned by the school to help us settle in, and he took Nicholas to his barber, who simply cut off all his curly hair. A scalped head wasn't how Nicholas wanted to start his new life in a new country, but we were desperate, and I was just grateful that it wasn't one of the girls. Of course, their turn came later, and the

battle with head lice would endure throughout our stay. "Nit picking" eventually became a part of our lives and the phrase "we want
to live like Egyptians and experience life as they do" came back to
haunt me. Be careful what you wish for!

ℰ

Brad had begun his evening classes offering conversational English
to adults in the community. Sister Heba was very helpful in organizing the classes and registering students. MCC has provided these
classes off and on for twenty years, though no one had been
assigned to Beni Suef in five years. This English program is sponsored by the Coptic Orthodox Church, with the goal of providing a
setting where Muslims and Christians can interact with each other.
Brad found that lots of folks were eager to learn English, even
though chances to learn it are limited in a town that few foreigners
visit. It seems that the lure of the Internet, especially e-mail and chat
rooms, is a major incentive for folks to improve their fluency.

After a month in Beni Suef, Brad's work was the one bright
spot in our life. The rest of us were steadily going downhill.

Nicholas, adopted into our family as a toddler, is biracial. His
rich, chocolate skin color allowed him to blend right in with Egyptians.
Brad, Rebecca, and Emily had the predicament of always looking like
foreigners. With my Italian heritage, I often "passed" as Egyptian and
could avoid the unwanted attention foreigners continuously have to
deal with. This meant we had a unique opportunity as a family to
experience how both foreigners and locals are treated. Nicholas's ability to pass as Egyptian would prove to be both a blessing and a curse.
Unfortunately we experienced the curse part first.

One evening I took the kids exploring down a narrow alleyway
where people were selling all sorts of cheap plastic toys and noise-
makers, nuts and beans, and other foods we couldn't identify, all laid
out on plastic mats with dirty, barefoot kids sleeping here and there.
The alleys were lined with colorful tents filled with turbaned men in
galabayas, who were rhythmically swaying to loud Qur'anic chanting.
Gas lamps lit the crowded streets, giving it a surreal and mystical
feeling.

I instructed the kids, "Don't say anything; we don't want to
attract any attention. Just observe with your eyes." We had only

gone a short way before a horde of boys followed us, shouting, "What's your name?" and other comments. First we decided to ignore them, hoping they would tire of us and go away. When that didn't work, and their numbers increased, I yelled for them to go away, *imshi min hina*, as our Arabic phrasebook had suggested. Hearing my feeble Arabic only encouraged more antics. The girls were particularly distressed by all the unwanted attention. What had happened to our fun evening out to explore the neighborhood?

Emily spotted a cotton-candy machine, and we headed there to get some respite. The vendor, annoyed at all the commotion these boys were causing, shooed them away. They moved back, leaving our family standing alone. But the vendor, mistaking Nicholas for one of those boys, grabbed him by the neck and shoved him, knocking him down on the dirty ground.

I was horrified and started yelling, "*Ibnee, ibnee da*! [That's my son!]" The man was quite surprised and helped Nicholas up, dusted him off, and kept apologizing. We bought the candy and left. I felt so bad for Nicholas, I would have bought him the whole machine if I could have. Afterward, he said what hurt him the most was that the other boys laughed when he was pushed down. This experience was the inside view of how annoying local boys are treated by adults. This would prove to be a constant struggle for us: the girls received special treatment because they are blond and light skinned, while Nicholas received the same rough treatment as his Egyptian peers.

How was I to handle a situation like that? I didn't want any person mistreating my son, or any boy, in such a manner. If we were being harassed again, would I ask an adult for help, knowing that violence might be the response? How could I protect my kids from all this excessive attention? How could we go about our neighborhood without being on parade? All those questions just made my head swim, as there are no easy answers when adjusting to a new culture and to a new set of rules, rules that can be revealed only through the passage of time and experiences.

That scene in the alley occurred during a *moulid*, a festival honoring a Muslim saint. These festivals, a mixture of Qur'anic chanting for adults and rides and games for kids, are officially condemned by Islamic sheikhs as violating true Islamic beliefs. Nevertheless they are immensely popular with poor villagers, who were streaming into Beni Suef and into our neighborhood. The next day, one of the colorful tents appeared on the sidewalk next to the school with a loudspeaker tied to the outside of the tent. An imam sang prayers and readings from the Qur'an in a rich, deep voice that was beautiful to listen to. One problem was that it was so loud, even inside our apartment we couldn't talk to each other, only read lips. Brad had to cancel his evening class because he could not compete with the noise; his students couldn't hear him. Seven hours later, at eleven at night, the imam finished. We were exhausted from the noise and tension. This would last for two more nights. There are no anti-noise laws in Egypt.

☙

I was nearing the end of my stability as a calm, reasonable person who can put up with a lot of inconveniences. I tallied my list of woes: occasional water, no hot water, sporadic electricity, three bickering kids crammed into an eight-by-eight room, constant loud "welcomes" from strangers on the street, curious school kids coming up to our floor during school hours, the dismal teaching and learning environment, head lice, the incident with the cotton-candy man, street noise, and now chanting that prevented me from getting a decent night's sleep. Plus we were still adjusting to strange food, hot October weather, and a different time zone. I was exhausted and stressed out but didn't realize it.

Then Sister Heba came to tell me that painters would arrive the next morning at ten to begin painting our apartment. I know I should have been appreciative, and I tried to show it, but then she said, "You'll need to move all your things out." Since August we had been living out of suitcases. In the last few days, I had decided that our place needed to look homey and what better way to do that than to decorate the bare concrete walls? So up went posters, wall hangings, and knick-knacks. Now all that, plus the rest of our belongings, would need to be put back into our suitcases and into boxes that we did not have. The painting would take at least two weeks, but I didn't even have the presence of mind to ask where we would live.

Brad was teaching and the kids were at Arabic lessons, and after seeing Sister Heba down the stairs, I was finally alone. What in the world was I doing here? What was I trying to prove? It had been easy to be confident about going overseas while in the comforts and familiarity of the United States. As I collapsed on the sofa, overwhelmed by reality, a young girl appeared in the doorway and asked for Emily. I curtly told her Emily wasn't there, and she scampered away. Treating her rudely only added to my depression.

"Good evening. How are you?" said a slim man with wispy black hair who was now standing in my doorway. I sat up on the sofa, brushed away my tears, and invited him to sit down.

"My name is Osama, and my daughter is in Emily's class." I didn't have the time to be annoyed about another pushy parent, as I had another worry. I was sitting in my apartment alone with a strange man, a Muslim at that. Warnings I had received echoed loudly in my head: don't be alone in your house with another man. What you are doing doesn't matter; it's what people think you are doing that matters, and people in Beni Suef will only think bad things.

"My daughter is in the car with my wife and we are going to the *nadi*, the club. You and your children are welcome to come spend the evening with us if you'd like." I looked at Osama, who was sitting calmly in the chair, explaining that his daughter was "infatuated" with Emily. It was a wonder he did not turn and run from me, with my face red from tears, my hair a mess, and wadded up tissues surrounding me.

I should have known that God would place angels here and there to rescue us when we needed it. This angel, Osama, had a name that before that moment had been associated only with evil doings. I knew that the best medicine for depression was to get out of the house and have a little fun.

The kids finished Arabic lessons. I went to Brad's class to tell him we were going out, and "Oh by the way, we are moving tomorrow. Don't worry, we'll deal with it in the morning."

4
Living in an Orphanage

"Welcome. Your family is welcome here. Our home will be your home," said Sister Maria, the director and "mother" of an orphanage for twenty-four girls.

One of my goals was to make contact with the local church-run orphanage, but I never imagined we would do it so intimately. But there we stood—Rebecca, Emily, me, and our little bags—looking like lost orphans ourselves. Brad and Nicholas were next door at the boys home. I joked with my girls that not only did they get to live like *Little House* but now like *Little Orphan Annie*. They barely tolerated my humor. But we were impressed with the warm greetings and welcome we received from Sister and the girls, especially after our frenzied move just that morning.

Sister Heba had greeted us. "Good morning. The painters will be here soon. We will help you move everything out." She pointed to some workers holding a few boxes. We had already packed our clothing and personal effects. We assumed all furniture and other belongings would be pushed to the middle of each room and covered with drop cloths while the painting was happening. We were wrong. When Sister Heba said that everything must go out, she meant everything—filing cabinet, beds, rugs, refrigerator, stove, washing machine. Only the proverbial kitchen sink remained.

We thought this was taking things a bit far; after all, weren't they just painting the walls? But there was no time for discussion; Brad woke the kids as the workers began disassembling their beds. It was pandemonium with so many people trying to move so much stuff in an hour's time. Organizing anything was hopeless. We just piled it all into the empty school hallway nearby.

"The problem is, where will you live now? You and the girls can stay in the convent, but the rooms are small with single beds only. And

45

Nicholas, Rebecca, and Emily with Sister Maria at the orphanage.

I don't know about Mr. Brad and Nicholas." Sister Heba, short and stocky in her long, gray nun's habit, directed orders with her cell phone in one hand and hot tea in the other. She was the same age as me, forty-one, but looked much older and more stressed, with a perpetually wrinkled forehead.

"Isn't there a home here for girls without parents and also one for boys?" I asked. Sister made the necessary calls and, half an hour later, there we were, standing in the courtyard of the girls orphanage. Situations that would be completely impossible in the United States could be relatively simple in Egypt.

The two orphanages were only a mile from the school near the nadi. For the next two weeks, Brad and Nicholas camped out in the boys home. The girls and I were next door, in the home for girls. The outside area was sand, strewn with rubbish, concrete chunks, scratching hens, playing kids, and large women congregating on doorsteps, drinking tea and eyeing us curiously. A large green gate separated us from the outside world. Sister Maria, the orphanage director, kept the girls well protected, letting them out only for school, church, and an occasional well-chaperoned outing.

The courtyard of the orphanage proved a pleasant refuge from the noisy streets. Large trees shaded two concrete patios, a small swing, and an outdoor sitting area offset with green plants. Lots of girls came out to stare at us, then smile at us, then greet us with the Egyptian female greeting—four kisses, two on each cheek. Let's see. Four kisses times twenty-four girls. . . . Oh, it was too much to contemplate.

Dimiana, a tall, pretty girl with a dimpled smile who was named for one of the Coptic Orthodox saints, showed us to our room. The bedroom had three single beds, a desk, and a cupboard for our clothing, definitely a step up from our cramped quarters at the school. The bathroom had a window that would not close, allowing the cool desert breeze to blow in, adding further chills to the cold-water showers. The orphanage girls all took showers on Thursday nights, and I was sure they endured the cold water and drafts without complaints.

We unpacked our bags and laid down to rest before we were called for dinner at 3 p.m., when the main meal of the day is eaten. Dimiana escorted us to a separate dining room from the orphans.

"Who cooked all this?" I inquired as my eyes scanned the table lavishly spread with a tureen of zucchini soup, a huge platter of rice, another platter of baked chicken, a plate of bread, and a tomato and cucumber salad.

Sister Maria smoothed out her habit and explained, "The older girls do all the cooking. Each day it is two different girls. I want them to know how to do everything so when they leave from here they will be good wives and mothers who can do all in the house."

We could hear the hens that had escaped the knife that morning on the other side of the wall. How could two teenage girls cook all this food, from scratch—no cans, no boxed mixes, no microwave—for thirty people every single day? I was amazed. None of the girls I knew in the United States could match this.

When we had finished eating, two girls cleared away the table, refusing to let us help. They were responsible for washing all thirty trays as well as pots in cold water. Rebecca and Emily, feeling shy around so many girls, went back to our room to read. Sister Maria and I were served tea and a large platter of fresh guava.

"What has happened that the girls live here instead of with their families?" I asked as I scooped out the guava seeds.

Sister took a sip of tea and answered in slow precise English,

"Some families are poor and cannot take care of all their children. Sometimes the parents have problems with theirs minds [that is, are mentally ill]. Some parents do not take good care of their children. Sometimes the parents die, and no one in the family can care for them. The children are brought to the bishop, and he decides if they should come here."

Over time, we were to discover that few children were orphans in the true sense of the word. About every six weeks, it was "family day," and parents, siblings, aunts, and uncles would come to visit. I was surprised to see mothers with children visiting their daughters in the orphanage and wondered how poor mothers decided which child to keep and which to give to the orphanage to raise.

While there are government orphanages, these boys and girls were specifically brought to the bishop to be raised by the church, much like young Samuel in the Old Testament was brought to the priest Eli. Sister raises them as if they are living in a convent, with daily morning and evening prayers and weekly Mass in the orphanage chapel. The girls also attend a nearby church for Friday school, the equivalent of Sunday school. They are also taught Coptic, which was the language of all Egyptians before Arabic. It is basically a dead language, except for its use in the Coptic Orthodox Mass.

I took advantage of the quiet time and probed more about the orphanage. "So the money for the orphanage comes from the church?"

"No. We don't get money from the church."

"Oh, from the government or private donations?"

"It's a gift from Jesus. Jesus provides."

And that would be the only answer I ever received.

GOD IS THE GREATEST!
I TESTIFY THERE IS NO GOD EXCEPT GOD.
I TESTIFY THAT MUHAMMAD IS HIS PROPHET.

I was suddenly jolted awake by the voice of the muezzin giving the predawn call exhorting all faithful Muslims that it was time to pray. It wasn't a deep, warm voice encouraging one to get up at

5 a.m. It was more like a grouchy, loud voice barking through a static-filled loudspeaker, carrying over the rooftops, right into our room. There was no point in sleeping after that. Besides, the chickens and roosters on the roof had been cackling all night and had now reached the peak of their own wake-up call.

I had made a vow that if I was awakened by the call to prayer, I would also use that time to pray. After all, we were all worshipping the same God, weren't we? For Muslims, the dawn prayer is a big commitment beginning with the *wudu*—washing the hands, face, and feet to be clean before God. Some devout Muslims even walk down to the neighborhood mosque and pray communally. As for me, I stayed in bed and prayed.

A short while later, I heard young female voices, pitched high and chanting, the sound wafting down the hall and into our room. Ahhh, the Christian call to prayer, at least in an orphanage. I reached the chapel door and nearly tripped over the pile of plastic *shipship* (slippers). Respecting their custom, I took mine off and observed the scene from the doorway. A small room filled with twenty-four girls, ages five to twenty-four, all standing shoulder to shoulder in their pajamas, with white lacy cloths on their heads and a prayer book in their hands. They were singing loudly, no one slouching or staring off into space. The walls were lined with numerous pictures of saints; a huge square altar adorned in faux gold and silver stood in the center; large incense burners hung from heavy chains; and lit candles were dripping wax into a clay pot of sand.

Dimiana brought me a white veil for my head. Taking me by the arm, she led me to her spot and shared her prayer book with me. I could follow the Arabic briefly; by the time I'd finished pronouncing two words, they had completed the verse.

One of the reasons Arabic is difficult for foreigners is that vowels are not written, and one has to learn which vowel sound goes between what consonants. In English it would look like this: ht. So, is it *hit, hut,* or *hat*? How can you pronounce it without knowing what the vowel sound is? I had been promised that I'd get the hang of reading as I studied the language, and I was eager for that magic day to arrive. After a half-hour, chapel ended and the girls filed out quietly. I went to wake up Rebecca and Emily for another school day.

ℰ

Emily buys roasted corn from a village woman.

Now that we were staying at the orphanage, each morning we had to negotiate street life as we strolled the mile to the school. Country women in their bright dresses and black net veils glided with erect postures gracefully down the street and stopped at a self-designated street corner to set up business. We watched one woman unload the large, metal pan from her head and neatly arrange on newspaper all her goods for the day: glossy purple eggplants, ripe red tomatoes, and zucchini so fresh that the ends still had unwilted yellow flowers attached. She sat next to a large woman who had four chickens hobbled and lying down. How did she sit in the hot sun on hard, dirty sidewalks all day long, waiting for someone to buy these measly chickens so she could buy food for her family?

Another woman had only a basket of grapes, which at first glance looked spotted, but the spots focused into flies. Her barefoot, one-year-old daughter wore a stained dress and was lying across her lap nursing. I made a mental note to try to swallow my hygienic standards and buy from these women. I admired their strength and determination to be out working in the heat and car fumes to support their families. As we would get to know Beni Suef better, we would discover there were hundreds of women like these, squatting on any available piece of street or sidewalk, selling the fruits and vegetables of their family's labor.

We turned onto a quieter street that allowed for a quicker pace. But there was so much to look at that I thought Egypt should market to another kind of tourist—"people watchers," who like to sit on a bench and watch the world go by. A loud horn honking behind me ended my daydreaming. We needed to be constantly alert while navigating the streets. We had gone from a town of twelve hundred people and one traffic light in rural Georgia to Beni Suef with nearly a quarter-million people and no traffic lights. The basic rule for pedestrians was simple: you have no rights and it is your responsibility to get out of a vehicle's way. Do not expect a car to yield to you. Furthermore, if a car hits you, don't expect any sympathy or help from the driver. There would be many times when we felt a car's outside mirror brush against our clothing, once even bruising Rebecca's arm.

We approached the end of the street, and the six-story school building loomed ahead. Cars and buses unloaded their little passengers; fathers dropped off kids they had bicycled to school. We greeted the three bowabs and guards who still guarded the school, even though we weren't living there. Four girls immediately grabbed Emily, pulling her in four directions while another group of girls complained to me that Emily wouldn't play with them. Rebecca played chase with her friends. Nicholas and some boys blew up plastic bags to pop in people's faces. All the running around kicked up swirls of dust that hung in the air. Teachers strolled in through the gate, talking with each other or on cell phones, the modern status symbol that defines one's importance to all within earshot. The bell rang, welcoming us to another day of school.

The final bell rang at 2:30—at least we imagined it did, as the electricity was off, a common occurrence throughout the school day. The kids took a *hantoor*, a horse-drawn carriage, back to the orphanage while I retraced our morning route. I wanted to check on the lady selling chickens. Sure enough, all four birds were still sitting beside her. I managed to avoid eye contact and turned aside from her desperation. Other times I wouldn't be so cautious and would end up buying all sorts of stuff I couldn't use, just because I hadn't the heart to say no.

By the time I arrived at the orphanage, it was chore time, and we needed to wash our clothes. I had seen an automatic washing machine but was told not to use it. "You must let Dimiana wash your clothes! She's the best clothes washer here," a chorus of girls enthusiastically assured me. Dimiana stepped forward with a big smile, as if she had just won a set of keys to a brand-new car. Since we had guest status, I knew all I could do was be appreciative. The girls were divided into two groups—the younger ones, who were still attending school, and the older, who had finished school and were waiting to get married. It was the latter's responsibility to hand wash, in cold water, all the clothing of about eighteen younger ones.

After chores and evening prayers, the girls gathered their note-books, set up tables and chairs in the courtyard, and began the nightly homework ritual. We did the same until I realized that none of the girls had their books open; they were all simply sitting, waiting for their tutors to arrive. We in turn would get a lesson on the underside of the Egyptian educational system.

Private tutors are not for slow and struggling students or for the elite students who want admission to a superior university. Tutors are necessary for the basic education of every student, regardless of learning ability. Tutoring isn't just limited to one or two difficult subjects but almost every subject the student takes, easily numbering six or seven. It seems the real education of students is not during the school day but in the evenings. I would even encounter parents checking out their children from school to begin private lessons at home.

The tutors arrived at about 7 p.m., mostly young women wearing typical "Christian clothing": pants, long-sleeve blouse, and hair pulled back in a ponytail. Whether Muslim or Christian, women always dress up and look neat and fashionable when they go out. The casual clothing that we often wear publicly in the United States would give neighbors much to gossip about.

One tutor sat nearby with two girls about eleven years old, who were hunched over their books, writing. The tutor would say something and the students would write. This went on for about half an hour, then it was time for the students to repeat back to the tutor word for word everything she had just said. To "help" a student's memory, the tutor carried a long switch and would not hesitate to whack an arm over a missed word. It wasn't a hard whack, but at an average of six whacks per minute—I timed her—how many do you need before you are so completely focused on the whacks that you can't recall anything that you just wrote down? The tutor, impatient with one girl's responses, began yelling and insulting, then reached out her hand to pull on the girl's ear. By this time the child had tears streaming down her red face.

I was not watching anything unique. This scenario was taking place in living rooms all over Egypt. While I considered it an abusive way to force rote memorization, Egyptians considered it effective education. The tutoring was like the teaching I witnessed during the day; there was no exchange of ideas, no questioning of students, no critical thinking, no analysis of information. Students simply wrote what the teacher said and regurgitated it word for word. The kids hated it and the parents lamented it, uttering this sarcastic proverb: "Egyptian children are some of the smartest in the world. Then they start school and it's all downhill from there." Yet no one knew how to reform the schools.

Supper wasn't served until 10 p.m., but Rebecca and Emily were already asleep. A new acquaintance telephoned to see how we were doing, and we chatted a bit until her doorbell rang. "I must go now. My children's math tutor has arrived. You know, I lived a while in the United States, and I know this way of learning is crazy. But what can we do?"

It was ten on a school night. Her girls were in second and fourth grades. They would have an hour of math tutoring ahead of them before they went to bed.

Č

Sister Maria had a lot of responsibilities raising twenty-four girls. She oversaw the cooking and household cleaning, supervised the girls' tutors and education, tended to health needs, greeted the numerous guests who'd drop by to visit, provided religious training, and maintained family relationships for those with families. But she also had the role of matchmaker, for the girls would stay in the orphanage until they were married, because it is impossible in Egyptian society for a single woman to set up her own household. The goal at the orphanage is not to raise girls to be independent; it is to raise women to fit into society as outstanding wives and mothers. Sister took great pride in the fact that "her girls" had exceptional skills.

One evening we were sitting in the courtyard while my girls did their homework and the other girls worked with their tutors. Dimania, a student in the College of Commerce, handed me a thirty-page study guide on economics and trade, all in English. I was mystified. She couldn't even ask me for a cup of tea in English. How in the world could she study this? It was all part of the memorization method of teaching, which was so perfected that students can be tested in a language they can't speak. They merely recognize the words.

Then Dimania popped her own question, in Arabic: "A man came to talk to Sister about a wife. I am twenty-two years old. But he is forty-seven. I think that is too much for me. What is your opinion?"

Wow, what a loaded question! My first thought was, Twenty-five years difference? Run! But I didn't think that would be very helpful to her. Besides, my Arabic was limited to grocery shopping, not marriage counseling. I took a long sip of my tea and looked at Dimania's dark eyes, waiting expectantly for some wise words. "Is he good? Is there love in your heart?" was the most I could manage.

The next day I had a chance to talk further about this with Sister. "How do you choose a girl when a groom comes looking for a bride?"

"I don't choose. God chooses. I talk to the groom and think about which girl can fit his personality, which girl can love him. I pray to God and God chooses the girl."

"What if the girl doesn't want to get married to him? Can she say no?"

Sister Maria was distracted by her cell phone, which was always in her hand. She answered the question a bit, then answered the phone. Another few words to me, then another call. Egyptians are constantly talking on cell phones, and no one would ever turn it off during a conversation. Interruptions aren't considered rude; they just roll with the dialogue.

"I tell the girl about the man and I wait for her decision. If she doesn't want to marry him, no problem. If she does, then I go visit this man's family and neighbors to find out about him, if he is a good person, a man of God who will be good to her."

The idea of a marriage arranged by someone else has always perplexed me. Coming from a place where boy and girl meet, fall in love, and may or may not have their family's blessing and approval, I had always assumed that in arranged marriages, a woman's parents forced her to marry a man for whom she didn't care. That is sometimes true, particularly for poor girls in villages without many options in life.

But Christine, a middle-class Christian, painted for me another picture that I think is more accurate. "My fiancé saw me at church and he likes me. He went to talk to my father, and my father asked me if I know this man. I say I have seen him but we have not spoken, but I would like to talk with him. My parents met with his parents, and they saw that they are good people, have a good reputation, are honest people, so we got engaged. I want a long engagement, maybe one year, so I can study him, and he can study me. Once we are married, we cannot divorce, so we should be sure this is a good thing."

That sounded like a reasonably well-thought-out plan. With the divorce rate in the United States as high as 50 percent, I wondered if there isn't something we can learn from Egyptian Christians.

A few days later, Dimiana told me she had refused the groom. Almost exactly a year from that time, we would attend her wedding to another young man. Closer in age, they seemed like a perfect match for each other. God would choose well.

☙

On another evening, while we were sitting in the courtyard, a priest walked in to visit. I had seen priests on the streets and was curious to know more about them, because they appeared quite different from the Catholic priests I knew. Priests in the Coptic Orthodox Church are called *abunas*, the Arabic word for "our father." This priest, Abuna Tomas, wore a poofy black hat and a full, bushy, gray beard as he strode into the courtyard dressed in a long, black cassock with a large cross swinging from his neck. The girls immediately gathered around and greeted him with a kiss on the hand. I just stuck mine out for a western-style handshake.

Abuna Tomas spoke English quite well and was in a talkative mood so I just jumped right in with my questions. "How does a person become a priest?"

"Priests are selected by the bishop," he said. "When we are growing up in the church, he sees we love the church and know its theology. We have good skills in leadership. When the bishop asked me to be a priest, it was a great honor. But I was not married." He chuckled and threw his hands up in the air. "All priests must be married. So the church found me a wife. But," Abuna Tomas stressed, leaning forward, "this cannot be any woman; it must be a special woman who wants to be married to a priest, because her life can be difficult. At my ordination the

A Coptic Orthodox priest.

bishop said I must serve the people and not myself. And he told my wife she can also be active in service, but she should not distract me from my work with the people and the church."

Priests must marry but monks, bishops, and nuns are celibate. This priest was also a veterinarian, a career he sacrificed for the priesthood.

"After we married, I left the next day for a forty-day retreat. I learned more about our church, how to celebrate the sacraments and the liturgy. And I had to grow a beard!" He laughed at my surprised look. I assumed the beard was to identify with the appearance of the early apostles.

"Afterward I was given a church parish. I am also the 'father confessor' for many people." At about the age of eight, each child is assigned a priest who hears his or her confessions periodically. This relationship can last for years, with the priest becoming both a spiritual guide and a family counselor by helping with employment, solving marital disputes, reconciling a rebellious teenager to the family, and of course dabbling in the ever-popular sport of matchmaking.

"Do you know about our church history?" Abuna Tomas asked.

"It's very interesting. We are one of the world's oldest Christian churches. Our history begins with St. Mark, one of the four gospel writers, during his visit to Egypt a dozen or so years after the death and resurrection of our Lord. St. Mark became our first martyr in AD 68 after Roman soldiers dragged him through the streets of Alexandria. This city is on the Mediterranean coast, and surely you will visit it as it is very beautiful." The priest paused to drink some tea brought by one of the girls.

Many Egyptians converted from paganism to Christianity and suffered tremendously during a period of persecution under Roman rule. To commemorate those who died for their faith, the Coptic Orthodox begin their calendar year in 284, calling it "The Calendar of Martyrs." The word *Coptic* originally meant "Egypt" but today refers only to Egyptians who are Christian. So Coptic Orthodox literally means Egyptian Orthodox, like Russian Orthodox and Greek Orthodox.

The majority of Egyptians were Christian until well after 641, when converts to a new religion, Islam, arrived at their borders. How most Egyptians converted over time from Christianity to Islam is a matter of dispute, depending on the religion of the person you talk to. A Christian account speaks of "conversion by the sword, where people's tongues were cut out for speaking the Coptic language and the streets ran thick with the blood of martyrs." This explanation is widely held and fits very well with the Coptic Orthodox Church's history of persecution. Muslims relate that the Christian church was suffering from corruption and political infighting, particularly regarding heretics, and that many welcomed the Arabs and the new religion. I was curious about the current state of affairs between Muslims and Christians and asked the priest about that.

"Officially, Muslims represent 90 percent of the population in Egypt, while Christians make up the other 10 percent. Some Christians are also Catholic or Protestant." He shook his head and set his tea back down, "There are a few good Muslims, and we know we must love them all, but many Muslims just wish we weren't here."

His fingers scratched through his bushy beard. "Our biggest problem is that we cannot build churches like we want to. Not just build them, we can't even get them renovated, and many are very old and in need of repairs. We must get permission from various government officials, including state security and, not exaggerating, the president's own stamp of approval." It was an old law dating from the 1800s that required a stack of paperwork. Proposals often entered bureaucratic limbo, shelved in some official's files, where the application could languish for years.

"I think if you will stay here for three years then you will see how we suffer."

Another visitor, who had been quietly listening to our conversation, piped in. "You can't trust them. Muslims, I mean. We know they want to convert all of us. It's one reason Sister won't let the girls go out by themselves. We hear too many stories of girls being kidnapped and forcibly converted to Islam and these girls"—she waved a hand toward the girls—"they are without families and are very vulnerable to that."

That sounded like a story worth pursuing, but Sister Maria interrupted. "I am friends with many Muslims because I love all of humanity, and God created us all and wants us to all live together and love each other." She pulled her habit down over her face, smoothed out her black hair streaked with gray, and pulled it back up again. "Do you know Rihaan? She teaches Arabic at St. Anthony's. I was the director at that school before coming to the girls home. Anyway, we used to walk down the street together—me in my nun's clothes and she in her *higab* (a loose, long-sleeve, ankle-length coat-like dress that goes over regular clothes), and people would say as we passed '*Watani wahda*.' Do you know what that means?"

I shook my head.

"It means one nation—the crescent moon and the cross, the symbols of Egypt's two religions."

"*BES! BES!* [STOP! STOP!]" Emily's screams interrupted our conversation. I ran to where the sound was coming from and found her buried under a pile of girls, arms flinging about as everyone tried to get a piece of her. I shoved girls aside and pulled Emily out. Her face was red and streaming with tears. She was screaming and having a complete meltdown.

"I hate it. And I hate all these girls. I just want to go home." And she didn't mean the home in the school apartment, but home to her friends in Georgia, who knew how to play with her and, more important, knew when to leave her alone. Sister came over and lovingly wrapped Emily in her arms, shooing the other girls away.

Lying in bed that night, I wondered if it had been a mistake to come to Egypt, giving up the good life we had. Could I have misjudged our ability to be flexible, resilient, and adventurous? Was I expecting too much of my children? There was no doubt that we were overwhelmed by the lack of privacy, the constant attention, the inability to communicate, and now the separation from Brad and Nicholas. We had stretched ourselves more than I thought possible and were simply yearning for a normal, boring, humdrum day. But that day was a long time in coming.

℘

At last! The painting of the school apartment had been completed, at least by Egyptian standards. The walls were freshly painted, but the floors were covered with drips of plaster, cement dust, and paint splotches. I surveyed the damage: fourteen windows were cracked or broken; our good cooking pot had been used to mix paint in; the ceiling fan had been reinstalled with the blades upside down. Brad regretted not bringing his toolbox to Egypt. Sister Maria had graciously thought to send four girls with me to help clean and that, along with duct tape, took care of the clean-up work.

Our friendship with the girls in the orphanage continued. Sister was true to her word that "this is your home." But it would take a while before we felt that way. Two of my assumptions about the kids were proving to be wrong: they weren't automatically bonding with foreign children, and they weren't effortlessly picking up the new language.

However, I did hope we were moving beyond "It's a Hard Knock Life" and entering "The Sun Will Come Out Tomorrow." Already the fresh, blue paint was lifting my spirits as we moved back into the apartment.

5

Blessings on Your Hands

"Ahlan wa sahlan! Itfadalu! Welcome! Come in, come in!"

Girgis, one of Brad's adult English students, swung open the door and warmly welcomed us to his apartment one Thursday evening. We were ushered into an immaculate living room decked out with gold and red velvet, Louis XIV-style furniture. In the center was a coffee table with a ceramic bowl filled with chocolates. There were no newspapers or magazines in sight. I wondered where the family relaxed and watched TV, as they clearly never "lived" in this room. Rather, it was the reception room, which all Egyptian homes, no matter how tiny, have to greet guests.

Girgis, in his early forties, had a head full of gray hair and an ever-ready smile. "Would you like a drink?" he asked. We were surprised, because alcohol is extremely limited in this Muslim-majority country. "I bought this whiskey in Cairo."

I declined, but Brad didn't get off so easily. Girgis had a good knowledge of English, so the conversation flowed. Settling down on the sofa, he turned to Brad and asked all the standard questions. "How are you and the kids? How are you liking Beni Suef? How is your teaching job?"

As the kids and I listened, I surveyed the wall hangings. Four pictures of bishops in the Coptic Orthodox Church decorated the wall. There was another picture with the Virgin Mary—blue eyes, white skin, and light brown hair—and a halo on her head lit up by tiny, colored lights. The infant Jesus, lying in her arms, mechanically moved back and forth. My eyes passed from a long, green, plastic plant trailing down the wall and a clock that didn't work to the door we had just passed through. On the back was a full-length mirror with a tall picture of the current Orthodox pope, Baba Shenouda, etched on it in red ink. It seemed both Christian and Muslim

Egyptians shared a love of gaudy and garish religious art and, while I did not share their sense of taste, their faith and devotion was impressive and humbling.

Girgis's wife, Noura, entered the room with a dishtowel in her hand. Apologizing for keeping us waiting, she exchanged handshakes with Brad and Nicholas and kissed the girls and me.

Their two boys, George, fifteen, and Jonathan, nine, joined us, and we all squeezed around a dining-room table loaded with food. We stood and faced east toward Jerusalem "because when Christ comes again, it will be in Jerusalem" and said the Our Father in low, mumbled tones.

Then we sat down and survey the feast spread before us: fried chicken, meat in a tomato sauce, macaroni with ground beef, rice with liver and almonds, vegetables cooked in tomato sauce, french fries, bread, and four different kinds of salad. Noura must have been exhausted from it all, but simply preparing one main dish would have not met her standards of hospitality. Family name and reputation were at stake, and the family's generosity was measured by the quantity and variety of dishes.

"*Daiman*," I said, "May your table always be full."

Weekends in Egypt are short. People work and kids go to school six days a week, leaving only Thursday night and Friday as a weekend. We had suggested visiting on Friday but that brought other complications for our Christian friends.

"Orthodox Christians in Egypt fast for 210 days of the year," Girgis explained. "Before all the religious holidays, and every Wednesday and Friday. What does this mean?" He ticked off a list on his fingers. "No meat, no eggs, no milk, no cheese, no chicken. Nothing can come from animals. And in the fifty-five-day fast before Easter, not even fish." From the tone of his voice, I could tell that, while fasting was a sacrifice, it was also a spiritual discipline of which he was proud.

In the center of the table was a bottle of water and two glasses. We came to learn that this is standard practice in all homes and restaurants. No matter how many people are seated around the table, there are only two glasses. One of my very thirsty kids shot me a glaring look.

"You can drink from your water bottle if you want," I said under my breath.

This is only one of the dilemmas we encountered as a foreign family used to a higher standard of hygiene. Do we whip out our water bottles, drink from them, and insult our hosts? Do we drink from the community cup, taking in the germs of everyone who has drunk before us? Do we not drink anything and suffer thirst through the meal?

For us, it was an issue of hygiene. For Egyptians, it was an issue of hospitality—they had failed us if we refused to drink what they offered.

After encountering this situation a few times, we had a family discussion but left the decision to what each individual felt comfortable doing. More often than not, we drank from the common cup, sacrificing hygiene to the sacred god of hospitality. Many things, from litter to violence, greatly challenged us during our three-year term.

As Girgis loaded my plate, I noticed a small cross tattooed on his wrist. Just as many western Christians wear crosses as jewelry, the tattooed cross is the standard symbol of Christianity for Egyptians. Indeed, many store clerks, upon hearing my answer "Christian" to their question about my religious identity, rolled up their shirtsleeve and proudly displayed their proof. After Girgis had served everyone, I asked him how old he was when he had his cross made.

"I was three and we were at a *moulid*, a festival honoring a saint," he said. "My father wanted to hold me, but I wanted to prove I was a big boy. So I stood, and the tattoo man held the whirring machine on my arm. I am sure I cried, but after a few minutes it's over and the pain goes away."

We later saw this in action ourselves at a moulid honoring the Virgin Mary. We heard the loud whirring of the tattoo machine, the scared and screaming children, and proud parents and relatives all looking on and smiling at the big event in the young Christian's life. While it seemed to us painful and even traumatic for a young child, Christians were very proud of this.

"Do you want to have a cross made while you are in Egypt?" Noura asked me while serving Brad another generous helping of meat. I had not really thought about it before. "No, it really isn't our custom in the United States," I said, thinking about the current American fads of tattooing and body piercing.

"You don't do this in the United States because everybody is Christian there. But here we want to show we are different from the Muslims," replied Noura.

This was a good time to correct a common misperception. "Actually, not everyone in the United States is Christian," I said. "There are lots of different religions, and some people with no religion. In fact, among Christians, there are many different groups with different beliefs. And many secular Christians."

This proved a bit much to digest for our hosts, who had grown up in a world divided into two groups, Muslims and Christians. Furthermore it is hard for Coptic Orthodox, who often have a sense of superiority about their religion, to accept the validity of Protestant faiths. Whenever I would attend a local Protestant church in Beni Suef, I would get disapproving looks and comments from the Orthodox, as though I were somehow betraying "the one true church." But having grown up Catholic in the United States, the idea of religious superiority was, unfortunately, familiar to me; it's not at all unique to Egyptian Christians.

Remembering the advice from one of our cultural guidebooks to always leave some food on one's plate, Brad put his fork down in a symbolic gesture that he was finished. It was also Girgis's signal to be a generous host and ply his guests with food, regardless of their protests. He squeezed into the chair next to Brad, put one arm around his shoulders, and picked up a piece of fried chicken with his other hand, poised to feed Brad. Brad put his hands up in protest, and the battle between host and guest was on. Girgis tried to convince Brad to take one more bite as Brad tried to convince Girgis that he absolutely could not. It was a battle we could never win. Brad reluctantly tore off a small bit and put it in his mouth.

The kids left the table to play games on the computer while Noura sent us to the living room. She cleared the table and prepared the tea and dessert. I no longer bothered offering to help clear the table; it would result in another verbal tussle and misunderstanding. While I considered it a helpful and friendly gesture, my host would feel insulted that a guest must "work" in her home.

As we sat in the living room, I thought about the differences between American and Egyptian hospitality. Egyptians say, "My house is your house" and Americans say, "Make yourself at home." The words may sound similar, but we learned there are fine distinctions between the two. For Egyptians, hosting does not mean acceding to your guest's wishes, but fulfilling the role of a good host, regardless of the guest's desires. In turn, being a guest doesn't mean doing what you want; it often means having to do what pleases the hosts. There were times when I had to sit in the stiff, formal guest chair rather than the comfortable cushion on the floor, which I preferred; I had to accept a soft drink when I preferred water; I had to accept a ride in someone's car rather than walk and do errands along the way. Being a guest could become tiring and burdensome. Over time, this diminished with some families, and I was always delighted to "graduate" from the stiff, formal living room, symbolizing "guest status," to the comfortable TV room, symbolizing "family status."

"Do you want a cigarette?" Girgis, like many Egyptian men, smoked frequently. But as nonsmokers, we politely declined his offer.

"Mr. Brad, where will you vacation this summer?"

"We are hoping to go to Israel, to see Jerusalem," Brad responded. Girgis's eyes lit up. We knew it is the dream of every Egyptian Christian to make a pilgrimage to the Holy Land. But it wasn't the lack of money that kept them from going.

"Our pope—you see him on the back of our door?" he asked, gesturing to the image on the mirror. "He has forbidden us to go. It is a way for us to give our support to the Palestinians. The Church wants Israel to settle this problem with the Palestinians. We fought several wars with Israel, the last one in 1973. And even though we signed a peace treaty, there is not much cooperation between us."

Girgis was referring to the Camp David peace accords signed in 1978 by U.S. President Jimmy Carter, Israeli Prime Minister Menachem Begin, and Egyptian President Anwar Sadat. Widely acclaimed in the west as a victory for peace and stability, the treaty was greatly criticized in the Middle East. Egypt was shunned by the Arab world and Sadat, a prophet without honor in his own homeland, was assassinated by one of his own army officers in 1981.

Noura brought in a tray of hot tea and a huge platter of fresh fruit. She added, "When Christian pilgrims return to Egypt from Israel, they might be interrogated by our security police. Our pope wants to avoid conflicts with the government, so he forbids us to go."

"And do Christians here listen to the pope?" Brad asked.

"Of course we do. He is our father and we are his children. He knows what is best for us, so we agree with him." I stirred sugar in my tea and tried to imagine the many religious leaders in the United States who would love to have such obedience from an unquestioning flock. But all faiths have dissenters. We had heard that some Christians who traveled to Jerusalem were excommunicated, and we knew of one couple that went but did not have any conflicts with the government or the pope.

"But listen, we are not trying to visit Israel. We are hoping to emigrate to America, to Canada. Even Australia; it's not so far from here. We have put in for the lottery, but so far, we are not successful." Girgis took a sip of his tea and shrugged. "*Rabina yeraktib.* [God will make a way.]"

For those without family connections, the immigration lottery is the main way to enter the United States. Every year fifty thousand names are drawn worldwide, and those who meet the strict qualifications are issued visas. Emigrating to the west is the dream of many Egyptians, and people looked to us for advice and assistance to make the dream come true. Some did not understand the process and naïvely hoped we could just whip a visa out of our back pocket.

Our response was actually quite simple and universally understood: "You know, after September 11, it's hard for anyone to get a visa. Especially from the Middle East." They would often complete the sentence themselves, shaking their heads at the injustice of it all.

"What attracts you about the United States?" Brad asked.

Noura passed out tangerines to the kids as she answered. "We want a better future for our kids. A better education for them. There are no jobs in Egypt. What can they do when they finish college?"

Such hardships are common. Unemployment is high, especially among college graduates. All young men aspire to good jobs so they can buy an apartment, marry, and raise a family. But the issue is not just economic, but social too, because if the men are not employed, the women cannot marry. With no jobs, many young men spend all day hanging out at the numerous *ahwas* (coffee shops), playing backgammon and smoking *shesha* (an Arabian water pipe for smoking tobacco). It was a depressing sight, highlighting that Beni Suef had nothing else to offer their aimless and unemployed youth.

"But there is another reason we want to leave Egypt," Noura continued. "We are persecuted because we are Christians. The Muslims all hate us and wish us to leave." All conversations with Egyptian Christians eventually led to the well-worn path of persecution. It was an awkward moment for me; Christians assumed that because I am a fellow Christian, I automatically agreed with them. We had originally seen ourselves as a bridge between western Christians and Muslims and were unprepared, perhaps naïvely, to hear the animosity of local Christians toward their fellow citizens.

"I don't know, Noura," I said. "The Muslims I know are all friendly and helpful. They invite me to their houses, and our kids play together. Many have told me they respect my faith, and we often talk about God and what we believe."

"Of course, they say that to you!" Noura responded. "You are a Christian and a guest here. Muslims don't tell these bad things directly to Christians, but we know it's true. I know one Christian girl that tried to get a job and she couldn't. Why? They told her it was because she was Christian. Muslims don't want Christians to work with them."

I set my tea down. A plate with a huge piece of cake on it distracted me as I contemplated what to say next. "Well, if it happened that way, then it's wrong. Many Muslims tell me they can't get jobs either. It is a bad economy for everyone. They say you have to know someone or have connections."

"True, but it is worse for us."

"Noura, didn't you tell me once that at your science lab you are the only Christian and that you all work together well?"

She smiled. "Oh, you remember that? We do work together good, but I know they would prefer all Muslims."

Prefer all Muslims. We had heard that, or a similar phrase— *prefer everyone to be Muslim*—from several people, and it was time to find out more about conversions. "Noura, why do you think a Christian would change his religion to Islam?"

Girgis, pouring himself another drink, answered instead. "We have poor times now and some people do not have money. If they change their religion, maybe they will get a better job and they will get money. And the person who helps them change their religion gets a big prize, maybe five thousand Egyptian pounds." In 2003, that was about 830 dollars, a huge amount considering that the average salary was forty dollars a month. "Many poor people want to convert someone to Islam so they can get money. This money comes from the Gulf countries—Saudi Arabia, Kuwait, Bahrain."

"Is it mostly men who convert?" I asked.

"No. Mostly women. They are not good women, and fall in love with someone who is Muslim. Maybe they are unhappy in their marriage and, as you know, we do not have divorce in the Orthodox Church." For Christians to divorce, special permission is required of the Orthodox pope and is usually granted only in cases of adultery. If divorce is granted, neither party is allowed to remarry.

"Do you think it is possible that Christians convert to Islam because they like something about that religion?"

"No!" they both answered quickly and decisively. "They are weak in their faith, and they are desperate for money and easily persuaded that their life will be better. Sometimes a whole family will convert because they have no money." That was the typical answer I got from Christians. Of course, there was a much different answer when I posed the same question to Muslims.

Our conversation and our time in the girl's orphanage highlighted an important fact for me. We have as much to learn about the Coptic faith as we do about Islam. Being a Christian in the United States and being one in the Middle East are vastly different realities, despite many things in common.

Fortunately kids are always a good excuse for having to leave and, after four hours, it was culturally acceptable to make our exit. Nevertheless it took another half-hour to convince our hosts.

"*Tislam eideeki* [Blessings on your hands]," I told Noura as we kiss goodbye.

"*Sharraftunna* [You have honored us by your presence]," she responded.

We visited with Noura and Girgis frequently during our first year and spent many evenings together at outdoor clubs along the Nile. But our frequent contact diminished dramatically after George, their older son, started high school. They were facing none of the things American parents encounter when their kids enter high school; George was not into sports or hanging out with friends or a girlfriend. He had begun a strict study regime of private lessons for exams that would take place a year later. All of the family's time, energy, and money was consumed on private lessons. This is

Neighborhood vendor selling roasted sweet potatoes.

the reality for every Egyptian family with high-school students. It's just one part of an educational system that makes many parents, like Noura and Girgis, seek opportunities abroad.

We left Girgis and Noura's bright, clean apartment and stepped into a dark, dirty stairwell. A plastic bag thrown from a balcony floated in the breeze until it became tangled in one of the few trees along the street. People felt no sense of ownership or responsibility for the area just outside their tiny properties and thus had no problem littering it.

We walked home past carpenters building furniture and tailors sewing curtains. Their workshops were on the sidewalks, forcing pedestrians into the street with the car and animal traffic. A young man hobbled in front of us on two uneven legs, but his disabled status didn't stop a taxi from nearly knocking him over. A young boy paraded a camel down the main street and tied it in front of a butcher shop, which advertised the coming meat special.

"*Tailu.* [Come.]" Our elderly neighbor raised her wrinkled hand. That week I had already passed up two of her invitations for tea; it would be rude and unneighborly of me to refuse again.

"Come and greet her," I said to Brad and the kids, who were greatly unenthused about my proposal, "then you can go on home while I visit with her a bit."

Greetings are an important part of Egyptian life, and I wanted my kids to adopt this custom. Several times I had hurried past the woman, and others, like a typical "in a rush" American. But gradually I shifted to Egyptian thinking, in which stopping to exchange pleasantries is much more valued than being on time.

Tayta (Grandmother) offered me a wooden chair with chicken dirt encrusted on it. But first she picked up a piece of newspaper thrown at the curb and laid it over the chair. She shuffled into her little, mud-brick house to put water on the one-burner gas stove that rested on the concrete floor. She had raised seven children in that house, and they now all live with their own families, except her youngest son, the one we previously saw sleeping on the roof with his family. Though she was in her seventies, Tayta did not spend time at a senior-citizens program, for no such thing existed. She made a valuable contribution to her family by sitting in a chair all day to make sure none of their sheep, goats, ducks, or chickens wandered out into the busy street. Like many others in Beni Suef, Tayta's is a farming family. But without land, they raised their animals on sidewalks and rooftops.

She returned and set the tea tray on a wooden crate. Our conversation was limited. Tayta, who had never set foot in a school, didn't have many teeth, and it was difficult to understand her. But her language, like everyone else's, was peppered with words referring to God.

"How are you today, Tayta?" I ask.

"*Ilhamdulilah.* [Praise be to God.]"

"How are your children?"

"Ilhamdulilah."

"How is your husband?"

"Ilhamdulilah."

"The weather is nice today."

"Not so hot. Ilhamdulilah."

For beginning Arabic learners, this one word can get you through a whole conversation! Her ten-year-old grandson came skipping up to greet me with a ball in one hand; he was holding his

The author and Tayta with farm animals raised on the sidewalk.

pants up with the other. He had Down syndrome and a permanent grin plastered on his round little face. While he didn't go to school—"he can't learn anything," his mother said—he played and helped the family sell their animals. When Christmas came, he would bound up the 105 steps to our apartment with a large bunch of bananas wrapped in newspaper. Breathlessly he'd call out, "For your feast!" It would surprise us to have so many Muslims greet us on the Christmas holiday and their generosity and thoughtfulness was touching.

We drank our tea, and I tried to move our conversation to a higher level.

"Tayta," I said, waving my hand toward the alleyway neighborhood of poor houses. "Do both Muslims and Christians live here, or just Muslims?"

Tayta knit her brow, pursed her lips together, and shook her saggy cheeks, "Muslims, Christians, we all live here."

"Well, wouldn't that make problems sometimes?"

She picked up her stick and scooted some wandering chicks back to the fold before answering. "All is quiet here, all is good. We are poor and simple people, but God is with us. Ilhamdulilah."

As time went on, I would find that her comments were the standard reply by both Muslims and Christians who were poor and lower class. It seemed that complaints I heard about Muslims came from middle-class Christians, who had a lot more invested in education and were seeking better opportunities in life. But the folks just struggling to earn bread for the day were less likely to perceive inequality and were not expecting much out of life.

Ç

One evening I was sitting outside on the breezeway of our apartment, watching the sunset. The big ball of sun, once a god worshipped by ancient Egyptians, was leaving for the day to light up another part of the world. As the last rays slipped over the horizon, one beam stretched over to the plain, white dome of the nearby Orthodox Cathedral, topped with its three-dimensional cross. The same ray continued over to the bright green dome of a nearby mosque topped with a crescent moon, one of Islam's symbols. As these two faith symbols shared a single ray of sunlight, one could easily romanticize metaphors of harmony and peace.

The goodwill and commonality between most Muslims and Christians dominated my impressions during our first three months in Egypt. But to get a true picture, I had to learn the right questions to ask. As I better understood the language and culture, it became clear that the relationship between the two faiths was more complex.

Christians frequently said Muslims persecuted them. In the west, *persecution* conjures up images of vicious mobs chasing and slaughtering Christians in the street. We often imagine massive numbers of Christians losing their jobs and livelihoods, and we envision ghettoized Christians living in cramped, crumbling housing. But many of the stories I heard were not about government policy to drive Christians out of Egypt. Rather they recounted acts of discrimination between individuals. The issue had been politicized because Coptic Christians who emigrated to the west often exaggerated their persecution in order to encourage western governments like the United States to pressure the Egyptian government into reform.

Christians proudly preserve their history of persecution and suffering. The stories of suffering saints were told weekly in Friday school. Videos showing the various ways that martyrs were killed—from burnings at the stake to having the hairs of their beards plucked out one by one—were regularly featured at church gatherings. Many people collect small cards depicting martyrs to line their mirrors and desks.

When our Arabic teacher gave birth to her son, she named him Marteer.

"Martyr?" I asked. "Oh gosh, I hope that doesn't happen to him!"

"Why not? It would be a great blessing!" she replied happily. Having grown up on this steady diet of the glories of martyrdom, Egyptian Christians today often perceive life's difficulties through the same lens. They have always suffered because of their faith, so religion, not social problems, must be the explanation for any current suffering. But when social and economic problems take on this religious tone, Christians find strength in their martyrdom history.

I realize this issue of persecution is a place where commonality with my fellow Christians ends. I am a foreigner and do not share the language and history of the Egyptian Christians. I cannot readily understand how they feel, because their persecution is not something I see or experience. But it was obvious they felt the persecution and discrimination deeply.

I had naïvely entertained notions of inviting Muslim and Christian friends over for dinner and dialoging about our faiths, all under the great umbrella of advancing peace in the Middle East. It didn't take me long to realize that the Muslims and Christians in Egypt had lived together for thirteen hundred years and certainly didn't need any help from me. In spite of all the negativity I heard from Christians, I found many positive things about the way Muslims and Christians live that could serve as a model for two other groups trying to forge a commonality—whites and African-Americans in the United States.

In Beni Suef, as in much of Egypt, Christians and Muslims lived side by side, in the same neighborhoods, in the same apartment buildings. There was not a "Christian area" or a "Muslim area." Children attended school together and played together on the same playground. Both groups spoke Arabic, and both used the same words for God—*Allah* or *Rabb* (Lord). Most people in the west tend to associate Arabic only with Islam, but it is also the language for Christians. Christians and Muslims read the same newspapers, watched the same soap operas on TV, ate the same foods, listened to the same music, and rooted for the same sports teams. We attended many Christian weddings and often saw Muslim women in headscarves who obviously were comfortable in a Christian house of worship. We attended funerals where friends and neighbors of both faiths came to offer their condolences.

Certainly there were limits and taboos between Christians and Muslims. Christians complained about job discrimination; the difficulties in receiving government permits to build or renovate churches; and the conversion of Christians to Islam, whether coerced or voluntarily. Muslim complaints? Many resent the "outside agitators"—Coptic Christians who've emigrated to the west and have lobbied the U.S. Congress and held conferences on the status of Christians in Egypt.

Many Muslims fervently stated, "All is well in Egypt between Muslims and Christians." This is not a surprising statement; Muslims are in the majority, and from their perspective, everything looks fine. Many are unaware of Christian frustrations because of an unspoken rule that the two groups do not discuss religion together. This taboo has kept people who live cheek to cheek from communicating on the topics that matter most in their lives, but it has also helped keep a certain peace and allowed the groups to share public spaces.

While we knew we could never completely identify with the Coptic faith, we discovered a role in Christian/Muslim relations—the role of the outsider. As foreigners, we were not tied to relating solely to one group. We were able to share with one group what we observed and learned from the other. "You know, Muslims have told me . . ." or "Many Christians think this is what happened. . . ."

While some people appreciate new insights, most aren't interested in anything that contradicts their beliefs. At the least, we had some enjoyable conversations and learned a great deal.

6

May Your Ramadan Be Generous

"*Ramadan kareem!*"

It was Mohammad, our ten-year-old neighbor who has Down syndrome, carrying a large tray full of different dishes, the main course being duck. Not just any duck but one of his family's own, raised on the sidewalk next to the school. We were touched by their generous gift, and in the spirit of *Ramadan kareem*—may your Ramadan be generous—we shared the meal with our guard and the gatekeeper.

It was 5 p.m. The sun had just set, and a cannon boomed loudly, signaling that Muslims could end their daily fast. The streets were completely empty, a sight we never thought we would see in Egypt. Evening prayers began, and then the fast was broken with lots of food, family, and friends.

Sitting on the benches in the dusty courtyard, licking our duck-sticky fingers, we talked about the differences we had noticed around us during Ramadan. One that surprised us was the change in schedule. For example, school began a half-hour later and ended a half-hour earlier, not that anyone warned us about it. This change was because by late afternoon, without any food or water, everyone is tired and grumpy and in need of a nap. At least the fathers and children nap; the women are in the kitchen preparing *iftar*, the meal that breaks the fast. Brad's English classes shifted to begin later to accommodate their break-fasting schedule.

The disciplinary aspects of Ramadan involve abstaining from food, drink, and other worldly pleasures—like cigarettes—from sunrise to sunset. Ramadan also involves more praying and Qur'anic reciting.

The kids witnessed first hand what this involved. "Well, my math teacher didn't have any makeup on today," Emily said. "And some girls in my class had on headscarves, even though they don't usually wear them. Some kids are even fasting, can you believe?" She was amazed that her fellow third-graders could do that. Most kids don't begin fasting until they are about twelve, but it usually depends on the religiosity of the family and the stamina of the kids.

"After playing soccer today," Nicholas reported, "when we were all hot and thirsty, some boys would just swish water around in their mouths and spit it out! Man, I don't see how they could do that. I was almost dying."

Rebecca noted that Ramadan isn't just about sacrifices, it's also a time of celebration. "The streets look like Christmas with all the bright lights and lanterns. And did you see all the big, colorful tents set up on the street? We should go see what's happening in them." After breaking the fast, the streets filled with people greeting friends, shopping, watching musical programs in the tents, and eating again. Some folks stayed home to watch the special TV programs called "Ramadan Soaps."

Islam means submission, and a Muslim is therefore one who submits to the laws and requirements of Islam. Fasting during Ramadan is one of the five requirements or "pillars." Ramadan is the name of the ninth month of the Islamic lunar calendar. Muslims believe that in this month the archangel Gabriel revealed the words of God to an illiterate businessman named Muhammad in a desert cave in Mecca, the heartland of Arabia. Years after Muhammad's death, these revelations were compiled into the Qur'an, which means "recite." The Qur'an is meant to be chanted aloud. It is viewed as a miracle because it marked the first time God was revealed to Arabs in a language they could understand. Because of that, according to Islamic scholars, the Qur'an must be read in Arabic; it loses flavor when translated into another language.

When I was writing this chapter and had the Qur'an open as a reference, a Muslim friend dropped by. I quickly removed a Post-it note stuck to the cover, and remarked, "I think this is considered an insult to the Qur'an."

My friend replied, "Yes, but that isn't really the Qur'an. It is written in English, so it is an interpretation. If you really want to read the Qur'an, you must learn Arabic." And he didn't mean the

Arabic I was learning and using in everyday conversation.

In a country like Egypt, where the illiteracy rate is 50 percent, the limitations of reading and understanding the Qur'an are obvious. Even for those who are educated, reading the Qur'an is a great challenge because the classical Arabic of the Qur'an is not the Arabic spoken by Egyptians or any other Arab group. When we told Egyptians that we wanted to learn Arabic, often the first question was, "Which Arabic?" Classical Arabic is taught in schools and is the language of the newspapers and news programs. Then there are the local dialects, but these are not written languages. Of course, we wanted to learn the local dialect so we could attend to our everyday errands.

I once read that "as Christ is to Christians, the Qur'an is to Muslims," meaning that Christians believe God reveals himself through Jesus, while Muslims believe God reveals himself through the Qur'an. The Qur'an is considered so holy and so revered that Muslims take care not to throw away any paper that has Qur'anic quotes on it. I once saw a mother reprimand her child for twisting a calendar that had Qur'anic verses written on it. "That's the Qur'an!" she admonished her child; it was not considered merely a calendar. They also do not place anything on top of the Qur'an and are careful about where it is placed. Emily would pick up this custom and chastise us for leaving our Bible on the floor or for putting another book on top of it. I was grateful for this lesson from Muslims reminding us that our holy books should not be treated casually but with respect.

Christians have a much different approach to the Bible. For us, it is a user-friendly manual. We highlight phrases with markers, scribble in the margins, insert bookmarks and photos, and jot down notes about a passage that is significant to us. We are proud that our Bibles look used and worn; it indicates the importance of it in our lives. This contrasts so greatly with how Muslims treat the Qur'an that I feared most would misinterpret our scribbling and highlighting as disrespectful.

Another difference between Muslims and Christians in their views of scripture can be seen in their respective approaches to new converts. When someone converts to Islam, one of the first things they do is enroll in Arabic classes so they can learn the language and read the Qur'an. This holds true no matter where in the world the convert lives. In contrast, when people convert to Christianity, they begin reading the Bible in their own language. Christians believe that the best way to experience God and the faith is to do so in our own language. Muslims believe that the best way to experience God is in the language in which he "sent down" the Qur'an—Arabic.

۲

Sometime later Tayta, the grandmother next door, invited us to her daughter's house for yet another Ramadan meal. I had wanted to proceed slowly with this family because I was a little dubious of their intentions. They were friendly and generous, but I was the "rich foreigner"—all foreigners are rich in Egyptian eyes—and they had asked me previously for money. They never repaid the amount, equivalent to eight dollars, that I loaned them when Tayta was in the hospital. I had rationalized that it was in exchange for the Ramadan duck dinner. But when they asked for money yet again, I suggested they cook me a meal instead, and I would pay them for it. I thought this was a creative solution, but the meal was a big disappointment. Realizing that I did not want to be viewed as their personal bank, I summoned up the courage to reply with a wimpy no to the next request. Later on, when asked to loan money, I learned from Egyptian women to say, "I'll ask my husband," and that ends the conversation sharply.

"Here's the microbus," Nicholas shouted as the vehicle swerved in our direction and screeched to a sudden stop. We hopped on to go to Tayta's daughter's house. *Microbus* seemed like such a fancy word for what they really were—beat-up, white minivans, jammed with seats and crammed with more people than could safely fit. Children sat on mothers' laps; others stood hunched over the narrow aisle, while four men stood in the open doorway, one of whom was a barker who called out the destination and yelled for more passengers to climb in. The driver was in front with other passengers; a few times we even saw a man wedged between the driver and his door in what looked like no space at all!

There were only two types of music played on a microbus—Qur'anic chanting or Arab pop. And there was only one volume—earsplitting. Microbuses raced down the street at frightening speeds, while the driver, with one hand on the wheel and the other holding a cigarette or a glass of hot tea, continuously blared his horn. We bounced up and down on the seats, swerving left and right as if in beat to the blaring music. It was a cheap form of transportation at a few pennies per person, entertainment included.

The microbus rambled over the Nile, the longest river in the world. The blue water is a lovely contrast to the green, fertile fields that sharply end where the brown desert begins. Egypt is 97 percent desert, so water is to Egyptians what oil is to many Americans—a precious commodity needed for daily survival. But both nations are equally lacking when it comes to conservation. We were mystified to find a water park on the outskirts of Cairo, where the view from the high slide is the surrounding desert.

The fruits of the Nile have provided life to countless Egyptian pharaohs and many foreign invaders, beginning with the Greek general Alexander the Great in 332 BC. He was followed by the Romans, Arabs, Ottoman Turks, French, and, never to miss a chance to colonize, the British. Egypt and the Nile have also been the backdrop for much biblical history: a pharaoh who imprisoned Joseph then made him co-ruler; the lawgiver Moses, who floated down the river in a wicker basket; Mary, Joseph, and Jesus, who trod on the donkey paths along the riverbank while escaping King Herod.

Tayta's daughter lived on the other side of the Nile in an area simply called The City. To handle the burgeoning population of Beni Suef, the government had developed this area out of the desert. With seventy-four million people living in Egypt on only 3 percent of arable land, the Nile looks as though God tossed it out as a device to help cities and villages cling to life.

We found out what "cramped quarters" really means one day when Brad took a walk around the perimeter of Beni Suef, a city of nearly a quarter-million people. It took only one hour. It takes longer to walk around my mother's neighborhood in the United States, which houses maybe a thousand people. The lack of living space here is a formidable problem, evident in the lack of infrastructure, housing, schools, and employment.

Reclamation—taming the desert to make it livable—is the preferred solution to overcrowding, and the City is a typical example of it. The skyline is dotted with one huge, boxy, concrete apartment block after another, a few tree seedlings, a few stores, and a few people. Sand is the one thing in abundance, leaving fine grit on everything and everybody. The government offers special mortgage plans to entice people to settle there, and the family we were visiting had just moved in.

"Welcome! Come in! You light up our house!" About seven people greeted us at the door as we exchanged handshakes and kisses. The father, dressed in a galabaya, greeted me by putting his hand over his heart, a gesture of welcome some men make when they are uncomfortable shaking a woman's hand. Centered on his forehead is a *zabeeb*, which literally means "raisin." A sign of piety, men develop the rough bruise, or "raisin," from rubbing their foreheads on their prayer mats while praying. The father sat back down and picked up his red, wooden beads. Some Muslims, particularly men, use the beads to meditate on the ninety-nine names of God found in the Qur'an, names such as the Forgiver, the Knower, and the Bestower of Daily Bread.

Several long, wooden benches with cushions lined the wall; we all squeezed in and accepted the drinks offered to us. We spoke the usual round of pleasantries, offered bags of fruit, and then the hard questions came. Questions that Americans would consider rude, or at least none of anyone's business, are all fair game in Egypt.

"How much money do you make?" demanded Tayta's daughter. I pretended not to understand so as to avoid an answer; to help my understanding, they all started yelling the question at me.

"We don't get money from St. Anthony's School but from a church in America." My tactful reply failed to satisfy.

"How much?"

"It's enough, ilhamdulilah."

"Why is his skin so dark?" demanded another family member pointing at Nicholas. I'd had this question posed to me by many strangers in stores or on the streets. My answers to them never seemed adequate. In the United States, a stranger looking at our family would assume either that I had been married before or that Nicholas was adopted. But these are unknown concepts in Egypt.

When we were still living in Georgia, an Islamic scholar, who is Muslim and has an adopted son, told me that Muslims were very accepting of adoption. "The Prophet Muhammad, Blessings and Peace Be Upon Him, was orphaned when he was six years old and raised by his uncle. There are many places in the Qur'an that stress the need to be kind to orphans and to take care of them. You should not have any problems with having an adopted son."

Although I learned the Arabic word for adoption, neither Muslims nor Christians knew what it really meant.

Another Egyptian friend explained to me, "We think this is very good for you to have adopted Nicholas and this is very pleasing to Allah. For us, the problem is that Nicholas's last name cannot be your last name, but he must keep his own. There could be problems later on when he wants to marry. Suppose his birth mother had other children, including girls. How do you know he wouldn't end up unknowingly marrying his sister? This would be terrible."

So that was the issue. It seemed like an odd excuse to me, as Egyptians do a careful checking of the family tree before committing to a marriage. The irony was not lost on me either that the woman I was talking to was married to her first cousin. I decided to tease her about this. "You know, in the U.S. we cannot marry our cousins."

Her eyes grew wide in shock. "That is terrible! How do Americans cope with that? You must be very sad and angry." She shook her head again in pity. "Really, Americans don't have as much freedom as you say you do."

"*Your son! Why is he so black?*" one girl shouted, startling me from my daydreaming.

"My mother is black," I finally said. It wasn't truthful, but after many different responses, it sufficiently satisfied her curiosity. And besides, I hardly felt the need to explain my family history to every stranger I encountered. While these people weren't exactly strangers, I didn't have the words to explain, and they didn't have the ability to understand, something as complex and foreign to them as adoption. Nicholas was constantly asked about his skin color, and he developed his own coping strategies by replying that one of his parents was Egyptian.

Several daughters spread newspaper on the floor and set down bowls of steaming food. Our family sat cross-legged on the floor with the father of the family; a few yards away the mother and teenagers sat with their own food. We never knew quite what the seating arrangements would be in a Muslim home because it often depended on the religiosity of the family. Rarely did we all sit together at one table. In families that were very religious, we would eat with the males while the women remained in the kitchen, cooking and serving. After the meal, I would be invited to join them in another part of the house.

"*Bismallah ir rahman ir raheem*. In the name of God, the Compassionate and Merciful," said the patriarch of the family, and with that we could begin eating.

There were no plates, no bowls, and no utensils. We ate from the serving dishes with our fingers. Tearing off pieces of pita bread and using them to scoop up food from the bowls was the best way. We kept glancing at the father to see how he managed to eat soup and rice without having a stream trickling down his elbow. After eating, one daughter brought us a bowl with water and a towel for cleaning our hands. The father gave the usual comments about our not eating much, but I had no doubt they would make good use of the leftovers for another meal.

I expressed our appreciation for the delicious food by complimenting the father, "Your daughters will marry, in sha'allah." Both Christians and Muslims use that ubiquitous phrase for "God willing." No remark about the future is complete without it. It's a constant reminder that all we do depend not on our will but God's.

We moved back to the sofas for tea and fruit. We had brought a ball as a gift for little Mohammad; we knew his had just popped while playing soccer in the street, which was often the only playground space available. Our kids went out to play with him as my eyes searched the room, wondering what we could talk about next. Their walls had the usual Qur'anic pictures and verses.

"Mama is going on the pilgrimage next month, in sha'allah," the oldest daughter said as she handed me a platter of grapes.

"Really? How long will you be gone?"

"Three weeks, in sha'allah."

"Three weeks? Where will you stay for that long?" That seemed like such a long time for a poor woman. How could she afford a hotel and food, not to mention the journey there?

"In Mecca, there are cheap hotels and food for pilgrims. I will go by bus and then boat to Mecca, in sha'allah."

The woman's shining eyes revealed her excitement. It was a lifelong dream. The pilgrimage is another one of the five pillars of Islam, and all able-bodied people should undertake it at least once

A mural commemorating a pilgrimage to Mecca.

in their life. For this woman, whose income depended on how much farm produce they sold, the journey was an immense sacrifice.

Perhaps "sacrifice" is a meaningful way to begin the journey, as the pilgrimage is made during the Feast of the Sacrifice. This feast commemorates Abraham's willingness to sacrifice his son in obedience to God's demands. Of course, in the end a ram was substituted for the son, but the identity of the son highlights another difference between Islam and Christianity. In the Christian and Hebrew scriptures, it is clearly written that the son to be sacrificed is Isaac. In the Qur'an, however, no name is given. But in following the customs of Arabia, where the eldest son traditionally receives all the blessings and the inheritance, it could only be Ishmael, Abraham's firstborn son, by Sarah's maidservant, Hagar.

"Will you paint your house when you return?"

"My children will, in sha'allah." After a pilgrim has returned from Mecca, family members often paint one side of their house with symbols of the journey: a ship or an airplane, depending on how the person traveled; the black Kabba stone; a person praying. It not only looks pretty, especially compared to the flaking, gray paint of the other walls, but informs outsiders that someone from the house has been blessed enough to make a pilgrimage. Even the person's title changes; our host would no longer be addressed *Abla* but *Hagga*. She would now be looked upon more honorably.

Arriving home from a pilgrimage is a great celebration, as everyone turns out to welcome the person home and receive gifts. Usually the gift is water from Zamzam's Well, a well that miraculously appeared when Hagar, cast out of the household by Sarah, wandered in the desert with young Ishmael. Dying from thirst, Hagar cried out to God, who not only made the well appear but bestowed blessings on her, her son, and all his descendants. The Arabs of Mecca trace their genealogy to Abraham through his firstborn son, Ishmael. Like Jews and Christians, Muslims are part of the Abrahamic faith of belief in one supreme God.

"Well, I need to go back out and sell more fruit. Please visit us again. Your presence has honored my family." The father was wrapping his turban tightly around his head. Even though it was a Friday, the Muslim holy day, for the poor, a day without work is a day without money.

We took advantage of his exit to make our own because we knew the family would have an early start the next day. During Ramadan, a man will walk through the neighborhoods banging on a drum or knocking on doors to wake people at dawn. Groggily, they eat yogurt, beans, and cheese and pray the dawn prayer. They will not eat again until sunset. We would participate in some fasting days but could never rouse ourselves from a good sleep to eat.

"We hope all goes well on your pilgrimage. We will pray for you," I said on the way out. I didn't know if that was the right thing to say or not; Muslims are a prayerful people but was it all right for Christians to say they would pray for them?

"Thank you, my dear. We want to see you every day."

"In sha'allah," I replied. I had also learned that this was a handy remark to say when you didn't really intend to do something.

The oldest son walked us outside, where we saw a horse with

a sack of hay tied around his mouth. "Let's take a *hantoor!*" the kids shouted. We climbed aboard our favorite mode of transportation.

The hantoor, a horse-drawn carriage, slowly and elegantly rolled down the streets, transporting us to the bygone days of another era. We listened to the clip-clopping of the horse's hooves and the jingling of the carriage bells, and we cringed with the crack of the driver's whip against the horse's back. We could relax, watch the crazy traffic around us without being a part of it, observe peoples' faces without being seen, and arrive at our destination refreshed. Then the haggling over money began, quickly ending our "de-stress therapy."

Hantoors, unlike taxis, have no set fare. One person told me, "The drivers look you over and see what you are capable of paying, and charge you that." Following the "all foreigners are rich" theory, we were seen as their lottery ticket cashed in. Over time, we developed the philosophy that we were willing to pay somewhat more than the local folks, but not the excessive fares of twice or triple the normal amount that so many greedy drivers insist on. Even while the driver would be yelling at me for more money or, worse, refusing to take what I offered, I would put the money on the seat and simply walk away. I was confident I had paid more than my fair share, and the driver should just quietly go on.

One evening I took Rebecca up on her idea of exploring the colorful Ramadan tents decorating the town squares. But we had one problem: how to do this without being the Pied Piper and having a stream of kids trailing after us? Rebecca came up with what sounded at the time like a possible solution, plus a lot of fun. "Let's wear scarves. That way we will look like everyone else. No one will see my blonde hair." We put on scarves and happily bounced down the 105 steps to the street.

We had a delightful time. It was a festive evening of bright lights, loud music, and streets filled with laughing, smiling people who had just stuffed themselves. Special ovens were set up on the sidewalks to make the desserts served only during Ramadan. Brightly colored baskets overflowed with imported dried apricots, cashews, dates, and almonds. It was the irony of Ramadan: people made up for their daytime abstinence by eating all the more in the evening. A month of fasting did not keep people from gaining weight!

We walked around a crowd of men in the street, standing shoulder to shoulder, shoes tossed to the side. They were facing the direction of Mecca and reciting evening prayers. Some men would stay all night in the mosque, listening to the Qur'an. Traditionally women pray in their homes, though mosques have separate entrances and prayer rooms for women. To the outsider that may seem sexist, but once I saw the positions of Muslims during prayer—the bending over, the prostrating—I could see why men and women prefer to be separated. Besides, all the Christian churches worship in similar segregation, with men sitting on the left side, women and children on the right.

We enjoyed our anonymous walk among the festivities. No one followed us. No one yelled out to us. No one asked us the time— the number-one annoying question asked only to hear a foreigner's accent. No one knew who we were or paid any attention to us.

All went well till we returned home and were "caught" by Magdy, the young man responsible for helping us settle in. He had some unsolicited advice. "I am going to tell you something and you can take my advice or not. If you dress like a Muslim, the Christians will not have anything to do with you. You are a Christian and should dress like a Christian. If Muslims see you dressed like this, they will think you are becoming like them."

His words hurt us, even though I knew it was the truth. When we had walked past the juice bar we frequented, the Muslim owner, upon seeing our heads covered, gave us the thumbs up. We did not want to imitate Muslims; we simply wanted to walk around like normal people.

"Christians wear headscarves too," I said defensively and not without a touch of anger.

"Poor Christian women do that, but you are not poor. We are a traditional society. Do you know what that means? It means we do things simply because that is always how it has been done, without any question, without any reason. And sometimes the stupider something is, the more we cling to it."

Magdy continued in a matter-of-fact voice. "Muslims have their way of dressing; Christians have another. Poor people have their own way of dressing and eating and the middle class another. You are middle class, so you should live and socialize with the middle class. I know America is a classless society but we are not."

I was too upset to correct his utopian ideals of the United State. I hadn't mentioned to him about our dinner outing with Tayta's family; he had already chastised me previously for sitting on the sidewalk and drinking tea with them.

"You work at this school. Who you are with and what you are doing will reflect back on this school. It is important for us to have a good reputation in this town."

In that case, wasn't it positive for someone from a private Christian school to befriend a poor, Muslim family? Is this not demonstrating Christian love and compassion? But that was not how my actions were perceived. Instead of "befriending," I was seen as "betraying" middle-class Christians.

Brad and I have always raised our children to mingle with a variety of folks. When we were directors of a homeless shelter, our kids frequently went with us to work. We lived with many poor refugees while ministering at Jubilee Partners and became familiar with different languages, cultures, religions, and levels of education and sophistication. We had one teenage boy from West Africa live with us for several months. We had even brought our children to visit with an imprisoned friend on death row. We did not look on any of this as a hardship or a social service project; all of these people and experiences brought joy to our lives.

Was I now going to have to betray my values to be accepted in Egyptian society? How much of myself would I have to give up? What values would I retain and challenge others with? This conflict hit us early on when Nicholas's friends, both Muslims and Christians, came to play with him. He wanted to play at the club right next to us, but because the church owned it, Muslims were not allowed. My gut reaction was to challenge what appeared to be discrimination and ask why Christians would not open their space up to all. But I held my tongue and after several months the answer became clear: many Christians felt the need to have their own space and just be themselves. Concerning our neighbors, I compromised and did not invite them onto the school property, including our apartment. But I thought I should have free rein to visit them in their homes.

Having the school dictate how and where I should spend my private time seemed a little excessive.

Suddenly I was no longer just a woman living in a foreign land. All that I did, rightly and wrongly, would reflect on every group from which I was perceived as representing: MCC, St. Anthony's School, my family, all western womanhood, Christianity, the United States of America. In this community-based society, my behavior and activities would be ever in the spotlight. And I was always being judged about whether I brought honor or shame to the groups I "represented."

I trudged up the stairs weary and disappointed that our fun evening had ended on such a sour note. But I also appreciated Magdy's frankness. We took off the headscarves; the girls would now use them only to play dress-up. I would buy several lovely outfits in harmony with Islamic attire, but I could not wear them. They were folded in my suitcase to wear when we returned to the States, where our dress would not indicate our religion.

7

Peeking Under the Veil

"You don't dress like an American—tight jeans and a little T-shirt. Egyptians get all their information about America from TV shows and movies. That's unfortunately the image we get. But you, you dress differently from what people see on their TV screens, so that's why people are surprised to hear you are from America."

"Well," I replied. "you know what the image is in the U.S. of veiled women, don't you? Forced to do so by your husband, oppressed women, intellectually inferior. Let's see, what else? Living in the Middle Ages."

Ola tossed back her head and laughed, "My hair is covered, not my brain!"

We were sitting at a table in the nadi (the club), with our friends, Osama and Ola, talking about stereotypes of Americans and Muslims. The Sports Club of Beni Suef sounds much more sophisticated than it is. In reality, it's basically a large area where hundreds of kids can play soccer or basketball, do karate, or swim. Because it is a private club and people pay an expensive yearly fee, I was surprised to see so much trash and broken glass on the ground. There was only one small restroom, which looked and smelled like it had not been cleaned since opening day years ago. It puzzled me as to why Egyptians never demand better quality and services for the money they pay.

We were sitting in the garden area, doing the "adult sport" of talking, drinking tea, and eating snacks while our kids played. Ever since Osama rescued me from the overwhelming stress I was experiencing right before we moved to the orphanage, our families had become friends, enjoying many activities together.

Osama is from Indonesia but married Ola, an Egyptian, when they were both working for the same nonprofit agency. International marriages are rare, and even though he is Muslim, the couple still had difficulties obtaining parental approval.

Ola once told me, "We had heard that some Muslims from other countries take their Egyptian wives back to their home country and the wife is never allowed to see her family again. Osama was not like that, but he had to prove that to my parents. When they saw he was a good man, and that we love each other and will live in Egypt, my parents were satisfied. My mother loves him very much, ilhamdulilah."

"So Ola, why do you dress like that?" I asked. "Like that" meant wearing the higab. Her long veil was wrapped tightly around her head, covering her hair and neck, and secured with hairpins.

"You know," she answered, "I just began wearing this two years ago. I had two close aunts who had recently died, and they were very influential in my life. It was after their deaths that I started wearing higab. I was nearing forty, and I think as a person gets older they get more spiritual, and I wanted to get closer to God."

"What did you think of her suddenly changing to wear the higab?" I asked Osama as he lit another cigarette.

"You know, all her friends were surprised I did not make her wear higab before. They think that because I'm from an Islamic country, I should force her to wear the veil. But it's her choice to dress as she wants. If I had any say-so in the matter, I would prefer that she wear regular clothes, but she did not ask me!"

They looked at each other, touched hands, and laughed in a way that married couples still in love after fourteen years do.

Ola took a sip of tea and continued. "My mother-in-law was very happy to see me wearing a veil. We visited her two years ago in Indonesia. I remember we were flying home on September 12, 2001, just after the terrorist attacks that struck your country. I was terrified that something would happen to our plane, especially when we were going over the high mountains that made the plane jump about. I took out the Qur'an and read it to comfort me. I knew if I died, I would be a martyr and go to paradise." How is it that the same Qur'an that inspired nineteen men to hijack planes and smash them into buildings was the same Qur'an that was offering Ola comfort and solace?

"When you were younger, did your mother pressure you into wearing the higab?" I asked.

"My mother always left the decision to me. She never pressured me, but it wasn't so common when I was a girl. So I decided I would do the same for my daughters. They can wear the veil when they want to. Nada is now thirteen, and many of her friends are veiling, but I think it is too young, as she will have her whole life to do it. You know these things are trends in our society; they come and they go. Twenty years ago you didn't see so many women veiled, but now everyone does. It even surprises me. As our life gets more difficult economically, people become more religious. It makes them feel more secure. Will we still dress this way twenty years from now? I don't know."

The sun had moved and was shining directly on her. Ola moved her chair to a shadier area. We kept playing "musical chairs" with the sun but, in double layers of clothes, she must have been broiling. I no longer ask women about the heat and higab, as their answer is always the same: "We are used to it. God gives us the strength."

Wearing higab is not merely donning more clothes but commitment to a certain way of life. It's how a woman dresses all the time, and it does limit activities. When our two families vacationed together in Luxor and were about to climb a desert mountain to reach the King's Tombs, I tried talking Ola into doing it with us.

"I climbed a mountain when I was in Turkey," she said. "But that was before I took the higab." This time she took a taxi instead.

I also observed that wearing a headscarf prevents women from wearing earrings. That sounds trivial, but in a land where girls get their ears pierced in the first week of life, it does become part of one's identity. I asked Ola if she had similar sentimental attachments. She shook her head and looked at me intensely. "Not wearing earrings doesn't bother me. I have gained so much more by putting on the veil. Ilhamdulilah."

ﻉ

One of the most striking things to us in Beni Suef was the number of women wearing veils. It was even more stunning when I realized this was not something mandated by the government but came from the bottom up, from the people themselves. President Mubarak's wife, Madame Suzanne, who is highly visible, never wears a veil.

This may be because she is upper class and doesn't feel the need or pressure to veil. It is illegal for female newscasters and TV personalities to veil, because the government does not want to be perceived as Islamic. Some newscasters sued for the right to be veiled on TV when it otherwise deprived them of employment in the profession. I heard they won their case but still, none were allowed to veil. Turning on the television, we often saw actresses with long, flowing hair, wearing tight sexy clothes, hardly reflecting the female masses on the street.

There are almost as many reasons for veiling as there are ways to wear one. From a simplistic view, it is fashionable for some women. "Muslim" for them is more of a cultural identification, not a religious one. They wear chic, color-coordinated veils and outfits complete with high heels, makeup, and jewelry. Appearances count greatly in Egypt, and wearing a veil does not distract from that. In fact, it's just the opposite, because the veil accentuates the face. Some veiled girls wear tight jeans and T-shirts—provocative apparel that totally contradicts the purpose of veiling.

One friend commented to me as we watched such a girl sashay by, "This is not Islam. We are supposed to wear loose clothing that covers your arms and legs, not show them off. These girls have not been raised properly."

For many females, taking the veil is traditional, the way their mothers dressed and the way they started dressing once they became teenagers. Others refer to the Qur'an, which offers two verses on the purpose of veiling: modesty and protection of women. In the United State, Muslim feminists declare that this referred only to Muhammad's wives, not to all women. It was not controversial in Beni Suef. "All Muslim women must wear the veil" was a phrase I heard repeatedly. Indeed a poster I saw glued to many shop walls shows a woman, and above her veiled head is the caption, "The road to paradise."

When France instituted a law that students were prohibited from wearing religious ornamentation in school, my Muslim friends were outraged. One summed it up: "Wearing a veil is not an option. If you are Muslim, you *must* do that. How can the French government prevent someone from practicing their religion? This is terrible."

The fact that Turkey and Tunisia, secular countries with majority Muslim populations, have similar rules went unmentioned in the media and is not a commonly known fact.

For most women, wearing higab means they are respectable and decent, thus giving them the freedom to be out in public and keep their reputations intact. Arab societies are based on honor and shame, and that comes through the behavior of its women. Long, loose dresses and veils preserve a woman's virtue and bring honor and respect to her husband and family. Many Muslims fear that relaxing dress standards will start people down the slippery slope of moral decay.

For some, veiling is a political statement. For others, it is a feminist statement: you will deal with me as a person based on my mind, not my looks and body shape. Lower-class Christian women veil, though in a different style, just like peasants from China to Bolivia do. Being a hot, dusty country, women have worn veils as protection from the elements at least since the time of Cleopatra.

My favorite reason for veiling came from my friend Doctor Negwa. "I want to look beautiful only for my husband," she said. "What do you prefer to buy—meat that is covered up or meat that is all open so that everyone can see it and touch it? No, you want something that is clean and has not been touched by others."

I understood her point, but the comparison is hilarious because that is exactly how meat is sold—on the streets, hanging bare from hooks and exposed to the heat, flies, dust, and kids. I wished the meat was covered as well as the women were!

Whatever the reason, my women friends made it clear to me that it was their choice to wear a veil, in keeping with their understanding of the Qur'an and their role as Muslim women. They became angry and defensive at the suggestion that it came from pressure by a father or husband. I never met any woman who showed any sign of jealousy about how westerners dress. Instead the questions I was often asked reflected their pity for westerners: Why don't Western women respect themselves? How can they go outside "naked" (meaning with exposed arms and legs)? Why don't fathers and husbands care how their daughters and wives dress?

ع

One evening I was sitting at the nadi, watching Rebecca and Emily play basketball with about fifty teenage girls. The coach, a tall, energetic man, encouraged the girls and enjoyed playing with them. The players were unlike any I had ever seen: all were dressed in nice, long pants, fashionable long-sleeve shirts, and veils hanging down their shoulders.

As they dribbled the ball on an outdoor concrete court, I got into a conversation with the coach's fourteen-year-old daughter, who was sitting on the sidelines:

> Me: Are you playing basketball this summer?
> Girl: No. I don't like basketball so much. But I do like swimming.
> Me: Are you going swimming after practice then?
> Girl: No, I started wearing the higab this summer.
> Me: Are you happy to be wearing it?
> Girl: A little. But a little sad too because I can't swim anymore. But all my friends started wearing it too, so it isn't so bad.

Whether they veil or not, there is a certain change of life for girls once they reach adolescence. Typically it means putting away a swimsuit and bicycle, because neither is seen as proper behavior once a girl reaches puberty. "All my friends started wearing it" made it easier for everyone to conform to cultural and religious expectations. It is the opposite advice I give my kids; I encourage them to express their individuality, think for themselves, and not to do as their peers do. But in Egypt, their peers were doing what society expected of them—to conform to culture so one fits into society.

We saw this conformity in unexpected ways. Egyptians wore winter clothing such as sweaters and jackets until the day after Easter. Hot weather begins in March but one year, Easter did not come until May. Our guards were suffering in their gray, wool sweaters until the magic date arrived. Brad dressed for the weather in short sleeves and heard many comments on "summering" before the official date arrived. People argued that the weather could get cold again, and Brad reassured them he would put on a sweater if it did. No one joined him in "summering" early; foreigners were the only ones to buck this tradition. Conforming to cultural standards superseded individual desires for comfort. The thinking was that if society could not control the trivial things like "summering," how could it expect obedience and loyalty to the more important issues?

❦

Abdullah, a student in Brad's English class, was eager for us to meet his family and invited us to his house for dinner one Friday afternoon. Friends had accompanied us to a doctor's visit and helped us put up shelves in our apartment, find our way around the town, buy stamps, and complete a hundred other tasks that render foreigners helpless and dependent. All of this greatly improved our lives as we gradually adjusted to noise, chaos, and disorganization—both in the school and on the streets—as normal. Being invited into friends' homes also gave us an intimate window to see how they lived and to teach us more about their culture.

Um Abdullah (mother of Abdullah) was of medium height and, like many of her peers, overweight. Her two teenage daughters wore cape-like veils that fit snugly around their full faces and flowed downward past their waists.

We greeted with the obligatory four kisses on the cheeks, but when Brad stood up to extend his hand, Um Abdullah said with a smile, "No, I don't shake men's hands." I knew we were in for a different sort of evening.

"Please, come to the table." Um Abdullah said, gesturing with her hands. The daughters had just laid several hot dishes on the table and disappeared.

"Are they coming back?" I asked Abdullah.

"No, they will stay downstairs, but you can visit with them after we eat."

Following Arab tradition, Um Abdullah had taken the name of her firstborn son. His father was Abu Abdullah (father of Abdullah). I found this custom troubling; giving up one's name seemed like giving up a part of one's self, like the western customs of a wife taking her husband's last name in marriage.

But a new father explained that changing names is not giving up one's identity but is instead changing a person's identity to reflect the new circumstances. "I was so happy when my son was born," he said, "that I wanted everyone to know me as Abu Mina, father of Mina. After his birth, to call me by my own name is like an insult." Egyptian women do not take their husband's last name but retain the name of their father, symbolizing that they still belong to their family of origin.

Abdullah was dressed like all young men, in tight blue jeans and a T-shirt. Islam does have some guidelines for male dressing, but they are not followed as rigorously as female guidelines. "FBI" was written on the front on Abdullah's T-shirt. On the back was the abbreviation's definition: "Female Body Inspector." We knew he didn't know what it meant, but was just enjoying the popular trend of wearing any shirt with English writing. But it contrasted so greatly with the conservative nature of his family that we chuckled about it for days.

While eating, Abdullah told us more about his family. "Three of my siblings and I were born in Kuwait. We enjoyed living there very much. When Saddam Hussein invaded in 1990, we had to return to Egypt. I was nine years old and was very sad to come here, as I had never been in Egypt before!"

A million other Egyptians were also forced to leave at that time. This put a great strain on the Egyptian government because remittances from workers abroad contribute immensely to the Egyptian economy. Plus, all the "returnees" needed a place to live, a job, and schooling for their children—essential things that Egypt could not adequately supply.

The family now has eight children, including one with Down syndrome. Abdullah explained, "My grandparents had this apartment, so we moved in with them. It is very big because it is really two apartments together. My mother will show you later.

"My father opened a coffee shop downstairs. It is very famous. Did you see it?" he asked us proudly. Abdullah, whose name means "slave of God," smiled brightly. We didn't have to go far to see the coffee shop. He just opened a window, and we saw the men drinking tea and smoking *sheeshas* (tobacco with a water pipe) at the numerous tables and chairs set up right outside the house. This was strictly male territory; no respectable woman would ever set foot in a coffee shop in Beni Suef.

We finished eating and went downstairs. Brad and Abdullah sat in one room to visit; the children and I in another. Initially, visiting in

Women are increasingly wearing the niqab, *but not all Muslims approve.*

separate rooms was awkward, but by then we had done it a few times and were comfortable with it. Gender segregation, like the higab, is another way to protect and preserve female virtue. I had been given plenty of advice from a variety of folks on what was acceptable interaction between males and females: avoid long eye contact with males I know; avoid all eye contact with males I do not know; do not give exuberant, warm greetings to males; wait until the man offers his hand to shake rather than offering my own hand first; in a room or in a crowd, sit and stand with the other females. Men were no longer simply people; they were males and I was female, and that needed to be uppermost in all my interactions.

It wasn't long before we heard the evening call to prayer and Abdullah emerged from his room, wearing a sparkling white, freshly ironed galabaya and a white, crocheted prayer cap on his head. He sat down and called for his sister Imani to bring his shoes to him, even though he was closer to them. His sister obediently got up and brought the shoes. I knew how my daughters would have surely responded to their brother: "Get it yourself." But Imani was following the role she had been raised in by submitting to the authority of her brother and father, and one day her husband. Conversely Abdullah demanded things from his mother and sister and, one day soon, his wife. Women often secured their position in the home by making the men dependent on them. Once dressed, Abdullah headed out to a nearby mosque for prayer, and Brad went home.

Um Abdullah and her daughters Imani and Hedaya walk in with tea, followed by her sister-in-law, who had dropped by to visit. I looked up to see a "black ghost." I tried not to express my surprise, but she was a startling sight. The sister-in-law wore the niqab (face veil), and was completely enveloped in long black dress and veils, including elbow-length black gloves, black socks, and black shoes. There was only a narrow eye slit in her veil from which she could view the world. I often saw these women on the streets, shopping with kids, running errands, working in clothing shops—and even a few behind the wheel of a car! They lived ordinary lives, but I couldn't imagine how they handled the heat and stifling attire. "God gives them strength to sacrifice" was a common refrain. But not all Muslim women approve of the niqab. "Dressing like this is not Islam," they would say. "It comes from Saudi Arabia, not from the Qur'an."

Once the sister-in-law was safely in the house and saw that no men were there, I expected her to rip off the face veil and fling it aside. But she didn't. She greeted everyone, sat down, chitchatted, and after about ten minutes pulled her face veil over her head, revealing an ordinary face. But because kids were still coming in and out the door and she didn't want to risk being seen by a man other than her husband, she went into another room to visit with her two nieces.

Sensing my curiosity, Um Abdullah volunteered some information. "Do you know why she dresses like that? She is a very religious person and does not want anyone to contaminate her. She wants to be very pure. I think in your religion you have women who are like that but they do not marry." It took some seconds for me to realize she was talking about nuns. "She is the same way, but of course she is married and has children."

"You know, in America, we think that Muslim women with covered faces are forced by their husbands to dress this way so other men won't look at their wives," I commented. After all we had heard and seen about the Taliban's repression in Afghanistan, this wasn't an unreasonable assumption.

"Maybe there are some like that, especially in other Muslim

countries," Um Abdullah responded. "But her husband is also very religious. Sometimes the woman wants to dress niqab but the man refuses her that right. In other families, the husband is very religious and wants the wife to wear niqab, but she doesn't want to. Of course, if her husband wants her to, she must. But maybe she will complain to her parents, and they will talk to her husband and to her husband's family, and he will change his mind."

Many marital problems are solved "family-style," with all the parents and relatives getting involved. Very little privacy exists, and getting into everyone else's business is a favorite past time.

As we were leaving, I invited Um Abdullah to visit with us in our apartment. She replied sweetly, "You come here and visit any time. I am always here. I never leave the house, so you will always find me here."

We continued to visit and found her statement to be true. The six sons were free to come and go; the two daughters went to school, but their free time was spent at home. But they were a regular family, and I sometimes witnessed the teenage daughters argue with their mother, then storm off to their room, slamming the door behind them.

Because Um Abdullah didn't go out, the world came to her. Her sons, friends, or relatives did all the shopping. Their place was always lively with children running up and down the stairs, in and out of doors. Something was always cooking on the stove, and we ate many midnight meals with them. The TV constantly blared over the noise, but it didn't seem to faze Um Abdullah. Having eight kids in the house and living above a coffee shop that was noisy until the wee hours of the morning was just normal. We watched TV and talked about our lives while the girls played Uno or braided each other's hair.

Um Abdullah had a twelve-year-old son who liked to play soccer with Nicholas. One evening we were listening to Egyptian music and trying to belly dance. Mohammed liked to rap dance and soon had us enthralled with his smooth moves. The American tape was only music—no words—until the rapper yelled out, "Mother [expletive]. Take your clothes off!" Nicholas and Rebecca quickly looked at me with wide eyes. I glanced at Imani and Isma who, fortunately, were completely oblivious to what had just been said, and I surely was not going to enlighten them.

Why is Um Abdullah confined to her house? It wasn't always that way. One day I was leafing through a family photo album and saw photos of her in the 1980s, before they left for Kuwait. She was standing next to a car that she drove to her nursing job. She was dressed in a knee-length skirt, a sleeveless top, and high heels, her hair blowing in the breeze. Emily brought the album to show Brad, who was sitting in the other room with Abdullah. Abdullah removed all the photos of his mother before passing it on; he did not want Brad to see her "exposed."

What is the journey that one takes from this style of fashionable dress, posed next to a car, the ultimate sign of freedom, to being constantly in the home, covered in higab, and catering to the needs of a spouse and eight children? Were they influenced by the ten years they lived in conservative Kuwait? Um Abdullah bluntly stated that her husband and sons wanted her and the daughters in the house "for our own protection, because we are so beautiful." She accepted her lot with humor and made the most of her situation. Did she secretly resent her way of life? I don't know, but I suspect she didn't dwell on it much.

"It is easier for me to stay home," she said. "I have much to do here." And she structured her life in a way that she had no need to go out.

It was rare to find housebound women like Um Abdullah. In fact, when I mentioned her situation to other Muslim friends, they all expressed surprise. "That's the purpose of the higab," one said. "It gives you the freedom to be out of the house and still be decent and respectable."

ت

I thought I understood about veiling, but then I met Amal. This happened frequently—I thought I had an aspect of culture figured out when along came someone who threw my theories out of kilter. On the surface, Muslim culture appeared monolithic, black-and-white. But there were always a few shades of gray, and Amal was one of those shades.

I met Amal through Brad's classes and, like Abdullah, she had also lived in Kuwait. But at age twenty-three, she still did not veil. She explained it to me one evening as we enjoyed fresh-squeezed lemonade at the nadi. "I want to wear the higab when I can commit to a life of goodness and am spiritually ready. Does wearing higab show I am a good Muslim? What if I wear higab and tight clothes like many young girls? I need to be clean in my heart, then I will know I am ready to take the veil."

"Do you get a lot of pressure from others to veil?" I asked.

"Sometimes. My mothers and my uncles [her father was deceased] keep asking me when I will take the veil. But I tell them I am not ready. If we lived in Cairo or Alexandria it would not be a big deal, but here in Beni Suef. . . . "

She shook her head. "Beni Suef is very conservative, so not veiling is unusual. Many people think I am Christian because I don't wear a veil and because I have many Christian friends. You know, people will even ask me my name to see if I am Christian or Muslim. But my name can be either one. So then they will ask me my father's name. People play games with me to try and find out my religion."

With perfect timing, Emily interrupted us and whispered in Amal's ear, "Are you sure you are a Muslim? You aren't wearing a veil!" Unfortunately it had not taken our family long to get into the mentality of using outward signs such as crosses and clothing to identify religions.

"You see what I mean?" Amal cried out. We both laughed and slapped our hands together as females do when sharing a common joke. "I get so frustrated with all these outward symbols to be a Muslim or to be a Christian. Why can't we just be God's people?"

8

Respect from a Switch

"Come," I said to Bessem, one of the English teachers. "I want to show you what I am looking at."

He was early for our English-teachers meeting, so I motioned him to the back of the classroom, where I was standing, looking out the window. Behind St. Anthony's School was a public middle school for boys. It had been a private school run by the Coptic Orthodox Church but was taken over by the government about twenty years earlier. No one seemed to want to say why, and from what I saw on the playground, it was obvious that the government school was not necessarily more competent.

Between our school and theirs was a large, dirt courtyard teeming with hundreds of boys running and jumping about while teachers, wielding long plastic sticks, swung liberally in efforts to get the boys into straight lines. Once they were in lines, the drums began and they did their exercises. *Up, two three, four. Down, two, three, four!* It reminded me of a scene from an old prison camp movie, except for the last rousing line—*Allahu Akbar!* (God is greater!)

It was one o'clock and their school day was ending, but several boys were still being punished. They were standing in the hot sun with their hands straight up in the air. The teacher, a fat, balding man I'd dubbed "the Sadist," sat in a chair in the shade, fingering his long stick. Every few minutes, as their arms started to sag from weariness, he got up and whacked each boy with a stinging blow on the backside. I had now been standing and watching this for twenty minutes.

"Do you see what this teacher is doing?" I asked Bessem, pointing to the Sadist. "I wonder what they think of him. Surely they must hate him and school."

"I'll tell you what they think of him. They love that man and

they respect him. Why? Because he cares enough about them to correct them. My father and my teachers beat me as a child, and I love
them for that, because I know they were teaching me the right way
to go."

"But did you feel that way as a child?"

"Of course. I know I did wrong. And their job was to correct
me—simple."

I shook my head in disbelief, doubting that as a child he really
appreciated those beatings. Fear can often be mistaken for respect.
Another glance at my watch told me that the other teachers were
not going to show up for our regularly scheduled meeting. No surprise there; I was usually pleased if one showed up.

My job was to improve the language of the students, and it
seemed the best way to do this was to work with the teachers. But I
wasn't having much success. I suspect one of the reasons teacher
meetings failed is that the teachers had no motivation to improve and
didn't want to share their knowledge with each other. Since almost
all the teachers at the school gave private lessons, they were in competition with each other for the same students. There I was wanting
them to cooperate to improve the school while they were competing
to boost their monthly incomes.

Sensing my disappointment at another no-show, Bessem suggested we go to the teachers room for tea. "I have something I want
to tell you."

The teachers room was a small room with chipped, white paint
dulled and dirtied through the years, a few wobbly, wooden chairs,
and one rough plywood table covered with a stained and faded
tablecloth. Since maintenance was not a priority at the school, it
looked about fifty years old instead of nine. The only thing hanging on the wall was a calendar from the previous year. There were
no schedules, no clocks, no announcements, no inspirational or
humorous quotes. Most teachers taught five classes a day, so there
was time for correcting notebooks, drinking tea, and talking on cell
phones.

Bessem went to get tea while I carefully sat down in a rickety
chair, having had two previously collapse underneath me. He soon
joined me, and we continued our conversation. "I used to teach in
a village school and got a small salary," he said. "I couldn't live on
that. I wanted to get married, so I needed money for an apartment.

I wanted a car, just normal things in life, nothing fancy. But I could not get those things while teaching at a village school, because there is no money. So I had to force the village kids to take private lessons from me." Bessem paused and took a sip of his tea, the steam fogging his glasses.

"What?" I asked. "How can you *force* kids to take private lessons?" I had often heard there was a lot of manipulation and coercion on the teacher's part but never knew the details.

"How? The students I am tutoring, I don't ask them questions in class. But I'll ask the other students and give them a hard time. If they answer wrong, they get hit with a stick. Eventually the child will tell his parents he needs lessons because he always gets everything wrong. So they succumb to private lessons. We have a joke: The teacher asks a student he tutors, 'What's the population of Egypt?' That's easy, seventy-four million. Then the teacher will ask a student he doesn't tutor, 'Name them.'"

We laughed and shook our heads. The students he did not tutor would indeed have a rough time.

"Then I left that village school when I was hired here at St. Anthony's. Being able to teach at this school is a gift from God. Before coming here, I had a conflict with my conscience. I hated forcing the students to take private lessons, because they were poor students, and I knew their families could not afford it, but I also had to survive myself. It was either my conscience or my survival, but at this school I can survive with a clean conscience, *ashkurak Rabb* [thanks be to the Lord]." St. Anthony's did not pay a higher salary, but because the student body was richer, parents could more easily afford private lessons.

Bessem went on to explain how he carried a switch and would hit students, admitting that it didn't necessarily change their behavior. "But they would not respect me if I did not hit them. Neither would my colleagues. Respect means power." He chuckled and tossed his hands up in frustration, "I was young and inexperienced; I didn't have a moustache. How can I get respect if I don't use a switch?"

The bell rang. Bessem returned our tea glasses to the small kitchen and we parted. I went home for dinner and helping the kids sort out their school day. Bessem went home for dinner, then into an evening spent going to four or five students' homes for tutoring lessons. My day was winding down; his real work was beginning.

The average school salary for government and private schools in Beni Suef was thirty-five dollars monthly. That barely covered apartment rental. Bessem would earn three times that amount in private lessons.

Private lessons had become a necessary evil because of examinations. Taking exams is the main purpose of schooling, and students are well trained for the rigorous process, which begins in first grade with monthly exams in ten different subjects. Once I was helping the computer teacher grade exams for second-graders when one of the questions caught my eye: "The computer printer is an output unit." The students were to circle "true" or "false."

"How can a second-grader understand what an 'output unit' is, especially in English? I hardly know what it means," I complained to the computer teacher.

"They don't have to understand it. We have them write this sentence over and over each day so they have it memorized. When they see it on the test, they know which one to circle." Indeed, they all had circled true.

In one of my meetings with the English teachers, I asked what their reasons were for becoming teachers. I had wanted to tap into that initial spirit and enthusiasm for a teaching career. After a few discussions, it was clear that no one had any long-term desires or dreams to teach.

"You mean no one influenced you to become teachers? Maybe a favorite teacher or an inspirational one?"

They all shook their heads except the lone woman. "My parents were both teachers, so it's my fate in life," she said.

The teachers had scored a certain level on the all-powerful high-school exams. The score determines one's field of study and future career. The top scores are reserved for doctors, engineers, and pharmacists. Ask the proverbial question "What do you want to be when you grow up?" to Egyptian children and likely they will reply "a doctor."

I remembered back to our first day of school when we got a tour by Sister Heba. We went in the fourth-grade class, and all the students stood up and in very loud voices recited, "Welcome to our class, 4B. We are happy to see you. We want to be doctors and engineers. Thank you." They were taught from a young age that this profession is desirable, respectable, and would bring honor to the family. It has led to the joke that Egypt has more doctors than diseases.

Unfortunately the teaching profession was near the bottom of the totem pole and did not garner much respect. One math teacher explained his predicament to me. "My father was an engineer and I loved following him and doing what he did." But his score on the high-school exam was way below the "engineering level."

"I hate this system because it would not let me do what my heart wanted me to do. I am okay for a math teacher, but I would be a much better engineer." With the current push for more standardized testing in the United States, I feared I was seeing the future of the American educational system.

But it isn't only low scores on high-school exit exams that could derail ones career; parents also had influence. One acquaintance confided that she wanted to be a teacher "but when I tested at the doctor's level on the exam, my parents wanted me to have a better career and opportunity in life." It is more important for the adult child to be loyal to parents' wishes than to pursue personal desires.

Even though the teachers complained of stress, low pay, and a poor working environment, one reminded me that more money was not the only solution. Mona, Emily's French teacher, was a contract worker who received payment only for the classes she taught. She and I were correcting exam papers when I asked her if she resented not getting paid for her work that day but having to pay money to put her child in daycare.

"You know, the lack of money doesn't bother me so much as the lack of appreciation," she replied. "No one will say, 'Thank you for being here today.'"

Mona's comment was a good reminder that we all have the common desire to feel valued and have our efforts acknowledged. Interestingly, when I shared her comments about appreciation with other teachers, anonymously of course, the general consensus was that one could only show appreciation secretively, because Egyptians are very jealous of each other. Honoring one teacher would create resentment and chaos and probably make the teacher lazy.

I shelved my idea of "teacher appreciation" recognition, and I was learning lessons in why my imported ideas would not work.

ट

Respect means power. How can I get respect without a switch?

Those words of Bessem explained why I was having such a hard time in the classroom. I brought a different set of values to the school, ones that I had learned while volunteering in my kids' classrooms in Georgia. Now as I stood in front of a group of fifth-graders, I spoke in a quiet but firm voice, telling them I would only call on students who were sitting quietly with their hands raised. The students were not impressed; they just ignored me. They were running around, eating sandwiches, playing with toys, slamming their heavy, wooden desktops, throwing paper out the windows, yelling, crying, and hitting each other. I was completely bewildered. The students at Comer Elementary never acted that way.

A passing teacher stopped by and gave everyone a good yelling at and a few swats for good measure. "*Inta zif!* [You are tar!]," he roared. It was my first Arabic insult learned at school, taught to me not by the students but by a teacher. The students sat quietly for a minute or so and then went back to the normal routine. I wasn't willing to do what the students expected me to do—yell and hit. Besides being against my beliefs in nonviolence, I saw from the other teachers' classes that it simply didn't work and often got the kids more riled up.

"Bad schools" in the United State are usually associated with drugs, violence, and promiscuous students. That was not the case at St. Anthony's. The students all had high morals and values and came from good, respectable families. What the students didn't have was playtime, because tutoring followed school. So when *was* playtime? Why, school time, of course! A steady stream of disruptive and undisciplined students made the days long and exhausting.

The solution seemed so simple: classroom rules, school rules, an organized system of teaching and learning. I discussed this with Sister Heba, the principal, who explained, "The educational authorities won't let us have any rules. You are supposed to love the students and be their friend, and they will be kind to you. Mrs. Jennifer, you need to get the students to like you."

That was not my concept of teaching. I explained about the necessity of rules and consequences, but all of my arguments were met with rejection. "If I make the students stay in during break time writing lines," she said, "they will complain to their parents, who will complain to the school authorities, and we could be fined for this."

It made no sense to me that students would complain about writing lines but not about getting hit, which, though illegal, was a common occurrence.

It would be too easy to say the classrooms were wild and disorderly simply because they were taught by females, for some male teachers did not command respect either. There were some teachers, like Bessem, who could just stand in the doorway and the students would magically stop the chaos, stand at attention, and chorus out a greeting. When asked what their secret was, the response was "strong character." Unfortunately that was not a skill I had ever developed. The irony was not lost on me that I, who came to improve the English teaching, had the worst-behaved classes and was learning from the better teachers how to manage them.

؏

Sister Heba wanted me to do a training session with the teachers after school. It was my first one, and it was doomed before it even started. Throughout the day, I had seen the teachers furiously using their cell phones, calling mothers or spouses to take care of their children after school. I had only one day of notice for the training session; the teachers had just been informed that morning.

When school finished, forty teachers crowded into Sister's office. About six shuffled in the doorway, making their lack of enthusiasm clear. No one was willing to translate. "Everyone here understands English," it was claimed. Not true. The non-English speakers spent the entire session having their own conversations in Arabic, completely ignoring my pleas for quiet. On top of that, I had to compete with all the noise from the street, because there is nothing soundproof about concrete walls.

Sister was not present for the meeting, but the assistant principal was. He was an elderly, sedentary man who sat behind an immaculately clean desk. He had two jobs. One was dispensing a stick of chalk to children who were sent by their teachers each day for it. His second was "motivating" children in the morning assembly, either by insulting them or by giving out prizes for perfect test scores. Being assistant principal was largely a ceremonial role.

The teachers settled in for what they thought would be the usual "lecture and criticize" training session. Instead we played a game. I passed out paper and asked each teacher to write one or two qualities about a favorite teacher from their own school days. On the back, they were to write the qualities of their worst teacher. Never having done something creative like this before, it took a while for them to catch on to the exercise. Meanwhile the assistant principal was continuously growling in the background, "You are lazy teachers. You are stupid teachers."

We came up with a good list. Some positive qualities they remembered were teachers who gave presents to students scoring 100 percent on tests; visited sick students at home; managed class in a positive way; and used a variety of creative teaching methods. The negative qualities were that teachers had favorite students; gave physical and "psychological" punishments; did not like female students; and were lazy and did not like to work. I intended my final point to be for them to look at the lists and see which qualities were true for themselves, but we never made it that far.

The assistant principal was loudly barking away at the teachers with insults; the teachers were talking, yelling, and milling about against a backdrop of noisy street traffic. The nearby mosque loudly broadcasted its third call to prayer for the day. It was pure bedlam; I had no control of the teachers, just as I had none of the students. I went home, took two aspirins, and crawled into bed, exhausted and emotionally drained.

Sister had a teachers meeting the following week that made mine seem like a gathering of peacemakers. The teachers had the usual same-day notice, and we all crammed into her office. I don't know what the agenda was, but the method and substance of communication—yelling, criticism, and insults from the principal to her staff—seemed more important.

The most stinging criticism I heard was, "Your parents must have not raised you with respect and manners." It was the American equivalent of yelling "Yo' mama," but here it was coming from their boss. The teachers' families had just been humiliated, so honor needed to be restored.

One young man began by immediately jumping up and yelling at Sister in a way usually reserved for parents of a rebellious teen suddenly deprived of the car for the night. His face was red, fists tightly clinched at his sides, as he furiously moved around in the space before her desk, shouting and demanding. It was frightening.

After about five minutes, when it was silently acknowledged that he had restored honor to his family, his brother physically moved him to the hallway. I took a deep breath and wiped my sweaty palms on my skirt. But to my disbelief, the brother came back in and took over where his sibling had left off, with the same posture, the same tone of voice, and likely the same words had I been able to understand them. After him a third man delivered the same performance.

I nervously glanced at the others in the room. No one seemed particularly upset by the spectacle. Some were looking at their feet, others were inspecting their fingernails; most were looking bored and wondering when the show would end so they could get home.

During the entire twenty-minute showdown, Sister, to her credit, sat quietly and calmly behind her desk and never uttered a word. She watched and listened with no expression. There was an understanding among all, except me, that the men needed to defend their honor loudly with exaggerated gestures, and Sister needed to quietly allow it. When the men finished, she automatically delved into her next point, albeit without any further insults.

This incident was beyond my comprehension. I could not imagine any situation in the United States in which an employee could rant and rave at his boss and not be escorted, likely under police supervision, permanently out the door.

I saw one of the "ranters" on the street the next day, and he offered his apologies. It seemed that many teachers were embarrassed that this took place in front of me, a foreign guest. No one seemed to think that the ranters were out of line. I don't know if this was a typical teacher's meeting or not. In the next three years, I never attended another.

ई

What exactly do respect and honor mean? The words are frequently tossed around in Arab societies, but their definitions differ from a westerner's. I had no doubt that if a teacher in the United States threw the tantrum I had witnessed, the result would not be the restoration of the teacher's honor. It would be just the opposite. The teacher would be humiliated and disgraced.

My ideas of respect are more romantic—offering a seat to

someone on a crowded subway, opening a door for someone loaded down with packages. These things do happen in Egypt, but there were other ways to show respect: greeting everyone individually when entering a room; keeping feet flat on the floor, as opposed to crossing legs; addressing the parent first and then the child; sons not smoking in front of their fathers.

There were times when I would be confused about someone's actions and interpret them as being rude, but according to the unwritten rule of conduct, the person was actually showing me respect and consideration. For example, once I was preparing for a special English activity and needed one of the male teachers to help me buy supplies. Two hours later, his little car was loaded with food and school supplies, and we headed back to my apartment. While we were unloading, the teacher, who knew Brad was at work, asked if Nicholas was home.

"No, he is at the nadi playing soccer," I told him.

"In that case, I'll put your bags here." And he proceeded to place the parcels on the guards' bed in the lobby. I was a bit stunned that I had to carry fourteen heavy, plastic bags to our apartment while the teacher just drove away.

"How dare he leave me with the heavy work!" I grumbled during the five trips I trudged up and down the stairs. But when I finally caught my breath and looked at the situation in the cultural context, I knew he had done the right thing. The teacher was actually showing me respect by not being in our apartment without my husband or son present, which would have made me the subject of gossip. It wasn't about carrying plastic bags; it was about protecting my reputation.

As one person explained, "Gossip can ruin a woman for life, so it is better to avoid the situation in the first place. Unfortunately forgive and forget is not an option for us."

One time at school, I was mesmerized by the fascinating traffic when suddenly the sound of screeching brakes pierced the air. I turned my head and saw shoes flying up in the air. An elderly man had been crossing the street but wasn't going fast enough to suit the oncoming driver, who hit him. Perhaps that's just what the driver said when he got out of the car and berated the poor man. His rage expressed, the driver drove off while bystanders helped the man up, dusting off his now dirty clothes and gathering up his shoes.

A teacher who had joined me at the railing to watch remarked, "I like having foreigners at our school. You respect each other and us. We Egyptians don't do that." Her voice kind of drifted off as if talking to herself. "I don't really know why."

It was as perplexing to her as it was to me, but that simple comment confirmed in some small way that I did have a purpose and something to contribute to the school. I shared that story with other short-term volunteers who were equally overwhelmed and baffled by the school environment. Perhaps we could not change the system of teaching and disciplining, but as foreigners we could model a different way of respecting the students and teachers. Because everything we did was noticed and remembered, perhaps the best we could do was set a good example.

The school was organized pyramid-style. Sister Heba on top dictated to the subjects below. Having one person as the authority over everybody and everything permeated everything at the school. One day I wanted to print something off the computer, but there was no paper for the printer nor was any conveniently stacked nearby. There were five people sitting in the office, all doing nothing, including the assistant principal, who apparently could not multitask effectively enough to distribute both chalk and paper. I asked for some paper and received the standard reply, "Ask Sister."

This response always frustrated me, because it meant leaving the computer to find Sister and ask for paper. She wasn't going to refuse my request, but neither could I or anyone else just go to the storage cabinet and help ourselves; all had to be done through her. What was the point of having advanced technology if a basic tool like paper was not readily available?

No teacher or staff person was given any real responsibility, so no one felt they had anything to contribute. When a problem arose, no committee was formed to discuss it and offer solutions. Instead everyone depended on the principal to solve or not solve the problem. Teachers did not offer any input, because their advice, opinions, and ideas were not solicited. I never heard phrases that characterize so many American discussions: What do you think about . . . ? Have you considered . . . ? Why don't we try . . . ?

Once when I was in a meeting with the science teachers, Sister Heba interrupted us. She fussed at them for some minor error—I think it was drinking tea in the science office—and then turned to me, "Are they good children?"

Children? Briefly stunned, I replied, "No, but they are good adults."

Sister corrected herself. "You are right."

It was not merely a mix-up with her English, which she spoke competently. Rather it reflected her view that she was the authoritarian parent, and teachers should be treated as children.

When I related this story to some Egyptian friends, they were all in agreement. "All our institutions," one of them said, "are run with this attitude of one person in charge and everyone else following orders, just like children do. People need to consider this when they talk about democracy. Because democracy is not just about elections but about working together. But how do you change this way of thinking?"

While Sister's management style was certainly different from any I had previously experienced, it was not considered negative or unusual. One teacher summed it up: "Sister Heba is a good director because she is strong and forceful. She tells people what to do. If you aren't forceful with people, they will be lazy and do nothing. Always the director must be harsh with people to get them to do things and to get their respect. Egyptians respect strength and power, not weakness."

It's not an exaggeration to say that St. Anthony's school environment was a microcosm of Egyptian society. If you exchange Sister Heba with President Mubarak, the above quote serves as a metaphor of Egyptian government and leadership.

Just as the teachers felt they had no ownership and no voice in the school, so citizens felt about their country. I had always imagined that authoritarian regimes made people angry and rebellious, but instead I found citizens just like the teachers: passive, apathetic, powerless. At this time during our stay in Egypt, the United States was putting political pressure on the Mubarak regime for democratic reform. But the government, like the school, is a system of patriarchal authority content to dictate from above while fostering dependency from those below. How can an authoritative, patriarchal government pave the way for democracy, a movement that should come from the bottom up? In a democracy, people work together to identify and solve problems, giving and taking to find some common ground. Education can be an excellent way to nurture democracy, but the Egyptian educational system is more focused on cramming things into the mind rather than opening it.

ẽ

When our first school year ended, Bessem, the teacher who had enlightened me on respect and power, went to the United States with plans to apply for political asylum.

"I am a Christian living with Muslims," he would tell us. "Because of this I am persecuted, and there are some Coptic Orthodox organizations in the U.S. that will help me apply for asylum. After a few years, I will come back to Beni Suef and find a wife, but we will live in the U.S. There is no future here in Beni Suef."

As for me, I gradually caught on that the school was not so much interested in my teaching ideas but in the fact that having a foreigner present in the school brought honor and prestige. The staff enjoyed attending my workshops, but no one had any intention of implementing my ideas. It wasn't important that I was productive, but that I was present. Sitting, drinking tea and chatting were not frowned upon and became an excellent way to get to know teachers and build relationships. It would be a long time before I could let go of the American need to be busy, productive, and efficient. But once I lowered my own expectations, my involvement in the school became more manageable and enjoyable.

9

Crossing over the Canal

"What do Americans think about Arab people?" Abdullah asked Brad.

"Well, most Americans have an image of Arabs as terrorists." As those words registered, a look of bewilderment and dismay came over Abdullah's face.

"But we're good people!" he exclaimed.

"Yes, you are good people. All the people I have met here have indeed been friendly and helpful. But that is not what makes the news. The news in the United States focuses on the terror attacks and the suicide bombers, and those images, which do involve Arabs, are predominant in most American minds."

Brad clarified that he was well aware how one-sided this TV image was. "It is a major reason why we have come to live in Egypt. We want to see and experience the other dimensions of Arab people, and then we want to pass on this bigger, fuller picture to our family and friends back home."

Abdullah's face broadened into a grin as he caught on to the significance of what Brad had said. He shook Brad's hand eagerly and said, "Welcome to Egypt! Welcome to my house anytime!"

Sometimes opportunities to share our reasons for being in Egypt came up spontaneously in conversations. Other times, we would be caught off-guard. Once Nicholas and I were shopping in a popular bazaar that sells everything from household items to lingerie, all under a big, colorful tent.

"How much are these three towels?" I asked.

"Ninety pounds," the seller responded.

"Perhaps eighty?" I asked hopefully.

"Eighty-eight."

"Eight-two" I countered. If I could inch my way up, perhaps

he would inch his way down and we'd meet around eighty-five.

"Eighty-eight and no less."

"Eighty-two and no more." We went back and forth over the price as I was absolutely convinced that buying three of the same item gave me some bargaining power.

"Eighty-two," he conceded with a weary sigh, obviously disappointed to have eight pounds less than the starting price. He wrapped the towels in a bag and handed them to me with a lighthearted comment, "That's why America is rich and Egypt is poor."

Ouch! That hurt, and he knew it would. We bought some cold drinks and sat on an empty bench to rest our weary feet. It was then that I recalled the advice from one friend, "We really don't bargain at the 'tents' because the prices are so cheap." I had forgotten that.

Bargaining in the Middle East is an ancient tradition, but there actually are some rules to the process; for instance, one person should not excessively triumph over the other. Most foreigners have a Wal-Mart mentality in which "bargaining" means "how cheap can I get this?" When I finally worked up the courage to start bargaining, that was my attitude, and I often walked away proudly holding my purchase as a trophy for my clever bargaining skills. But I was now less concerned about saving money and more concerned about presenting Americans as fair and honest people.

"Nicholas," I said, "what do you think the towel seller will think of Americans after his work day is done?"

"That we have a lot of money but don't like spending it?" he guessed, swatting the flies away from his face.

"Is that the kind of impression we want to give him about Americans?"

"Not really."

"Well, what do you think we should do about it?" We discussed some options and agreed on giving back some money, enough for the seller to have made a reasonable profit and enough for us to feel we still had a bargain. I put five Egyptian pounds in my hand, meandered through the crowd back to the towel seller, and found him sitting in a plastic chair, snuffing a cigarette on the wooden table.

"Here," I said without any fanfare.

"*Merci*," he replied simply.

The relationship was restored and we parted, each feeling satisfied with the deal.

After about three months in our cubby-hole apartment, the back of one of our chairs fell off. Brad is an excellent handyman, but he didn't have the tools to repair the chair, nor would it have been a good thing for him to admit to others that he had made some basic household repairs. Egypt is a class-conscious society, and because we are educated and middle class, we were expected to contract out all our repair jobs. So Brad brought the chair to a welder whose workshop was the sidewalk in front of his house. The welder was soldering a metal tool together, without protective eyewear, while flying sparks narrowly missed pedestrians and a horse standing nearby.

When the job was completed, Brad, still not quite sure about the khalli (no charge) routine, never heard a specific price. So he thanked the man and left without paying anything. As he walked away, he could hear some bystanders snickering and laughing at the welder. We later translated their remarks to mean, "You fool! Don't say that to a foreigner—they believe you!"

Of course, we should have paid something! Wanting to keep a good reputation in this town, Rebecca and I set out to find the welder and pay him. We knocked on his door and went through the same khalli routine, until he finally relented and said one pound, about fifteen cents. When a service was this ridiculously cheap, I would think to myself, "Come on, you know we are foreigners. At least charge us double so I don't feel like I'm taking advantage of you!" I already had two pounds in my hand to give him, so I just handed it to him.

But he could not leave the situation as it was. I had been generous, and now he needed to respond in kind. He invited us into his small, dilapidated, mud-brick house, about the size of one room in our apartment. The door edged open slowly, and right in the entranceway was a small wooden bed with his white-haired mother lying in it. She sat up and welcomed us to sit on the only available space, her bed, and talked as if she always had foreigners coming in to disturb her rest.

A few minutes later the welder reappeared with two drinks, which cost nearly two pounds. It was the law of unintended consequences—I was thinking how magnanimously generous I had been for giving him double, and he went and spent the money right back on us. This was a new skill we would keep learning—not to protest a person's generosity but to graciously accept what a poor person had offered us.

There were also opportunities for us to learn the value of relationships and the responsibilities we have to others, whether we know them or not.

One holiday we were vacationing in Alexandria on Egypt's Mediterranean coast. It was about eleven at night, and we were walking with a throng of other folks through a popular market with vendors selling all sorts of cheap, "Made in China" items. We could barely keep our family together as we got swept along with the bargain hunters.

It never fails in these situations that a car will try to drive through a congested crowd as if the driver were playing a modern-day Moses and hoping the crowd would miraculously part. A driver of a shiny, new Mercedes slowly meandered his way through the crowd, furiously honking the horn. Suddenly we heard a loud wailing and turned around to see a thin man in his twenties, hands raised in the air, his face distorted by anguish. At his feet was an old, battered basket that had been filled with small clamshells, which were now scattered about: it was his day's catch, and he was on his way to the fish market to sell them. Apparently the car had hit his basket and now his "daily bread" was strewn on the streets, ruined.

The driver reluctantly got out into the midst of the gathering crowd and berated the fisherman unmercifully for a full minute. Without taking any responsibility for the matter, the driver got back in his car and drove off, leaving the other man inconsolable. But that did not mean the gathered crowd could just walk off. One bystander called out something and began walking among the crowd. We noticed people giving him money. I put some money in Emily's hand and she made our contribution to the cause. The bystander then brought the collected amount to the aggrieved man; it was his "insurance compensation" for lost wages. He accepted the money, gathered up his torn basket and a few scattered clams, and went on his way. The crowd went back to its shopping and milling about. The whole incident lasted about ten minutes, a small part of the daily flow of life on a crowded street.

We were to learn the value of the relationships we had developed when we tackled our next challenge: finding a new apartment.

౼

We had just survived winter. Winter? In Egypt? Somehow these two words had never connected for us. We associated Egypt with hot deserts. But it also has a good three months of cool days and colder nights. While the temperature isn't so significant, it's the houses themselves that make the weather seem colder, because the concrete walls do not insulate. If we wanted to be warm, we went outside and sat in the sun. Muslim women, of course, are snug in their headscarves, but Christian women wear neither scarves nor hats in the winter.

The coming of our first spring was enjoyable, with only an occasional dust storm blowing in from the desert. But a week later, summer hit us like a wool blanket—suffocating. Living on the top floor of the school meant we were right under the sun. We could see it glistening off our metal chairs, which by noon were too hot to touch. We braced ourselves for summer in an apartment that felt like a convection oven.

Fortunately our MCC country representative, James, had a better idea. "Why don't you consider getting an apartment away from the school? You won't have to hassle with the bowab telling your friends to leave at a certain time. Plus you'll have a lot more privacy than living in a school and likely a lot less noise."

James, along with his wife, Linda, were our "bosses," and more important, supporters, confidantes, and friends. Over the past nine months, our two families had grown very close; their three children were roughly the same ages as ours and acted as siblings. It was the instant bonding that sometimes happens among Americans living in foreign lands. We shared similar values, life experiences, and parenting skills that were constantly being challenged in the new culture.

James and Linda had met fourteen years earlier when they were living in Cairo. Romance blossomed. They married and later bore their eldest daughter while living in Beni Suef. After serving five years in Egypt and four more in Palestine, they were experienced with life in the Arab world. Besides that, they knew how to cross a

Cairo street and drive through the craziness of Cairo traffic, scary but necessary skills that foreigners living in Egypt try to achieve.

We were sitting in the breezeway outside our school apartment, reviewing with James and Linda the ups and downs of our lives. The kids were off playing in the classrooms on the floors below. This was one benefit to living in the school: endless hide-and-seek opportunities during after-school hours. Another benefit was the convenience of getting to school on time, though Nicholas, who had only to descend three floors to get to his classroom, often managed to fumble that advantage. But I was ready to have some neighbors and a more normal life.

"So, how do we go about getting an apartment?" Brad inquired. "We haven't exactly seen the Yellow Pages around here." This was true; though we had a phone, we had never seen a phone book.

"It's all word of mouth," Linda told us. "It's not completely true to say that Egypt isn't an information society; it's just that things are not written down. Part of the reason is that landlords don't want to rent to just anyone, but to someone who can be vouched for as trustworthy through a third person. So it's not a simple matter of 'letting your fingers do the walking' through the Yellow Pages but rather your legs walk through the desired neighborhood. All those good relationships you have been building up the past few months will come in handy."

With that advice, we explained to Magdy, the young man assigned to help us settle in, what kind of apartment we were seeking: three bedrooms, furnished, walking distance to the school.

His immediate response was, "I will take you to the Moqbil area, because a lot of Christians live there."

"Uhh, Magdy, that's kind of far. We want something close to school so we can all walk to school when we need to." The American real-estate mantra "location, location, location" was uppermost in our minds.

"But you should rent from a Christian landlord," Magdy explained. "It's just better. Muslims are always trying to take advantage of us, and we have to watch our business dealings with them very carefully. Some of them are good, but you can't trust most of them."

I sighed. We simply wanted to rent an apartment. Why did religion have to figure into so many things? We later found that religion has little to do with this issue. When it comes to money, most Egyptians automatically distrust each other and assume they will be taken advantage of.

Brad, Magdy, and I strolled through a new area, where apartments were still being built near a field in which a few camels still grazed. Yet it was near a main road that would be convenient for shopping. Brad tried a new approach. "We want to look in this area because it is quiet and there aren't many people."

"No, you don't want to live here," Magdy said. "This could be dangerous."

"Dangerous? How?" Brad asked as he looked around at the tree-shaded street, envisioning our kids riding bikes around because there were hardly any cars or people.

"Look!" Magdy said, getting a bit exasperated at our ignorance. "There are no cars, no shops, no people on the streets. It's not safe to be in an area without people."

For Americans, few people and few cars spell safety; for Egyptians, the rule is that people keep other people honest. It was one of the reasons there was so little crime—many eyes were always watching, and people often dispensed justice on the spot.

The summer days ticked away with no apartment in sight. We joined the nadi, and the kids did karate and swimming. Family swim time (meaning pre-adolescent boys and girls) was from nine p.m. to midnight; friends told us it's too hot to swim during the day! We adopted the Egyptian schedule to cope with the heat: nap all afternoon and stay up until the wee hours of the morning. We found several apartments we liked, but when it came to paying the deposit, we would be mysteriously rejected. It was beginning to seem like a futile search.

Prodded by a combination of courage and desperation, I went out by myself to ask around a neighborhood one morning after Brad had headed off to his summer English class. This in itself presented a problem: while I had more Arabic than Brad to make apartment hunting possible, it is definitely a "man's world" and that put me in an awkward position.

"Good morning," I said to the street cleaner as he scooped debris into a flimsy palm basket. "How are you today? I'm a married woman with three children and am teaching English in St. Anthony's School. My husband and I are looking for an apartment with furniture. Do you know of one near here that might be suitable for us?"

It was important that I explained a little bit about who I was and established myself as a married woman; a single woman wandering the streets asking for an apartment just might be told to take the first donkey out of town.

The garbage collector thought for a moment. His day was spent going in and out of many apartment buildings, so he always had an eye open for empty ones. He motioned for me to sit, then walked across the street to consult with a shop owner before disappearing down the street. I peered into a shop window of an electronics store and saw four boom boxes, each with "Panasonic" spelled differently. The shopkeeper, noticing me through the glass, walked out of his shop, carrying a chair and a glass of hot tea for me.

Not long after, a figure in bright orange came shuffling down the street. "A woman around the corner has a three-bedroom apartment with furniture," the garbage man said. "She says you can come look at it after noon prayers. The building is on the left side of the street with a light pole in front of it and a red car parked nearby."

With few street names and addresses, that was about as good as any directions got. I thanked him and slipped him some money to express my appreciation.

Brad and I returned in the afternoon and found the apartment delightful. The landlady was friendly and helpful in answering all our questions; we had the usual conversations about our work and ourselves. We made an appointment to return later that night so the kids could see our new place. But when we showed up, she would not open her door.

"My husband says I cannot rent to you," she said.

"But why?" I stammered, absolutely shocked.

"I'm sorry."

I wanted to bang on the door and plead, "But I had nothing to do with the war. I protested against it! I had nothing to do with Abu Ghraib." All summer long the newspapers had been filled with the horrid photos American soldiers took of themselves torturing and abusing Iraqi prisoners at the Abu Ghraib prison. I couldn't believe what I was hearing now from this landlady, and in my desperation, that was the first reaction that popped into my head. Was she rejecting us because we are Christians? Americans? Or something more mundane, such as previously having a bad experience renting to foreigners? My heart plunged to my feet. There was no "fair housing board" to which we could complain. Her husband had said no, and the matter was settled.

ع

"Daddy, tomorrow we'll be in Egypt for one year. We need to celebrate with a special breakfast—bacon!" So said Rebecca with her usual big smile. Bacon? A pork product in a Muslim country? Well, after a year in a place, you learn your way around. We had discovered a Christian-owned grocery store in Cairo that had bacon, not sitting openly in the meat case, but available upon request.

During our celebration, we recognized our achievements and all the relationships we had cultivated with families whose kids were classmates with ours. That was an unexpected bonus; having kids in a family-oriented society opened many doors for us.

We were still living in our cubby-hole apartment atop the school, but the children would no longer run down the stairs into their classrooms. We had decided to home school, a decision that surprised even us, as it was never my intention to be a home-schooling parent in a foreign land. It was a big step away from our original motto of "living as much like Egyptians as we could." One year in the school seemed manageable, but I feared after three years our children would lose their love of learning. Plus Sister Heba had informed us that the kids must stay in their classrooms all day instead of retreating when they needed to. We were concerned about the heavy emphasis on memorization of facts and monthly exams, and the minor emphasis on orderly classrooms and thinking skills. Whenever we told people that our children studied at home, we were always asked the same question: "But how will they take exams?"

Another big change was the arrival of a British family who also worked at St. Anthony's and the girl's orphanage. Another MCC worker had come for a one-year assignment at the Coptic Orthodox retreat center across the river. Beni Suef was becoming international, and it was exciting to have people with similar faiths and interests. Our lives had definitely improved since those early frustrating months.

By then we had walked through so many streets with various

friends that we feared our pickiness and general bad luck in finding an apartment would strain our friendships. With a new burst of
energy, Brad called our friend Girgis to ask for help. He came the
next day, which happened to be an Egyptian national holiday. We
appreciated his generosity of time, being sure he preferred to spend
the day like everyone else—sleeping in and watching TV.

Girgis immediately took Brad to a *simsar* (real estate agent).
His "office" was a plastic chair on a sidewalk under a tree. A crude
piece of board with SIMSAR written in fancy Arabic script was
nailed to the tree. We had heard of this service but in our zeal to be
independent, had never really considered it. Before hot tea could
even make its inevitable appearance, Brad was standing in a new
apartment that fit our needs perfectly.

Brad immediately came to get me and the kids; we were spending the holiday at the girls orphanage. We were all excited and anxious not to lose this apartment. When we went to see it, Girgis met
me outside and cautioned, "Don't show that you like this place. If
you look pleased they will give you a big price, but if you look like
you are not too happy, they will make a lower price." I went along
with him, but I suspect the reason we paid double the average
monthly rent had more to do with our nationality than our facial
expressions.

ẽ

It was a day for celebrating, as we had found a new place! It was
also a day of terrorism, shock, and mourning. Several men in the
distant Sinai desert loaded a truck with explosives and rammed it
into a hotel, killing thirteen Egyptians, ten Israelis, and fifteen other
foreigners. It was the first act of terrorism in Egypt since our arrival,
and we were surprised by the lack of reaction to it. We expected to
see candles and flowers commemorating the deaths, and people
marching and protesting against terrorism. But the folks we encountered in our daily life did not say much about it, and I assumed we
missed much of the conversations due to our limited language. As
time went on, we found that most Egyptians believed it was an
extension of the ongoing Israeli-Palestinian conflict and thus didn't
really involve them.

But the bombing was personal for us: Nicholas's American

friend was vacationing with his mother in the hotel at the time. Though his mother was not hurt, Nicholas's friend was injured, treated in Israel, and returned back home to Cairo, recovered but badly shaken.

𝕮

After everything with the new apartment was signed and paid, we packed and moved. Actually it didn't happen that smoothly. Though I was anxious to move, I suddenly became paralyzed with the thought of relocating to a new area and having to learn new street routes, new places to shop, new directions to give taxi drivers. Our territory around the school was familiar; people knew me, knew my accent, and often knew what I wanted when I didn't have all the right words. That is a great source of security and comfort when living in a foreign country. "You can walk a year along a canal and never cross it" is an Egyptian proverb that accurately summed up how I felt: no courage to take the risk to the unknown on the other side. I just couldn't gather up the energy to start over again.

But we were not alone. At times like this we needed our community of support, and MCC came through for us. James offered good suggestions and comfort; Linda helped us pack and organize our new apartment. The kids were all excited about the move, and even I rallied and bought an item that symbolized we were truly in a neighborhood: a wicker basket. The kids tied the basket onto a long rope attached to the balcony railing. Now whenever a donkey cart vendor came plying his wares down the street, we would simply lower our basket to receive our orders of bananas or eggplant.

It wasn't long before we discovered lots of conveniences on our new street. First, was the *makwagi* (clothes ironer). He used a true iron—the kind that holds open a door in an antique shop—heated by coals. His method was quite entertaining. First he took a swig of water. Then he tilted his head back, and *whoooosh!*—a fine spray covered the clothes. I could have six pieces ironed and delivered for less than a dollar, tip included. The only drawback was that deliveries came around one in the morning. Never tell anyone to just "drop it off when you're finished."

Our other discovery was the milkman who rode his motorcycle

Our milkman, who delivered to us twice a day, always greeted us with a smile.

all day with a big metal can of fresh milk strapped to the side. His first delivery had him ringing the doorbell furiously. Brad got out of bed, wondering what the commotion could be, and found the milkman standing in his sparkling white galabaya, holding up two plastic bags of milk, a smile of satisfaction on his face for having found the right address. All Brad could do was groggily shake his head and close the door: it was 3:30 in the morning. Was it just us, or did Egyptians normally have their clothes and food delivered at the wee hours of the morning?

Our three grandfatherly guards moved with us. Before being able to rent the apartment, the security police had to inspect the neighborhood and make sure it was suitable for foreigners. Any place too crowded or poverty-stricken—the stereotypical "breeding ground for terrorists and terrorism"—was off-limits. Actually we frequently walked through these areas but lately had avoided them but for a completely different reason: the elderly women in bright peasant scarves whom we sarcastically called "the tea terrorists." They sat all day outside their doorways and beckoned us to stop and drink tea whenever we passed. We occasionally did, but the girls got tired of the scratchy, hairy chin when "grandma" pulled them down to her for a kiss!

We bought some plastic chairs and had a bed made for the guards so they could sleep in the apartment entranceway. One of the guards immediately struck up a friendship with the fruit and vegetable seller across the street. One morning when I was buying some fruit, another customer, after hearing me speak, complimented me on my Arabic, then turned to the guard to ask where I was from. It was common for me to be ignored and left listening to people talk about me. It was annoying, so I felt no obligation to correct the guard when he replied, "Germany." Either the guard was being really clever by guarding our nationality, or he had never been briefed by his superiors about who he was guarding and why. I had no doubt the latter was true. While the heavy police presence in every village or city gave the illusion of security, it was generally a government employment scheme that provided jobs to lots of men at very low salaries.

The kids' goal in their new neighborhood was to have bicycles, but the idea took a while to grow on me. By my own unorthodox calculations, whenever I was in the street on some errand, I narrowly missed being hit by a car at least four times. If I moved out of the way to miss a car that had just swerved right in front of me, then I would step in the path of a bicyclist whom I did not know was quietly coming up behind me. Just a few days before, I had witnessed two boys on a bicycle collide with three boys on a motorcycle, causing the driver, who was perhaps twelve years old, to ram his motorcycle into a standing horse. They were not going fast and no one was hurt; bystanders dusted off the kids and sent them on their way. But I kept visualizing my kids in that situation.

It was important for us that, while avoiding hospitalizations, the kids had positive memories of their time in Egypt. It was impor-

A typical close call between two bicyclists. These kinds of near-accidents made us cautious about letting the kids ride bikes.

tant to the kids that they could easily travel to St. Anthony's, the orphanage, and the nadi. In the end, we got one bicycle with a seat on the back, which they all shared. The arrangement worked out fine. As for my coping methods, I found the best thing was to just not look when they were riding down the street. I was picking up the Egyptian habit of surrendering to God and fate, for there was little I could do about the Egyptians' erratic driving habits.

After about a month, the kids discovered we had neighbors. A small woman and her young sons were out on the balcony one morning while we were hanging out the wet laundry. We exchanged smiles, waves, and a few awkward "how are yous?" She held her son up so we could see him. Wow! What a surprise to see a mass of curly blond hair, brown eyes, and light skin.

Over the last six months of apartment hunting, we had received plenty of warnings and advice about neighborhoods and landlords. Looking back, though, I now wonder why no one mentioned a common Egyptian proverb: "Choose your neighbor before choosing your house."

10

Choose Your Neighbor

"Wahlahi, wahlahi, wahlahi. Yababa, yababa, yababa!"

Oh my God! Oh my God! Oh my God! Oh daddy, oh daddy, oh daddy!

Our neighbor's screams pierced the silent night. I sat up in bed to listen. Why can't they just go to sleep at night like normal people do? I got out of bed, glancing at the clock—3:40 a.m. Should I go any further? The woman's screams got louder. I grabbed my robe off the wall, walked out of the apartment, and stood in front of their door.

I had talked to her earlier that morning while I was getting clothes off the clothesline. She was on her balcony with her two-year-old son, her right arm in a makeshift sling. She talked a lot about her husband, and I gathered he had something to do with her arm being in that condition. She mentioned about going to her mama's that night but evidently had come back.

She had also told me that her husband's father was the owner of half the apartment building, not our landlord but probably well acquainted with him. That was going through my mind as I stood in the hallway outside her door, arguing with myself. I had seen this woman only a couple of times; I didn't yet know her name. If I knocked on the door and interrupted their argument, would her husband turn his anger on me and possibly take revenge by telling his father something about his new neighbor? He could probably have us booted out of the apartment before I could say "tenants' rights."

What was I doing standing outside their door anyway? What did I think I could accomplish? If I were in the United States, I would know what to do: call the police about a "disturbance," hardly having to roll out of bed, hardly having to get involved. But I was in a foreign country where I didn't know the rules. Should I wake Brad? No, he wouldn't know any more than I about what to do. Should I wake the guard sleeping in the entranceway two floors down? No, he was there to protect us from "terrorists," not wives from their husbands.

While I didn't know what to do, it was clear I could not go back to bed and pretend nothing was happening. I had previously witnessed an abusive situation involving a teacher and students, but I had cowardly watched in silence. I had vowed then that even though I was a foreigner, I had to "speak truth to evil" when I saw it. If I spoke out against the war in Iraq, I should also speak out about the battle taking place in this living room.

"*Wahlahi, wahlahi, wahlahi! Yababa, yababa, yababa!*" Another loud scream jolted me from my internal debate. I said a prayer and knocked on the door. Complete silence. I waited. Nothing happened. Good, perhaps they won't open the door; they'll just know that someone else knows and go on to bed. I turned to leave; the door opened. It was the husband.

"Uh, is there a problem? I heard some noise," I said.

The husband looked at his feet and blathered on with whatever lying husbands caught in the act of battering say.

I went back to my bed. What did he go back to? I couldn't hear anything anymore. Was he beating her again for being so loud? For having a nosy neighbor? It really didn't matter. Had I not knocked, he would have hit her anyway. I chided myself for not being more clever. "I'm baking a cake and don't have any eggs," I could have said. "Could I borrow two?" It's not unreasonable in Egypt to be cooking in the middle of the night! Or I could have just knocked on the door then gone back to our apartment without waiting for him to answer.

I thought about her mother, who surely knows her son-in-law is abusing her daughter. I wonder if she ever heard her scream like I did? I pictured my own lovely daughters asleep in bed and wonder how a mother lets her daughter go back to an abusive husband.

"*Allahu akbar!*" The sunrise call to prayer had just begun. We lived surrounded by three mosques, and no longer did I need an alarm clock. The prayers were amplified by loudspeakers on all four corners of all three mosques, but they were not synchronized to begin at the same time. The first mosque's call was lovely. The muezzin had a deep, melodious voice that would beckon anyone to arouse from sleep and thank God for the dawning of a new day. Unfortunately, after about thirty seconds, he was drowned out by another who believed the way to arouse the faithful was to shriek and bark commands, rattling our bedroom windows. After another half-minute, all the mosques had joined in and it was just a cacophony of competing noises. I remembered my vow to pray if ever awakened by the call, but I must confess I longed for one night of uninterrupted sleep.

But sleep did not come. I still heard the screams of my neighbor silently echoing in my head. Soon it would be time to get everyone up, as we were going into Cairo for the weekend. I said a silent prayer for my neighbor because it would be several days before I'd see her again.

🌙

"*Hamdillah salaam!* [Thank God you have returned safely!]" called out our neighbor when we returned from our trip to Cairo.

"*Allah yisalimik!* [May God keep you safe too]," I replied. This is the normal greeting after any journey is taken. We exchange names; she was Fatma.

Fatma was standing outside her door, directly across from ours, with her two boys by her side. Garbage from plastic bags, ripped open by the stray cats that wandered through our building, was strewn about the hallway, giving off a funky odor. Her foot had a bandage on it; she pulled up her pants leg and showed me her swollen knee.

"I knocked on your door a few days ago," I said awkwardly.

"Yes, I know."

Hmmm. I can't read anything from that response. Was she glad that I had knocked, or did it just make matters worse?

"I was afraid your husband would be angry."

"Don't be afraid of Nadir. He likes you and your children." Somehow her words were not very comforting, but she smiled, exposing a chipped front tooth. She called my kids over to exam her wounds. I preferred that they not know this aspect of my neighbors' life, for I had not told them anything about that disturbing night. But I remained silent. She had a need to share her pain with someone.

"I'm going out to buy some groceries. Do you need anything?" I asked. It was an expression I had picked up from Egyptians who always end their conversations asking if the other person needs anything.

"We don't have anything," she replied before turning to yell at her kids to quit climbing on the metal gate that covered their door. The wooden door had been kicked open so many times that it no longer closed properly, so the iron gate was added protection. Fatma took me by the hand, and even with an injured leg she had enough strength to drag me along into the kitchen.

I was dreading the sight, and reality didn't disappoint. The walls were stained with grease and the stove caked brown with years of burned grease. The sink tap leaked and the constant drips of water slid over the edge, ran down the side, and landed in a growing puddle on the floor. She lifted the lid from a pot on the stove. Inside the burned pot was an inedible chicken leg and an onion. A plate on the floor had beans and a piece of bread. She turned to the counter and opened one jar after another.

"No tea, no sugar, no oil, no salt." These were the staples of an Egyptian kitchen. "Nothing," she yelled, hitting her hand hard on the counter.

I left her house without promising anything, feeling a bit resentful. The proper response to "do you need anything?" is "no, thanks." But she didn't follow the game as I had intended it. When I asked her if she needed anything, she should have said yes and given me money to pick up a pound of bananas. I would have gotten them for her, and it would be finished. We would be good neighbors on even terms. Instead she took me by the hand and led me into her kitchen, into her misery, where I did not want to go.

☙

Throughout the next several months, over many glasses of hot tea, Fatma poured out her tales of sorrow. She was greatly animated, and her voice would rise high with shrill outrage then drop low to a whisper that I had to strain to hear. Her hands waved about, slapping her leg to make a point, or her finger wagged in my face to make sure I understood the impact of what she had just said.

Fatma had been married for seven years, beginning when she

was eighteen, right after she finished high school. Her parents did not want her to marry Nadir.

"They wanted me to marry my cousin," she said. "But I couldn't do that. He is like a brother to me." A friend knew a man who was ready to marry, introduced them, and it was love at first sight.

"After we married, relatives came to visit us. I prepared sweets, served the guests, and sat to visit with them. Nadir got angry. 'What are you doing with them? You should be in the kitchen preparing food for our guests, not out socializing with them.' That made me mad," she said cocking her eyebrows up. "I told him, 'Am I your servant? I gave up college to marry you, and you want me to stay in the kitchen and be your servant?'"

She got her first punch in the face. The relatives heard and tried to intervene but, "on the life of our God, he is as fierce as an ox. He then said, 'I divorce you.'" For Muslims, that usually means the wife returns to her family or at least the couple doesn't share a bedroom together until both families resolve the dispute.

The story got worse. Between the birth of her two boys, her husband was in prison "for stealing something before we got married." Fatma and her baby lived with her parents during those four years. Judging from the age of her youngest child, Nadir had been out of prison for about two years. Unemployed and rarely at home, he preferred to spend his time with his friends in the *ahwahs* (coffee shops). There wasn't much of a relationship.

I took a good look at her. Fatma was only twenty-four years old and probably not any wiser than when she married at eighteen. She would have looked cute in her jeans and pullover sweater, but her face looked tired and worn, giving the impression that she just didn't care anymore. Her large brown eyes, with permanent circles under them, filled with tears as she described the time her husband held her hand in hot oil. I recalled her earlier comments about marrying her husband because of love. How do you love someone who treats you worse than the cats roaming the streets?

"Feel that? And here." She took my hand and ran a finger over the scars on her hand, emphasizing each one. Fatma was the perfect "poster child" for advocating arranged marriages by parents. I could just hear Egyptian parents: "See what happens when young people decide these things for themselves?!" Surely the cousin selected by her parents could not have been any worse.

After a visit with Fatma, it helped to go for a walk around the neighborhood. Our family was still getting acquainted with different neighborhood stores and services, when I discovered a plant nursery. Seeing a pile of clay pots strewn in front of a bamboo fence, I poked my head in and felt I had been transported to another place. Flowers! Bright, pink bougainvilleas grace the entranceway to rows of marigolds and mums. The air was punctuated with the sweet smells of jasmine, rosemary, and basil. Yellow, pink, and red roses lined the fence. It was a feast for the eyes to behold such a panorama of colors. My nose, long accustomed to inhaling car fumes and the stench of horse manure, delighted in the sweet scents as I strolled about inhaling deeply. When living in a foreign place, you often don't know what you have missed until you encounter it again.

"I want a bouquet of flowers about this big," I said to the seller, using my hands to describe the size. I also enjoyed the friendliness of a gardener, who didn't have many customers coming by.

"Tomorrow is an American holiday, and I am having a lot of guests and want something pretty for the dining room table."

"What kind of holiday?" he quizzed as he reached for his pair of scissors.

"Well, it's a day when we thank God for our food, family, and friends."

"Uh huh. And do you thank God for your new president?" It was November 2004, and George W. Bush had just won reelection in the United States. While no one was surprised, neither could Egyptians understand how Americans could so naïvely reelect this man. All summer we had heard loud and lengthy conversations about the dangers and fears of President Bush. For Egyptians, who focused mainly on foreign policy, especially regarding Israel, Palestine, and Iraq, the matter seemed so obvious. I often left those discussions wondering why Egyptians were so intensely debating a foreign president's policies when I never heard any discussions about their own government's policies. Is it because President Bush had more of an impact on their lives or because after having the same president for twenty-four years, there wasn't much more to say? And how much freedom was there to say it?

"Every day so many Iraqis are killed and are suffering. Why is this happening?"

"Well . . ." I kind of hemmed and hawed. Political questions have no easy answers, and people didn't often expect them anyway. They mostly wanted to air their frustrations, which were often very similar to mine. "We're hoping the war ends soon. We want to have peace."

"Why does your president not like Muslims? He says that we don't like Americans and that isn't true. Do you want some greenery with the flowers?" He mixed in basil with roses and mums then set the bouquet on the ground. "We are like this," and he clasped his two hands together. "Muslims like Christians. Christians like Muslims. This is good."

I fished around in my purse for some money before he held up his hand, "No money. This is a gift for your holiday. Best wishes to you."

"Thank you," seemed like an inadequate reply.

🐾

About a week later, as we were sitting down to read, we heard the neighbors coming up the stairs. Their voices reached our floor before their bodies did. They had gotten into the habit of, before entering their own apartment, automatically ringing our doorbell.

"Oh no!" groaned Nicholas. "Right when we are at the best part of the story!"

I gave a weary sigh. I had pledged to the kids not to let Fatma and her crises control our family time, and I reassured them that we'd make this visit brief. Emily opened the door.

"Mama!" she shrieked. I tossed the book aside and we hopped up from the sofa.

There was Medo, barely two years old, standing calmly with blood all over his face.

"*Tante Gigi* [Aunt Gigi, my nickname], I want a towel."

I was wiping his face with a wet towel when Fatma walked in. "What happened?" I asked, carefully wiping the blood from around his eyes. "Did he fall down?"

"I tell you what he did, that naughty boy. He dragged the clean sheet I had just washed down the street. I hit him in the face, and his nose started to bleed. It's the only sheet I have. What are we going to sleep on tonight?" She yelled some more and raised her hand as if to strike him again.

Our neighbor Fatma with her children, Mumtez (standing) and Medo.

The sight of the little boy's face covered in blood stunned us, though it wasn't as bad as it looked. He had rubbed his eyes because he was crying and that smeared blood all over. But he had been hit hard enough to make his nose bleed. I was just getting accustomed to the idea of having a neighbor who was abused and sorting through all the personal and cultural mess that involved. While I knew that spouse abuse often isn't the only violence in the home, I wasn't at all prepared to witness her abusiveness to her own children.

To help me get a better perspective on the situation, I discussed the incident with one of the English teachers at St. Anthony's. I had already caught on to the difference in how something like this incident was viewed—I called it abuse; Fatma and many others called it discipline.

"When she hits her child so hard that he bleeds, what can I say to her?" I asked the teacher.

"Tell her that the boy doesn't behave that way to make her angry; he does it because he is a child. She needs to be patient with him. But many people think that hitting is the right way to teach children correct behavior."

I explained that if that happened in the United States, I would be obligated by law to call the police and report the parent's abuse.

"No, you can't do that here," the teacher informed me. "Maybe there are laws against child abuse but, for most people, this isn't abuse. And people don't interfere with what is going on in the home. If the husband is beating his wife, that is his business. And if they are beating the child, that is also their business. The husband is the master in his house, and no one will argue with him. Your neighbor is poor and ignorant and hasn't been taught any better way than hitting. But you should simply tell her that it is wrong."

It was good advice. Another day, Fatma came over to borrow a cup. I gave her one and followed her to her apartment with a bowl of popcorn I had just made. Mumtez, the seven-year-old, was in our apartment playing computer games with Nicholas. Medo lay sleeping on a mattress on the living room floor. I peered closely in the dim light and could see black and blue bruises all over his little back.

"Who hit him?" I asked.

"His father," Fatma said. "Kicked him too." She laid her hands gently on his curls, caressing his face.

"Look," she said, turning him over so I could see the bruises on his stomach.

I didn't bother to ask why; whys didn't really matter anymore. "You know, Fatma, my kids are bad too. Sometimes I get really angry at them. Sometimes I want to hit them. When I am angry, I make them go to their room so I don't have to look at them."

"Why don't you just hit them?"

"Because I think it is wrong. My husband doesn't hit me, and we don't hit our kids."

"But if you send them to their room, do they still keep doing the same bad things?"

"Sometimes. I have to talk with them and explain why they did wrong. Sometimes they know why and still do it anyway!"

"That's because you don't hit them," Fatma said. "If you hit them, they wouldn't do it again. They would be afraid of getting hit again, so they don't do it. If they do it again, then you know that you didn't hit them hard enough. Simple as that."

"I just don't like hitting people. I think it is wrong."

And so the talk went on. It was a small effort to show another way of handling problems. Husbands abusing wives and parents abusing kids both stem from a patriarchal culture that allows dominance of the male over women and children.

Violence isn't just a result of culture but also of poverty, and it is exacerbated in poor areas like Beni Suef where there are limited economic opportunities. People who struggle to survive day to day often live on the edge of their tempers. Loud arguments and gruff, angry voices frequently erupt in the streets during the simple exchange of buying food. Often a crowd gathers to supply a restraining force, making sure that reason or justice prevails, but not excessive violence. But where is the "restraining force" when the violence is in the privacy of one's home?

The message from the schoolteacher was not to dismiss violence and get sucked into calling it "part of the Egyptian culture," for that would imply acceptance or tolerance of it. Yet the responses I heard from several women were disturbing. "Gigi, some women are bad and need to be corrected. They cannot just gossip about others and go out dressed in a bad way. This brings shame on the whole family. What husband would allow that?"

People made a distinction between discipline, which was socially acceptable, and violence that leaves a person battered and bruised. Regardless of the fine line between the two, there were no sanctions against either. Had the guard posted two floors down heard Fatma's screams, he would not have interfered. There was no reason he should, because spousal abuse was not recognized as a problem.

I also tried to consider what our involvement should be with Fatma's husband. I had a hard time drumming up compassion for him, but viewing him as a vicious brute would not improve matters. When I shared this incident with John, an Egyptian who worked with MCC, he told me about his former neighbor, who drank alcohol and beat his wife. While John never interfered with the abuse at the time it was happening, he did make friends with this man, intentionally sharing his views on nonviolence. Over the years, the man eventually quit drinking and abusing his wife, who credited the change in her husband to John's influence.

It was an inspiring story, but our situation did not lend itself to the same solution. For one thing, we had no relationship with the husband. We only saw him coming and going from his apartment. I would smile or mumble a hello, but he rarely looked up. Brad did not know enough Arabic to hold a conversation with him. While language wasn't an issue for me, the cultural restrictions on personal conversation with men would have immediately raised suspicions of my true intentions. I could just hear the gossip that I was trying to seduce Nadir away from Fatma!

I was also concerned about the impact of the violence on my own family. We enjoyed having the boys at our house, and it was good for them to see how another family interacted. Sometimes Fatma left the boys with us while she ran errands. She never asked me for permission to do this, but instead asked Nicholas. Culturally this made sense. Brad was not home, so the next person in charge was not me, but my thirteen-year-old son.

It wasn't long before Nicholas caught on to the power he thought was granted him by the culture. One day Medo broke something in Nicholas's room, causing him to angrily declare, "I'm the man of the house when Daddy isn't here, and I want them out!" I had to remind my son that I was the one in charge. I looked at the culture from a distance, objectively observing what Egyptians were doing, but my kids lived the culture and, for better or worse, absorbed all they saw and heard.

☪

"How are you, Um Nicholas? How are the kids? How is Mr. Brad?" Um Amzat yelled joyfully. She stood up from her wooden stool and extended her arm over the basket of oranges to greet me, careful not to knock over the box of hot peppers. Her long, blue galabaya was soiled from the day's work of handling fruits and vegetables. Though poor and disheveled, she wore huge, gold loop earrings that dangled from her stretched ear lobes. Gold jewelry was her wedding dowry and now served as her "insurance policy" for financially hard times.

She and her husband rented a small stall across the street from us. Each day they set out tables and baskets filled with a garden variety. Empty crates were stacked on the side next to a box of rotting food covered with flies. An old fashioned scale with weights

Nicholas buys bread as Um Amzat praises God.

rested on a table. The dirt floor was covered with debris from the parsley, carrots, and dill she chopped.

"We are fine, thanks be to God," I replied while clasping her stained hand and kissing her cheeks. She patted a chair for me to sit on, then turned her attention to a burner heating water for tea. While she snapped green beans, we exchanged the news of the day. Her son had returned to his job in Pakistan that week; her daughter-in-law, who lived above her, "doesn't speak to me, I don't know why." Her grandson was sick; her daughter's upcoming wedding brought on multiple worries; her baskets were full of ripe fruit, but there were not many customers. After telling each mishap, Um Amzat raised her hands to heaven and called out, "Thanks be to God." She kissed her hand front and back to symbolize that God is thanked for all things, the good and the difficult.

"Do you know my neighbor, Fatma?" I asked. "She has the two little boys." That was on my agenda for the day—to find out what others knew and thought about Fatma. Not gossip, I told myself, but a genuine interest in her welfare.

"Oh, that girl. Yes, she's always smiling and waving to us. Comes here sometimes to say hello. God be with her." Snap! Snap! Her fingers flew as they snapped the beans.

"I think her husband beats her," I said while adding lots of sugar to the small glasses of tea.

"Why? What does she do to him? May God make it easy for her." Um Amzat stood up and poured the boiling water into the tea glasses.

"I don't know, but he really hurts her." I stirred the tea around, swatting away the flies from the dropped sugar pieces.

"Some men are like that. May God forgive him. God is present." Um Amzat set her glass down to handle a customer's order of cabbage. A couple passed—I had dubbed them "Mr. and Mrs. Islamist," because they seemed to be devoutly faithful but not fanatical and violent. The man wore a white galabaya, a crocheted prayer cap, and a trim beard—a sign that one is religious. His wife, completely covered in yards of black polyester, wore the niqab (face veil). But it was her black-gloved hand that grabbed my attention, for it was clasped with her husband's. They chatted quietly to each other as they strolled down the street. It was not the clothing that was startling, but the signs of affection between them, for I rarely saw public displays of romance, even among married folks.

More customers dropped by, so I made my exit. Um Amzat called out, "Go in peace, Um Nicholas. God be with you."

Though it seemed I had heard little information, I did learn two things: the responsibility for the beatings was on Fatma, and invoking God's name was a good solution, for it was becoming clear that no one else was going to help her.

All of this occurred in December and January, when Christians were celebrating the birth of Christ, the hope of light in a dark world. How would Jesus want me to respond to our neighbor? I was cognizant of the great command to "love your neighbor as yourself." I wanted to be generous but feared making Fatma dependent on me. I wanted to be kind and loving but feared being taken advantage of. My hope was that one day she would look back on this dark hour of her need and remember that it was a Christian who gave her food, bandaged her wounds, listened to her woes.

As for my own spiritual inspiration, I turned to a prayer posted on my wall: "May God bless you with discomfort at easy answers, half-truths, and superficial relationships, so that you will live deep in your heart."

11

The Priest's Wife

"One of Nicholas's friends found a picture from a lingerie ad," I commented to a friend. "And he refused to look at it. He said 'If I look at it, then I will have to tell it to the priest, and I don't want to admit such a shameful thing, so it is better not to even look at it.' The fear or shame of confession prevented this young man from temptation. I was impressed with his self-discipline."

"Yes, but I would say he should go further than that. He should not resist temptation because he has to tell it to the priest, but because he has to tell it to God. He must remember that God sees him in all that he does and in every place he goes. I tell my children, 'God sees what you do in your bedroom, in your classroom, even if you hide under the bed, because you cannot hide from God.'"

I had to pinch myself to see if I was sitting in Doctor Negwa's living room in Egypt or in my seventh-grade religion class with Sister Judy putting the fear of an all-seeing God in us to restrain our adolescent urges. I was visiting with Negwa, whom I'd met through St. Anthony's School and whose oldest son was in Nicholas's class.

She continued, "Muslims are always saying, 'Forgive me for my sins for the hurt I do to others.' All day long people say this under their breath."

"Why? Why do you have to say it so often? How do you know you are forgiven?"

"Because not to believe that God forgives sin is itself a sin. It means you don't trust God, that you don't believe God loves and created you. We believe God loves to forgive people and wants to be merciful and wants his people to ask for forgiveness. And if you don't ask God for forgiveness, God will send something your way that will make you go to him for forgiveness. Because God wants to be merciful."

The discussion was a mini theology lesson. While Christians believe their sins are forgiven through the sacrifice of Jesus, for Muslims, sin means "forgetting" God. They atone for their sins by "remembering" God through sincere repentance and performing good works that will earn them merit.

One day Negwa, a gynecologist, picked me up from school and brought me to her woman's clinic, where the main function was family planning, though never by abortion. At the clinic, we flipped through a picture book that showed a field of corn with stalks standing so close to each other that the leaves were wilted and brown. The next picture showed another field with a few stalks evenly spaced, looking green and healthy.

"We use this book to explain to illiterate people the necessity of spacing out their children," Negwa explained. "These pictures are simple explanations that uneducated farmers can understand."

Her clinic received money from AID—Aid for International Development—as part of a two-billion-dollar package of U.S. assistance that also supplies Egypt with military equipment. "This," she said waving the book, "is what we need from America! More programs like this to help our people, not wars in Iraq and Afghanistan."

"Do you have problems with some religious authorities about the use of contraceptives?" I asked.

"Not often, but sometimes a religious sheikh will make a statement condemning contraceptives. They do this because they are ignorant and uneducated, and it makes our situation very bad because a lot of poor women listen to them. The sheikhs have great influence on people, and sometimes that can be used for good."

The population in Egypt increases by one million every nine months. During our three-year term, the population will increase by four million!

Negwa laughed loudly, interrupting my thoughts. "And I'm not such a good example myself with four children. But my husband loves girls and wanted at least one, so I said we will give it one more try and, praise be to God, she was a girl."

Negwa and I met regularly. She took on the role of mentor and wanted to make sure I understood the differences between Egyptian culture and Islam. She liked to toss around generalizations like "Americans are practical people; Arabs are emotional people. We have different habits. That's all."

Negwa's goal was to hire a Qur'anic teacher to help her memorize the Qur'an. Many of my friends aspire to this, and children often spend the summer under a Qur'anic tutor. Education began in the Islamic world over a thousand years ago with the three Rs: reading, 'riting, and reciting the Qur'an. Gradually the Qur'an was supplemented with science and math books in the modern education system, though the main way of learning—memorization—hasn't been modified in favor of modern teaching methods.

Early on, Negwa gave me several books in English about Islam. Fearing that she was hoping for a convert, I decided to be upfront from the beginning, and said, "I'll read these books, but I want you to know that I am very happy being a Christian."

My fears were unrealized. "And I am happy being a Muslim," she replied. "But we can talk about our faiths and what God means to us."

And we did.

Negwa did not need to work for financial reasons. Her husband was a judge in Cairo, and his salary supported the family. Her salary, she told me, "is put in an Islamic bank. In Islam, the husband is responsible for the family, not the wife, so her money can be put in a separate savings and it is for her own personal use."

A very generous allotment, I thought, but I wasn't sure how many families could exercise that option. Most folks we knew needed both salaries and more to make it each month. But it was one of the advantages often raised when discussing how Islam gives women many rights, freedoms, and protections.

"You know, that is not the impression women in the west have of Islam," I commented. "They think all women here are oppressed and suffering."

"No, Islam is a very good religion for women because it is not just a religion that occupies a few hours of our time one day a week. No. It is not just a religion but a complete lifestyle. How can I best describe this?" she asked, looking around.

We were in her living room, which had just been painted a pretty mauve and still smelled of new paint. "Islam regulates all that we do, from how we pray to how we use the bathroom. Yes, it controls all aspects of our lives." She looked at her hand and ticked off a list: "What we eat, how we dress, how we marry and divorce, how we raise our children, custody of our children if there is a divorce, remarriage, how we use our money, and many more things. Even how we are buried! That which is permitted in the Qur'an is called *halal*, and that which is not permitted is called *haram*. These two words govern our lives, and that is good because this keeps us on the path to God."

It sounded kind of stifling to me and contrary to the spirit of Christ, who came to free us from restricting rules and regulations so we can love one another more fully. As if reading my thoughts, Negwa continued, "I think people in the west see these rules as against freedom, because you like to do as you wish. But we say Islam gives you freedom by giving you the things that are good for you in life and prohibiting the things that are bad for you."

She was right, of course. Individualistic, free-spirited North Americans don't like anyone else defining for us what we can and cannot do. "We call these laws of what we can and cannot do in Islam *shariah*."

"Shariah? The same as the word for street?"

"Exactly. Street—for that is the way that leads to God."

Americans familiar with shariah are likely to think of extreme punishments, like having a hand chopped off for stealing. But such extremism is often practiced in places that follow a strict Wahhabist sect of Islam. Though 90 percent of Egyptian law is based on shariah, it does not mete out such sever punishments, which were abhorrent to the Muslims we knew.

I wanted to hear Negwa's perspective on stories about young Christian women being forced to convert to Islam. It was a hot topic among Egyptian Christians, often discussed in muted tones of secrecy and shame. "Did you hear about the two girls in . . . ?" one would hear in whispers. Stories abounded among the Coptic community, often fueled as much by rumor as by fact, but there were enough common threads to suggest some grains of truth. Many of these stories were a prime reason for Christians' fear and suspicion of Muslims.

"La'a. La'a. [No. No.] That is not true." Negwa emphatically shook her head and put down her tea to free her arms for expression. "Why would we force anyone to convert if it is not sincere in their hearts? There is no compulsion in Islam. God would reject that. They would not make good Muslims if they are forced to be so."

"But, Negwa," I argued, "I have heard stories of young girls being kidnapped by men, drugged, forced to marry them, and forced to convert. Many are later abandoned by these men and have a miserable life because they are rejected by both Muslims and Christians." But one never knew the truth of such allegations. Were these unsuspecting girls tricked and forcibly taken to be converted, as many Christians alleged, or were they young women in love with Muslim men and following their heart's desire, abandoning family and faith in the process?

I carried on. "I have heard that money is involved in conversions."

"They do get money, and I will tell you why that is," she responded, conceding one point. "The money is not for the Muslims but for the Christians. Why? Because they need to start a new life over. They need an apartment, a job, food, maybe medical care or clothing. As you know, Christians lose everything when they convert, so we must help them in their new life." To Muslims, it is a resettlement fee; to Christians, it is a bribe to convert. "I think people convert because they are unhappy with their life; their religion does not meet their needs anymore. Maybe they have heard something from one of the sheikhs, our spiritual leaders, on TV. Perhaps they read something in the Qur'an, and God opened their heart and mind to Islam. I know several Christian women that converted because the religion of Islam makes sense to them. It's a practical religion."

"But don't you think some men can entice and seduce women to convert?" Every religion seems to have a few unscrupulous people, I'd noticed.

"Like what Christians say happened to the priest's wife?"

"Yes, exactly."

Just the month before, prior to Christmas, Egypt had been embroiled in a religious crisis that became known as the incident of "the priest's wife." The wives of Orthodox priests sacrifice much for their husbands' church position, and while they must give their consent for their spouse to become a priest, it's unknown how many over the years continue to joyfully embrace or begrudgingly endure their position.

We don't know how much pain, if any, Wafaa Constantine, endured in her marriage to Father Youssef. All we know is that one morning the forty-six-year-old mother of two college students went to her job at an agricultural office and did not return home. She was reported missing to a local police station. Her husband, a diabetic, was in Alexandria on the Mediterranean Coast, getting measured for a new prosthetic leg.

The villagers sounded the alarm that she had converted to Islam. The story of how she had disappeared and converted depended on whether you were a Christian or a Muslim. Muslims claimed she was in love with her boss and eloped with him. Christians claimed she was abducted, drugged, and forced to convert.

Our question was, "Isn't her religion and love life her own business?" which just showed how naïve we were about the power of religion and sex in Egyptian society.

Enduring the humiliation of the conversion of an esteemed priest's wife proved too much for many Christians to bear. Muslims in the village ridiculed the Christians over it. The Christians demanded her return, and when that did not occur, hundreds descended on the cathedral in Cairo, which is the papal seat of Pope Shenouda.

The ever-present and ready security forces far outnumbered the protestors and showed up in riot gear to contain them and prevent them from spilling into the street. Chanting "abduct us or kill us, you will never change us," the Copts called on Pope Shenouda to stand up for their right to be Christians and demand the return of Mrs. Constantine. The pope was often in the precarious position of having to represent his Christian flock and keep peace with the government and the large Muslim population. When security officials refused to return Mrs. Constantine, the pope protested by retreating to a monastery in the desert and calling on Christians to fast and pray.

After a week of tension and high-level meetings between government and church officials, the matter was finally resolved by contacting President Mubarak—yes, the president—who was on official business in Kuwait. The central security apparatus swiftly moved into action, and Mrs. Constantine was returned, not to her husband, but to church officials. According to an English-language Coptic newspaper, she confessed to the officials that while she had "been passing through a cruel personal crisis, 'Christianity was—and is—in the core of my heart.'"

After a full week of protests, the demonstrators went home, and the thirty-four Christian men who had been arrested for "fomenting unrest" were released. Christians could finally breathe a quiet sigh of relief, but Muslims were not satisfied with the outcome. They were angry that security had returned Mrs. Constantine, which was not the usual procedure. When a person converts, the conversion is reported to state security. In the name of protection and security, the new convert is not allowed to meet with his or her family, which is devastating to Christians who want to hear directly from a child that he or she willingly converted to Islam and was not coerced. Usually a meeting is held with the new convert and the bishop, but as a nun once explained it to me, "the person is drugged and the bishop only has that one time to convince them of the disastrous consequences." The Christian family then disowns their converted son or daughter, and the mother wears black, symbolizing the "death" of her child.

Is state security protecting the new convert to Islam from the wrath of the Christian community, as Muslims claim, or is security helping "the kidnappers" hold the newly converted against his or her will, as the Christians claim?

"Gigi, doesn't the priest's wife have the right to become Muslim if she wants to?" Negwa asked me. "Some friends told me they saw her on television, reciting from the Qur'an. She has been studying it for some time."

Suddenly Muslims became the defenders of religious freedom, a freedom they would not extend to one of their own should she or he exercise religious freedom to convert. Conversions are an offense in Islamic law but not in Egyptian criminal law. While the legal status of the convert is important, the more serious issue is the rejection of family, faith, and culture that results from converting. The conversion inevitably causes conflict; it becomes a criminal offense, not because of the conversion itself but because of the violence it may trigger. In some places, Islamic governments view conversions from Islam to Christianity as treason and apply the death penalty.

"Does that ever happen?" I asked one acquaintance.

"It's not necessary," he replied. "The family would do it first."

Muslims believe the Qur'an was revealed to correct the imperfections and "corruptions" of the Bible, a concept that often brings a look of surprised amusement to Christian faces. Since the Qur'an is considered the last of God's revelations and Muhammad the last prophet, Islam is believed to be the final true religion. Therefore, apostasy—abandoning the faith—is a great sin. Why would someone abandon the truthful religion to spend eternity in hell? So in order to save a person from himself, his blood is considered halal (permitted) to be shed.

Christians, especially those in traditional villages, can also endure the same repercussions from hostile family members. According to Negwa, "Some new converts to Islam are put in jail for safety and protection from their own family."

I was always under the impression that these severe reactions to conversions originated with Islam and Arabs, but a careful study of Coptic martyrs reveals a longer history. Some Egyptians who converted from paganism to Christianity were killed by their own family, who rejected the new religion; Roman rulers killed others. This happened hundreds of years before Islam developed. The reason for killing the newly converted is the same today as it was then: restoring honor to the family that was humiliated by the conversion.

Conversions in Egypt are a main source of friction between Christians and Muslims. This is primarily because religious identity is a societal issue, not a personal decision between God and one's conscience. Conversions involve more than religious authorities. The new converts must register at the police station and declare her or his new religion. It affects all aspects of life—marriage and divorce, relationships with family members, inheritance, child custody, and identification cards. The person even takes on a new name reflecting the new religion.

A Muslim once asked me how I would react if one of my children wanted to convert from Christianity. It wasn't a question I had put much thought into, but I responded, "I want two things for my children: for them to be happy and to have a relationship with God. I would love for that to happen through Christianity, but if my child found another way to relate to God, I could come to terms with that."

He smiled and shook his head at what was obviously, in his opinion, confirmation of my weak faith. I viewed religion and faith as a personal, private issue; he viewed religion and faith as a communal, societal issue. In his view, if I truly believed in the absolute power of God, it was a belief worth defending, and if necessary, killing for. He argued that "killing those who convert from Islam is necessary to stop the disease before it spreads."

For those familiar with Christian history, that rationale sounds familiar. Murderous defense of one's faith was some of the same reasoning behind Christendom's Crusades against Muslims in the Holy Land during the Middle Ages. Some western Christians today support Israel and the war in Iraq for the same reasons. Didn't President Bush initially refer to the "war on terror" as a crusade?

༂

Was the priest's wife kidnapped, forced to convert to Islam, then kept in a drugged stupor away from her church and family by security officials and religious sheikhs? That is what I heard from many Christians, though no Muslim could imagine any of it to be true. Or did the priest's wife, wanting to divorce her husband, find consolation in the Qur'an and in the arms of her Muslim boss and willingly change her faith? That is what I heard from Muslims. No Christian could ever image a priest's wife sinking to such low levels. Neither Christians nor Muslims could even concede the possibility that the other's explanation might have some validity. Issues were black or white, right or wrong, true or false. Though always searching for the common ground, I often found that with many issues between Muslims and Christians, there was none.

The story of the priest's wife had all the ingredients of a soap opera: religion, sex, power. People continued discussing it. But the truth about what happened during her absence has never been sufficiently brought to light to the satisfaction of either side. God and Wafaa Constantine are the only ones who truly know, and perhaps that is how it should be.

Negwa and I obviously weren't going to agree either. But she apparently had her own agenda to bring up. "Muslims can pray any time and in any place," she said. "We even see Muslims praying next to churches (usually the guards assigned to protect it). But Christians don't ever pray. You can only pray in a church, but Muslims are free to pray anywhere."

"But we do!" I cried out, surprised to hear her conclusion. "Christians can pray in any place they want to—in church, in school, on the street. The Bible tells us we should pray in secret and not do it publicly to gain the approval of others. Praying is talking to God, and we can do that in any situation."

Oops, I was concerned that I said the last bit about talking to God too casually. Muslims view God as omnipotent and to be approached only in awe and fear, not in conversation. "Where did you get the idea that Christians don't pray?"

"I really don't know," she said with a surprising lilt to her voice. "I suppose because we never see them do that."

Negwa's confusion makes sense. Muslim prayers are at five set times each day and are highly visible. Prayer time is announced on the loudspeakers at every mosque. Television shows are briefly interrupted; store clerks and employees leave their workspace and go to the area reserved for praying. Muslim speech is sprinkled with references to prayer: "I'll deliver the milk after the night prayers," or "Basketball practice will start after the Friday noon prayers." No time needed; everyone understands the reference.

I always thought Muslim praying to be cumbersome. One needs to wash, to have a prayer mat, and to discern the direction of Mecca. But that wasn't an issue for Muslims; it was simply routine. Yet I could see Negwa's logic—since they never saw Christians pray, obviously they didn't do it.

"We are waiting for Jesus to come again," she said. "Then all our problems will be solved and there will be peace in our lives."

Come again? Did I just hear a Muslim woman tell me that she is waiting for the second coming of Christ? Seeing my surprise, Negwa continued, "You don't believe me? There was a sheikh on TV the other day, crying and begging for Jesus to come and end our miseries."

It gave me hope that we had more to share between us than obstacles to divide us.

12

Angels in the House

December 25. A day so special in America and the western world is just another ordinary day in Egypt, with people working and kids in school. It was disorienting to be in a place where all the familiar trappings of the season were absent. No bright holiday lights, no Christmas parades, no "Jingle Bells" or "Silent Night," no signs in shops advertising holiday sales. We gathered with other MCCers and created our own Christmas spirit.

December 31. The day we always know as New Year's Eve had somehow become associated with Christmas in this corner of the world. Even our school had a party with the gym coach dressed as *Baba Noel* (Santa Claus), who gave out goodie bags, complete with whistles, to 350 kids. Our ears rang all day. Baba Noel faces and "Habby New Year" signs appeared on some store windows, accompanied by little artificial trees with lights on them. (Since in Arabic there is no distinction between b and p sounds, people often confuse these two letters when writing in English.)

New Year's Eve isn't celebrated, so Brad gave his final English exam to his class that night. Christians celebrate—where else?—in the church. The friends we went with to a Protestant church service said, "We know December 31 was really the night Jesus was born on." There was much singing and reenacting of the Christmas story. We were even asked to sing, and we stood—to Rebecca's mortification—at the altar with microphones, in front of about two hundred people and sang "Joy to the World" and "Go Tell It on the Mountain." Though God didn't bless us with musical abilities, the congregation seemed to enjoy it.

We left the church at 11 p.m., though the congregation would be there for another couple of hours. We went to Noura and Girgis's house, where about twenty folks gathered, all relatives except us. As midnight approached, all food and drinks were taken from our hands, and we stood up as the lights dimmed. We were expecting yells, kissing, and fireworks. Instead we all faced east, the direction of Jerusalem, "because that is where Jesus will come again," and recited the Lord's Prayer. It was an unusual but lovely way to greet a new year. The next day—January 1—was not a day of football, shopping, and good dieting intentions, but a regular day of work and school.

January 7. This is the day that the Coptic Orthodox Church celebrates Jesus' birth. If it seems confusing to have different dates in one country for recognizing the birth of Christ, imagine how it must seem to Muslims.

ट

"Get up! Hurry and take the child and his mother to Egypt! Stay there until I tell you to return, because Herod is looking for the child and wants to kill him" (Matthew 2:13).

Egyptians believe their country is blessed and protected because of the Holy Family's presence. Though the Bible does not elaborate on how Mary, Joseph, and Jesus spent their time in Egypt, stories and traditions abound: the Holy Family sought shelter at night in a cave; a palm tree lowered its branches to provide dates; a well miraculously sprang up to quench their thirst. All of these spots are marked today by a church or monastery and are sacred places of pilgrimage where thousands of Christians gather. Muslims, who also revere Mary and have stories in the Qur'an about the sojourn in Egypt, also visit these holy sites, seeking healing for incurable diseases or blessings for bearing children.

"Please come to the school office on Christmas Day about ten in the morning. We will go and greet the bishop." This was an invitation from Sister Heba, and while I understood her English, I did not understand what she really meant. Aren't people at home on Christmas morning, opening presents and having a big breakfast with family?

Nevertheless I walked into her office with the family, and we were surprised to see about ten other teachers, half of them Muslims. "What are you doing here?" I whispered to one. "Isn't today a holiday?" The school was closed, but were Muslims expected to work?

"We're here to greet the bishop," one woman answered, as if that explained anything. Why would Muslims come to greet the bishop?

A few minutes later, Sister, the teachers, and our family were walking past the spot where the fish sellers camped out each night, selling the catch of the day. It is a good business during the Advent season, for Christians fast for forty days from meat and dairy products, making fish a good alternative. Cats were licking up leftover fish scrapings. We held our breath from the permanent fish odor and rounded the corner into a dirt alleyway. Chickens pecked about; a goat ate a piece of paper; an elderly woman in black, sitting outside her rickety wooden door, greeted us.

"Emily, go give her one of our goodie bags," I directed. The night before, we had filled about twenty bags with apples, oranges, chocolates, and nuts to distribute to people on the streets—garbage men, doorkeepers, traffic police, and elderly women on doorstops. It isn't an Egyptian custom, so people were delighted to have a surprise treat.

The cathedral—home church and residence of the bishop—is a huge, gray structure surrounded by a wall and guard posts that give it a fortress look. The courtyard was always crowded with Christians attending Mass, going to weddings, or discreetly making eye contact with the opposite sex—the young people, that is. Four uniformed and armed guards were lounging out front. Police guards were posted in front of all banks and churches, though not mosques. Did anyone consider the irony of Muslim guards protecting Christian churches?

There are no Masses on Christmas Day, but hundreds of Christians come to the cathedral to greet their bishop. He sat in a large parlor surrounded by lots of priests wearing black hats and long beards. As we moved quickly through the line, Christians kissed the bishop's hand and Muslims shook it. What's important is not how long one stays but the fact that one makes an appearance.

We had gone to Christmas Eve Mass the night before, and the church had been packed—standing room only. The atmosphere was a feast for the senses: the chanting of the choir, clanging cymbals, drifting smells of incense. Suddenly, before the homily was read, there was a shuffling noise when an entourage of officials and security filed in to the seats reserved for them up front. It was the governor of Beni Suef, a Muslim. Various other local dignitaries, including several Muslim sheikhs, identifiable by their red caps and white turbans, accompanied him. It was tradition to show respect to Christians by being present on their feast days. The bishop reciprocated during the Muslim feasts. The broader message projected by the leaders of two faiths being physically together was that Egypt is a country where Muslims and Christians can live harmoniously.

We spent our first Christmas noticing the vast differences between how the holiday is celebrated in America and in Egypt. Most notable—and greatly appreciated by us—was the absence of commercialism. Exchanging gifts was not part of the Christmas tradition. No one asked, "What are you getting for Christmas?" No foods are special to this day. In fact, Christians break their Advent fast after the midnight Mass by going home and feasting on a variety of meats from which they had been abstaining for the past month. We did miss Christmas carols and fir trees. The kids improvised by turning over our green, plastic wastebasket and inserting leafy green branches they had cut from bushes in the schoolyard. They hung a few ornaments made from paper cutouts and proudly admired their homemade creation.

Just looking at the December calendar of a typical American Christian family can be exhausting, as it usually reveals a frenzy of shopping, church activities, parties, and social gatherings, much of it accompanied by excessive eating and drinking. None of this is present in Egypt because Christians there spend Advent fasting from "worldly pleasures." They spend more time in church with special Masses and all-night prayer services.

"We want to empty ourselves of all things bad so we can accept Christ again in our lives," was how one man explained the buildup to Christmas Day. I couldn't help but wonder how American Christians would feel after the Christmas holidays if we shared this approach to the season of Advent.

ॐ

After seeing the bishop, our group went to greet residents at a home for the elderly, the school for the disabled, and the orphanage. Emily and I occasionally stopped to pass out goodie bags, lingering behind the others when our attention was distracted by two men and a woman struggling with a big, old-fashioned television. The two men wanted to keep it balanced between them but found they could only shuffle slowly in that position. One man tried carrying it by himself but found he could not grip the sides easily. I was wondering what combination they would try next when the woman pulled a scarf off her neck, twisted it, and coiled it in a circle to make a pad on her head. The two men lifted the television, balanced it on her head, and without hesitating, the woman walked into the maze of traffic. Where did the idea ever originate that women are the weaker sex?

We rounded the corner past the shoe cobbler, whose shop reminded me of something in a Charles Dickens novel. Strips of leather shaped like bow ties hung from the rafters as the ancient machinery rattled and wheezed along, giving testimony to a profession that was nearly extinct in the west but thrived in Egypt. The cobbler waved me over to give me a holiday greeting and asked, "Where's Nicholas?" It was a familiar question heard from the sweet shop, the sporting goods store, the computer shop, and just about any other place he frequented. They all remembered the friendly boy who looked Egyptian; what he lacked in Arabic, he made up for in charm.

"Happy holidays! Merry Christmas!" We had arrived at the girls orphanage and were met by a group of beautiful girls. Like everyone else, they were dressed in the holiday spirit of new clothes and new shoes. I complimented them on their outfits and wondered who had managed to buy so many different sizes and styles, because they fit as if each girl had selected her own. I got the usual answer: the clothes were "gifts from Jesus." Their black hair, thick and curly, had been pulled back into braids, decorated with bows and barrettes, and shone radiantly. Some girls had on eye makeup and lipstick—right down to the five-year-olds. This was a festive occasion indeed!

Lots of tables and chairs were set out for the many friends of the orphanage expected to drop by. Some girls had families who also came to share in the festivities. Most of their mothers were from the poor countryside and were dressed completely in black, indicating that their husbands had died. They would buy new black clothes for the holidays. No matter how young the widow was, it would be her outfit until she died.

A balding, middle-aged man whom I had never met stood in front of me with a pleading expression on his face. "My wife like to see your daughter. Please, bring her? Please, this way."

I had a suspicion what he wanted and asked why.

"She pregnant."

Just as I thought. We made our way through the crowd, waving to friends, making mental notes of who to go back and visit with.

His wife held Emily's face in her hands squeezing her cheeks. "Oh, let me look at you! You are beautiful!"

Folklore that probably stemmed from the times of the pharaohs holds that if a pregnant woman looks into the eyes of a child she admires for her beauty, the woman's baby will look like that child.

Emily rolled her eyes and gave me a look that said, "Mom, get me out of this!" She was a good sport for tolerating Egypt's old wives tales.

The courtyard was full of beautiful little girls with brown skin and gorgeous black, curly hair, yet they selected Emily with her light skin and limp, light brown hair. Why? It was the same reason that our school displayed posters of chubby white babies instead of dimpled brown ones that would reflect the student body. It was the same reason skin whitener creams lined the shelves of pharmacies and beauty shops. It was the same reason the summer family swim time was at night. In a country where the sun's bright rays shine almost year round, no one wants to be in the sun; no one wants to have dark skin. Dark skin is bad and ugly, the locals said. Just as American females invest much time and money to obtain golden, bronzed skin, Egyptian females do the same to acquire creamy, unblemished, white skin.

Is it universal among women that what we desire is that with which God did not bless us?

Sherry, the pregnant woman, introduced herself. "You are from America? Last year President Mubarak made this day a holiday for Christians. We don't know why he did this. We think he had pressure from your President Bush."

"I don't know about that," I answered truthfully.

People were always suspecting President Bush or America behind any new law or idea. "In our country," I continued, "minorities like Muslims and Jews don't get a paid day off on their religious holidays. It's up to their boss and usually means a day off without pay. So you see, while Christians are a minority in Egypt, they sometimes have more rights than minority religions in America."

"Are you sure? I assumed that all religions had freedom in your country."

"Well, in America you have the freedom to practice your own religion, but that doesn't mean that all religions are treated equally. Our yearly calendar revolves around the Christian year."

"You shouldn't let Muslims practice their religion in America, because of what they do to us here," Sherry replied emphatically, much to my disappointment. I had briefly wished that a member of the minority religion in Egypt could be sympathetic to members of a minority religion in the United States. But that was unrealistic. Most people assume that the United States operates on a fair, equal basis for all, including minorities. They are startled to hear about any discrimination based on race, gender, or religion. Their sheltered life, and perhaps the speeches of a few rosy-eyed American politicians extolling the wonders of democracy, give them the impression that America is a utopia of freedom and justice. Many Egyptians conclude that Egypt is unique in discriminating against minorities.

Sherry was originally from Beni Suef, but she said she put up with the crowds and pollution of Cairo "because the schools are much better there." Much to my surprise, Sherry, a Christian, was also an Arabic teacher. All the other Arabic teachers I knew were Muslim, because they teach the Arabic language by using the Qur'an.

"Christians can teach Arabic up to third grade," Sherry explained. "After that, Arabic is taught from the Qur'an so it must be by a Muslim teacher. I teach both Muslim and Christian students and enjoy it very much."

Religion is taught in all Egyptian schools, whether the school is run by the government and or is private with a government-approved curriculum. When it is time for religion class, the normally integrated classroom divides. Muslim students go to one room and Christians to another.

"Can you teach Arabic from the Bible?" I asked Sherry while trying to balance a glass of steaming tea, perfect for warming my hands.

"Not officially, but I do it anyway. I find in the Bible verses similar to what is in the Qur'an and teach them to the children. In the early years, the concepts are simple, so there is much similarity between the Bible and the Qur'an."

Sherry confided that in eleven years of teaching, she had never had any Muslim children complain to their parents about teaching from the Bible. "The children love me because I am firm with them but also very creative."

How refreshing it was to meet a teacher who liked her work! As we continued talking I realized I had actually visited her school in Cairo and had been so impressed by the orderliness of the classrooms and the modern teaching methods that I'd brought a group of teachers from St. Anthony's to expose them to this other way of education. But after observing classes with children sitting quietly in their desks and teachers explaining concepts in a regular voice, they could only conclude in disbelief, "These children aren't Egyptian. This could never work in Beni Suef."

ع

A sudden clatter drew my attention to a group of people sitting around the coffee table examining a new product that seemed to appear out of nowhere—a bag of Doritos nacho chips. "It has a strange, spicy taste, but it's good. Have some," one man told another as I hoped the bag would soon make its way to me.

Near Beni Suef is an Egyptian air force base that has numerous American-built fighter planes and American personnel to maintain them. The United States gives Egypt nearly two billion dollars each year, most of it in military aid used to purchase American planes and equipment. Who Egypt needs to be protected from is unclear; since signing a peace accord with Israel, Egypt has no obvious enemies. But all aid has strings attached, and perhaps the larger reason is not so much about Egypt's security but that a good portion of the aid money is contracted back to American military and businesses. Many Egyptians also suspect that the aid keeps their government compliant with American interests in the region. The food at the airbase is not Egyptian food locally purchased but imported American food, courtesy of the American taxpayer.

This year the airbase donated cases of food—hotdog buns, hamburgers, Doritos, even bacon—all slightly past the expiration date.

"Perhaps if I had these chips, I wouldn't mind fasting," I

quipped to no one in particular as I took the last one from the bag.

"Oh? Do you fast during the holidays?" It was Mark, one of the science teachers from St. Anthony's School. He was a devout man, and we often spent tea breaks together discussing the latest issues in the Orthodox Church.

"Only for a few days," I confessed. Fasting for the Orthodox means abstaining from all animal products: eggs, milk, cheese, meat. As I viewed it, except for meat itself, fasting didn't mean "giving up anything," but just being more creative in the kitchen. For example, instead of baking cookies with eggs, Rebecca could make a delicious chocolate cake that had no eggs. Perhaps the biggest sacrifice for us would be not having milk with our morning cereal, which was one of the few American rituals we held onto.

"I guess I really don't understand the fasting," I said. "Fasting is more meaningful to me if I go without any food all day rather than refraining from certain foods."

"Like the Muslims?" he sneered. "They only fast one month out of the year. They do not eat all day, but then they can eat all night long!"

I heard the opposite comment from Muslims: "Christians can eat during the day but we go without even a drop of water on our dry tongues." What I admire and appreciate about both Muslims and Christians is their commitment to fasting; comparing whose fast was more sacrificial seemed to me picky and immature. Isn't the purpose of all fasting to discipline ourselves and bring us spiritually closer to God? Is there only one way to do so? Apparently so, I learned as I continued to describe American-style fasting.

"Some Christians fast in the United States," I told Mark, "but mostly before Easter, not Christmas. But we see fasting as a personal sacrifice. Each person gives up something that is important. For example, giving up chocolate or soft drinks, if it is something you eat a lot of. But lately, people have been giving up other things too, like TV or computer games."

I was about to give a few more examples of things that interfered with a relationship with God, but the look of disbelief on his face stopped me. "That's wrong," Mark said, giving a sympathetic smile of pity. "That's not the way to fast. The Holy Bible, it tells us, the Bible says how to fast—what foods we must not eat. We should give up the foods, like meat, that make us strong. Baba Shenouda, our pope, tells us that we fast correctly. The purpose of fasting is that everyone does it together and the Christian community is strengthened. It's not one person doing one thing and another doing something else."

He shook his head, baffled at how western Christians individualize faith rather than live it communally. "It's easy to fast when everyone fasts from the same things. I know when I go to a friend's house, they won't have cooked with butter. Why do you fast like Muslims and not Christians? You aren't fasting the right way."

I had never thought of fasting without food as a "Muslim fast," mainly because my world was not divided into Christian and Muslim behaviors. I had thought Mark would appreciate alternative ways of fasting, perhaps not adopting it for himself, but at least willing to understand the principles of it.

Conversations like this often left me feeling my faith and beliefs were completely invalid. I usually assumed people weren't inquisitive because they were products of an educational system that doesn't encourage curiosity and independent thinking. But neither could I discount the role religion plays in limiting people's openness to other beliefs and ideas.

I recalled a story the director of the orphanage, Sister Maria, had told me about a "reconciliation feast." She had had conflicts with the director of the boys home for several years but decided this Christmas would be different. The girls labored for two days to make pots of stuffed cabbage leaves and grilled fish.

"When we brought the food to the boys home," Sister Maria told me, "they were so surprised! The boys set up tables and chairs and all sixty of us sat down and ate. Yes, Gigi, this is a good story of forgiveness and coming together. We should tell everybody about Jesus' love."

We returned home, drained from a hectic but fun Christmas day, eager for some quiet relaxation. But the clang of our neighbors' metal gate foretold another scenario. Brad picked up a book and disappeared into the bedroom, his retreat place whenever they visited. So absorbed in her own misery, Fatma wasn't even aware that today was a holiday for us. The kids were playing basketball in the house when I heard Mumtez admonish Rebecca, "Don't bounce the ball in the house. You'll disturb the angels!" The image of angels flitting about the room seemed a fitting one to end a delightful day.

Nicholas plays a drum with girls from the orphanage.

About a month later, the girls from the orphanage cashed in our Christmas present to them—a boat ride on the Nile River. It was a beautiful February day. The distant desert mountains faded behind us as we drifted on the water. Nicholas brought his wooden drum, another girl used a table as her drum, and they led us in singing religious songs with a pop beat.

Sister Maria, rarely in exuberant health, was in a festive mood—literally swinging from the rafters. She jumped up, grabbed hold of the boat rafters, and swung back and forth, her gray veil and habit flapping a beat behind her. While walking on one of the islands, Sister took off her black socks and shoes, hiked her skirt up to her knees, and splashed her feet in the water like a child. Later she sat in a small fishing boat along with some of the girls, wildly rocking the boat to the rhythm as Nicholas pounded his wooden drum. "Nicholas!" she called out. "I want to buy your drum."

"It cost me forty-five pounds," he said. About eight dollars.

Ever clever and quick on her feet, even when they were muddy, Sister responded, "I'll trade you for a carton of American chips."

Nicholas did not even need to do the math. Any trade for a carton of his favorite snack food tipped in his favor. "You got it!" he exclaimed.

Back at the girls home, we claimed our carton of chips. "We don't like this," one girl said as she tossed in three squeeze bottles of mustard. "What about these? We don't know how to cook it." It was packages of bacon and sausages.

We were all delighted with our Christmas gifts that day.

13

The Heaven of a Stranger

"Just because a person lives alone doesn't mean he or she is doing anything bad."

"It does in Egypt. Why live alone when you can live with your family, who will protect you from bad things? Look at the Internet. There are all sorts of sexual things on it. If people see this, they will think it is normal to do these things. The bishop tells us to take care with our children and our computers to prevent these things. I cannot do these bad things if my father or brother is around."

Angie and I were sitting in a café in a monastery looking over the Nile River. The Monastery of the Virgin wasn't a functioning monastery anymore but a retreat center. Most monks live in monasteries in the desert. For Christians, this was a holy place where they come on weekends to get *barakah* (blessings). They spent the day picnicking and visiting, transforming a quiet place into a lively playground. A lovely painted mural on the wall depicted its significance in religious history: baby Moses is in a basket surrounded by tall reeds with a princess and her handmaiden looking on in surprise.

"So living alone means you can do things that you shouldn't do?" I asked Angie. I had heard this argument before, that everything a young person needs is in the home—food, clothes, comfort. Missing from the equation is sex. The logical conclusion, then, is that young people leave home for sexual freedom. Living on one's own for the sake of independence and privacy are not even considered possibilities.

"It is the role of fathers and brothers to protect you from harm," Angie explained. "And the only reason people want to live alone is to escape this protection. If I were to do that—live alone—the priest would visit me and tell me to go back home for my family's sake, for our honor and reputation."

The only possibility for young people to live away from their families is an out-of-town university. Even then, the girls stay in dormitory rooms with a chaperone and an eight o'clock curfew; boys may have a little more leeway, but both spend the weekends with their families.

"Do you have any marriage possibilities yet?" I asked, changing the subject. Angie was a kindergarten teacher at St. Anthony's and had one of those bubbly, cheery dispositions that good kindergarten teachers often come with.

"I was engaged, but it was broken during the negotiations. Do you know about the engagement process?" She explained it to me: "Well, in the first session the boy's and girl's parents get to know each other—who your people are, characteristics of the boy or girl, the family reputation and background. The parents send out other people—what shall we call them? Spies? Something like that—to ask questions about your family. Then if all that goes okay, the boy and girl can meet each other in church or at a park, always in public of course.

"Since there isn't dating, the young couple gets engaged first, and it's during the engagement period that they get to know each other and decide whether to marry or end the engagement.

"Then in the second session, the families meet to discuss where the couple will live and who will pay for what. Everything is spelled out—from the household furniture to the beauty shop visit on the day of the wedding."

The customary way to marry is for the man to first have a good job and an apartment arranged. Once this has been accomplished—a tricky task in a poor place with few jobs and few available apartments—his family lets the word out that their son is searching for a bride, and the dealing begins. I described to Angie how Americans went about setting up a household: the engaged couple pools their resources, buys cheap or used furniture, starts out with an apartment or "starter" house, works and saves money till a few years later they can get a bigger, more permanent house.

"In Egypt it is the opposite," she explained. "You must have the apartment and the furnishings arranged before the wedding. No father would let his daughter marry someone who cannot provide a good place to live. And even though our economic situation is difficult these days, our culture does not change, no matter how impractical it is."

I expected Tevye from *Fiddler on the Roof* to come any minute and hop up on the wobbly table to belt out "Tradition." To challenge the system and allow young people to marry without having everything arranged would be a move into an unknown area. And in traditional societies, the unknown is invariably feared. For once that "right" is permitted, who knows what young people will clamor for next?

The third session often determines if a marriage will take place at all. "That is the most important meeting because it determines how much the *shabka* will be." The shabka is the set of gold jewelry from the groom to the bride, demonstrating his esteem of her. It is her personal asset, and she is free to sell it in hard times. In the case of Muslims who can divorce, it would be her support should the marriage fail. Every evening we saw whole families crowding into small jewelry stores with the bride to select her shabka while a nervous-looking groom fingered his thick wad of cash. If a satisfactory selection was made, the bride paraded around, showing off her gold elegantly laid out in a red velvet box. In celebration of the happy occasion, women tossed back their heads and roll their tongues against the roof of their mouths, emitting a trilling sound of jubilation.

Parents can call off the wedding if the shabka isn't satisfactory, but other things can break an engagement too. "I loved my cousin and he loved me. He is my mother's sister's son. His family had a big apartment—six rooms. His mother, my aunt, wanted to live with us. That was okay with me. I love my aunt; she is like a mother to me. I am at work all day. It's no problem. But my mother wanted me to have privacy, to have an apartment of my own."

"So this was between your mother and her sister?"

"No, really it was my father who objected, so my mother could say nothing," Angie remarked flatly.

"And you? What about your opinion?" I asked, remembering that she was twenty-four years old when this occurred.

"Some families would listen to their daughter and respect her opinion. But my family wanted me to have better. But it didn't matter to me." She said this so calmly, without any bitterness in her voice.

"Weren't you angry?"

"Yes, of course. I did not speak to them for one week. I came home only to sleep. They knew where I was, of course—church or teaching at school. But I kept silent to express my anger."

And that was about as rebellious as Angie or any other girl would get. This willingness for an adult—at least that is how I view Angie—to so easily submit to parental authority is a conundrum for me. As a social worker, I learned that the task of adolescence is to rebel, break away from parents, and establish one's own independence. But it seemed in Egypt that as adolescents turned into adults, they became closer and more dependent on their families. I know Angie respected and loved her parents, and her parents sought the best for her. But isn't it human nature to want to control your own destiny, especially when the passion of love is the issue?

"But this is not to say that my father was wrong," Angie continued. "When you are in love, you can only see what is in front of you—the boy. But your parents can see all around, and they can see things for our future that I cannot see. My father is wise in many ways, so maybe he is also wise in this respect." There was none of the know-it-all arrogance so common among western youth toward their parents.

"You know, in the United States, we don't marry cousins," I told her. This was always a fun comment to make, if for no other reason than to capture the surprised look.

"Really? Why?" Angie's facial expressions did not disappoint as her eyebrows shot up and her eyes enlarged, as if I had just told her the pyramids had crumbled.

"Genetic reasons. We fear the child will have some kind of retardation or birth defects."

"I have heard of that, but you can take a blood test. If there is complex blood between the boy and the girl, then they cannot marry."

"Will you do that test?"

"Oh *no*! I am afraid of what the results would be."

No surprise there. Blood tests before marriage are a good idea, but no one does it, not even educated people like Angie. Some believe that "cousin marriages" are best because the personal characteristics and financial status of each side are known and trusted. It also keeps the inheritance of dowries and land in the family. A common proverb states, "The hell of a relative is better than the heaven of a stranger."

Surprisingly, most of the "cousin marriages" we knew of did not result in birth defects in children. Others told me that the defects, if any, would manifest in the next generation, meaning their grandchildren, as if that somehow justified the marriage risk. But Angie was like many others where "fear rules the roost." Why depend on medical evidence when one can avoid the situation and rely on what really matters—fate and a destiny determined by God?

"Did you think, Angie, about marrying your cousin anyway? Or begging and pleading with your father to reconsider?"

"Marry without my father agreeing to the marriage?" Her eyebrows darted up again in surprise. "Oh no. Who would do a thing like that? That would be like, how can I describe it?" She fished around in the air for a word. "Suicide. Something like suicide. Yes, it would be like ending my life."

She ticked off a well-rehearsed list on her fingers. "I am young. I don't know much about life, about men, about relationships. I need my parents' advice and support so they will stand behind me all my life. If my family is not there to take care of me when I need help, then who will?"

I waved the waiter over. Even though I had invited Angie to come, I knew she would insist on paying because I was a guest in her country. "Where are you from?" the waiter asked while clearing off the drinks from our table.

"From America, but we live here in Beni Suef."

"Welcome. Which one is better—America or Egypt?" It was a common question that I had a ready reply for, but it was still a difficult one to answer. I appreciate Egypt's friendliness and the laid-back attitude with which people take time to greet and speak with one another. I like its family-friendly atmosphere, in which children are always welcome and people are so eager to help us out. But what could I say about the rude comments from young men on the streets and loud, boisterous people who shove their way in front of me as if I did not exist? No one ever asked me what I didn't like about Egypt and neither did they want to hear it. When it came to this question, the only correct answer was flattery.

"People here are friendly. I'm happy here, and I was happy in America. My family and friends are there. I thank God for my good life." It was a truthful and simple statement that worked well.

The waiter pondered that for a few seconds then added, "Yes, but America is rich and Egypt is poor." People couldn't quite figure out why we would give up "the promised land" to live in this poor place.

We hopped on a waiting microbus and took the wild ride home, winding through the dirt streets of the village, dodging kids, animals, and bicycles. Before going into our apartment, I wandered over to Um Amzat to pick up some pomegranates.

"*Ana zalana minik!* I am angry with you!" she exclaimed.

"Why?" I was completely bewildered by this sudden flurry of anger.

"Yesterday, you bought fruit from someone else. I saw it in your bag. Why do you do that? We have fruit here. You buy only from me. If I don't have something you want, tell me and I will get it for you. Understand?"

I explained that I sometimes bought from her, but I also wanted to support the women sitting on the street corners with their babies who also needed money. But Um Amzat was not interested in my socio-economic theory of justice. She wanted customer loyalty.

Whenever I learned a new word or phrase, I would hear it all the time. "I am angry with you" became a common one as I developed deeper relationships with people. Its sharpness initially distressed me. ("Can't I do anything right?" I wondered.) With a little more experience under my belt, I realized people were merely blowing off steam without storing up a grudge. Besides, it was a good sign that my relationships with people were moving beyond the "polite" stage to a more authentic level. Indeed, as I made my purchase, I noticed Um Amzat put an orange in the bag.

About a week later, I was standing in front of Um Amzat's rough-brick apartment. Two men were sitting on the sidewalk, hunched over huge burlap bags of cotton and material, making mattresses. This is the last item required for a new household; the wedding was next.

"Um Nicholas, you will come tonight, won't you? To Marina's henna party?" How could we refuse? We had been to lots of henna parties, held the night before the wedding. The bride and groom have separate celebrations with their respective family.

At nine that night we took a *hantoor* (horse-drawn carriage), to their neighborhood. We found the correct alleyway by following

Um Amzat and daughter Marina at Marina's henna party.

the sound of music blaring from huge speakers. Lots of family and friends had gathered in the alley. On a small table was a three-layer, chocolate cake with candles. At least that is what we thought it was. Kids kept going by and taking huge swipes of the icing, but instead of licking it, they were rubbing it all over their hands. It wasn't chocolate but "henna cake." Henna is crushed dry leaves that, when mixed with water, makes a dark paste that leaves the hands stained orange for the next few days.

We sat in wooden chairs, fascinated by the dancing. Muslim girls in headscarves danced with Christian girls; large women in galabayas shook their ample hips with confidence; young men in jeans and T-shirts joined in. Everybody felt comfortable getting up and shaking loose. Belly dancing is not just limited to women; men can shake their hips in a way that would shame Elvis. The magic seemed to be in a scarf tied around a person's hips, rendering them loose so they could shake each and every body part, separate or together, as the occasion required. Others gathered around, clapping and cheering the dancer on.

Because Um Amzat's family was poor, the dancing took place in the streets. Because they were Christian, both males and females were present, though they would not dance with each other.

It was astonishing to see how free people felt to belly dance when its graceful hand and hip movements were so seductive and sexual—from my American perspective, at least. At wedding parties, we often saw young girls—six and seven years old—placed by their parents on top of small tables to shake their hipless hips. Oh, I could just hear some in the United States calling this the "sexploitation of children." But belly dancing was accepted as a time-honored tradition that even the radical religious fundamentalists could not snuff out. The more conservative, middle-class families simply had their parties indoors.

I looked over at Um Amzat, amazed at the life differences between she and her soon-to-be-married daughter. The eldest of nine children, living in a one-room, mud-brick house, Um Amzat never went to school. Her father, a poor farmer, married her off when she was eleven years old, "after only one month of bleeding," to her husband, who was "twenty or twenty-five years old; I don't know." Now, a generation later, her daughter, Marina, had graduated from high school and was marrying at twenty. Education for Marina and family planning for Um Amzat had improved these two women's lives tremendously.

Um Amzat offered me a soft drink, the only refreshment available, because their money had been spent on furnishing a new apartment. Food wasn't the focus, but rather dancing, clapping, and ululating to celebrate this next milestone in a young person's life. After attending many henna parties, Rebecca astutely concluded, "The poorer the family, the more fun the party."

About a month later, Marina was visiting with her mother at the fruit stand. I joined them for tea and flipped through her wedding album, stopping at a picture of her and her husband dancing at their wedding reception.

I asked, "Was this your first time to—"

"Hold hands? Yes, when we were dancing at our wedding."

"Even after you were engaged? You didn't hold hands?"

"In Beni Suef? No. We could only link arms while walking."

"When you became engaged, did he kiss you?" I quickly added, "On the cheek?"

"Shame! I would have slapped him if he had disrespected me like that."

"But you were engaged!"

"Oh, indeed! I would have broken off the engagement if he treated me like that." Her face was red, but she gave a slight smile.

"What about Mr. Brad? Did he kiss you when you were engaged?"

I suppose my knowing smile was sufficient answer.

14

Fatma on the Roof

Tuesday morning was Suad's regular day to clean our apartment. Cleaning meant taking an old galabaya dress in her hands and beating the dust off our furniture and coffee tables. So many vases and knick-knacks broke that it became the family joke to say "Suad did it," even if she wasn't there. Over time, she became valuable to me less for her cleaning skills—though they were appreciated—and more for exposing me to another side of Egypt: the village life of poor peasants and farmers.

She also heard plenty from my neighbor Fatma about her miserable life, and shared her own insights with me. "Not all men beat their wives," she once told me. "I have six sisters and only one was beaten by her husband."

We had more than an employee-employer relationship. She greeted me with kisses, and we always ended her work time with tea and chatting. That's how I found out she was buying bread that particular morning when a worker swung a huge, hot, metal pan around and hit her arm, causing a burn about the size of a quarter.

"Did you say anything to him?"

"No, there were too many people around. He didn't even know he hit me."

Any other woman would have given him a good yelling at, but Suad was more reserved. Yelling is often the only recourse in these matters; the poor take their bruises, and life just carries on.

I was about to launch into Fatma's latest dramatic event when Doctor Negwa unexpectedly arrived at the door. She joined us for tea, and I proceeded with the story of what had happened the week before.

It was Friday night, and I had been planning on a relaxing hot soak in the tub. But I heard the sounds of young children and bags shuffling up the stairs, and I knew it was Fatma and the children returning home after a month's absence. Our place had seemed a little too quiet, and I was surprised to find myself happy to see them back. They had been living with her parents, just a few blocks away. I didn't know what spurred Fatma to return, but I did know that a quiet, relaxing evening by myself was over before it had even begun.

Her two boys came into our apartment and busied themselves with toys I kept on hand just for them. Fatma stood outside on the landing. I could see by the dim stair light that her eyes were red and swollen from crying. "My father has put us out of the house" was all she said.

The door to her apartment was padlocked, and she had no key. So Fatma picked up the black plastic bags stuffed with clothes and walked up two more flights of stairs to the apartment roof. I followed with the rest of her bags, inquiring as to what she was planning to do.

"Sleep on the roof," she said unceremoniously. The roof was covered with mounds of dirt and debris, such as broken glass and tiles, animal poop, trash, stray pieces of wood, discarded bottles, and clay bowls used for feeding pigeons. Rooftops are open-air attics, a storage place for the family's junk that has no other place. We dropped the bags amid the mess, and I went back downstairs to brief the family on the situation.

"Do we feel okay about letting them sleep on the roof, or do we want to offer something else?" I asked. It was a short discussion because Brad and the kids were headed out the door to see a movie at a friend's house. I only remember hearing that we weren't responsible for her problems, which is easy to say when you are walking out the door. The voice that I heard in my head said that perhaps one day when her life is better, she'll look back at this dark moment and remember that it was a Christian who helped her when all else had fallen apart. At a time like that, one can only hope that something better lay ahead for her.

Fatma sat on the sofa, Mumtez was playing a computer game, and Medo was chewing on an apple core. I offered to fix them sandwiches, but Fatma protested. "No, we'll go out for *tamiya*." Those cheap, fried-bean-patty sandwiches were a staple food among the poor. She pulled six Egyptian pounds from her pocket, a little less than a dollar. "Look. This is all I have."

"Fatma, you can't sleep up on the roof. That isn't right for the kids." I took her by the hand and showed her our enclosed balcony. "You can sleep here. I'll put out some blankets and pillows."

"*Ukhti* [my sister], you are crazy. I can't do that." I expected this refusal. Nicholas said she refused my offers out of pride. Perhaps, but I also wondered about other cultural implications—sleeping in the house of a man to whom you aren't related was definitely taboo. While she and the kids went out to get something to eat, I took a shower and contemplated her situation.

Fatma and boys came back at about eleven p.m. with my own kids trailing behind them. Heeding Nicholas's warning that she wouldn't accept anything from me, I turned the situation over to him. Here's his account of what happened next:

"Fatma led me to their roof, which has a dirty shelter underneath the pigeon coop. It smelled so bad that I brought her to our side of the roof. It wasn't as junky and we had cleared out a section and made a nice sitting area. Fatma agreed to sleep on our roof.

"I went back to our apartment and got some heavy blankets and pillows. They thanked me multiple times and were very happy but cold. I looked around, trying to think of something to keep them warm and remembered our fire circle. We had lots of wood, kindling, and paper. It was very hard to get the fire started because it was windy, and the match kept blowing out. Fatma told me that in the morning her son had school, and she didn't have a watch to tell her what time it was, so I gave her mine, plus some cheese to go with her bread.

"Finally, we got the fire going. They were happy for the time being, but I was afraid the wind would blow the fire to our canvas roof canopy. But it was midnight; I decided all was in God's hands and went back downstairs."

About mid-morning, Fatma was at the door, a pile of blankets in her arms and a male relative with her. Her eyes were red and swollen from more crying. She hugged me and thanked me and said she was going to her father's house.

With Suad and Negwa I concluded, "That was four days ago, and I haven't seen her since."

Suad rubbed her burn mark and looked up. "She must have done something wrong for her husband to put her out the house. But her father can't do that."

Negwa, who had previously counseled with Fatma after a harsh beating, explained further. "This is a rather complicated situation. They are poor and uneducated people. They say there is no room in the mother's house for Fatma and her two boys. Women cannot live on their own in our culture, so she must live with her husband. How to explain this? In our culture, women don't belong to themselves. We are not individualistic like Americans. We belong to someone else—to our father, to our husband—and most of the time this is good. The family makes the decisions for her, but this is a poor, simple family who cannot do much for her. We don't have social programs like in the west to help her, because that is what the family is for. This family is an exception, but we have no programs for the exceptions."

"Can't she divorce her husband?" I asked. "Fatma tells me she is afraid to because he could take the boys."

"She can leave him, but when the boys turn ten, the father can take them to live with him. They are supposed to be changing this law and making the age older, like fifteen, but we don't know if this law has come about. But Gigi, even if she could leave him, where would she go? There are no apartments, or they are too expensive. And you know our economy here. There are no jobs."

Suad was standing in front of the mirror, assembling three scarves on her head. "You will come and visit us in our village soon?" she asked hopefully.

"In sha'allah," I replied. I saw her down the stairs before rejoining Negwa at the table.

"You know, Negwa, her situation is really depressing. Be honest. Would you send your daughter back to her abusive husband?"

"Absolutely not. I told you before this neighbor will make a lot of trouble for you. Believe me, most Egyptians are not like this. Perhaps you should consider moving. She also doesn't pray, and that's a problem too, because God can help her when no one else can."

This seemed an opportune moment to ask Negwa something about which I had heard varying comments. "Negwa, in Islam is it permissible for a husband to beat his wife?" I thought her response would be trustworthy.

"The Qur'an tells us that if a wife does not obey her husband, he should talk to her and try to reason with her. If that doesn't persuade her, then he should refuse to sleep in the same bed with her.

If she is still being stubborn, then he can lightly, and *lightly* is the correct word, hit her. But that is the last resort, only after everything else has failed. He must persuade her to obey him." She waved her hand to the door. "But what this man is doing, beating his wife like this, no, this is not Islam."

Negwa took off her glasses and continued, "But this situation is strange. It is something we expect to hear from the west, where men don't protect women like we do here."

Fatma did not belong to herself. It does not matter if you are male or female, Muslim or Christian, eighteen or thirty-six, the tradition is that you live with your parents until marriage. If the marriage falls apart, the woman goes back to her family's house which, for many, is a good arrangement because it provides her and her children with security and comfort in difficult times. That, of course, is the ideal situation. Fatma's father had no option but to take her back, and she had no option but to go back.

I had always kind of scoffed at the notion of parental approval, because it seemed to make adult children so dependent on their parents. But I could now see the wisdom of it. Marriage in Egypt is not about two individuals falling in love but about two families joining together. If the families approve of the marriage, then they have a stake in it and are responsible if things fall apart. While a father would not force his daughter to marry someone against her will, he could prevent his daughter from marrying someone he did not approve, like Angie's father did.

Sometimes fathers give in against their better judgment. I recall a conversation with a Christian friend who had met her husband at a university and fallen in love with him.

"My father said he would not stand in the way of my marriage, because he could see I was in love and he did not want me to be angry with him," she told me. "But he also told me from discussions with my fiancé that he would not let me work nor pursue my own activities. My father said he would be overbearing and controlling, and that has all proven to be true."

The conversation with Negwa drifted to raising children, and some differences in our approaches became apparent. "Gigi, in a few years your children will be eighteen and will want to leave the house. How can you let them do that when that is the time they need you most? How can anyone decide something as important as marriage and careers without their parents' involvement and advice?"

She knew I loved my children and took good care of them, and that conflicted with the prevalent image of westerners as callous, uncaring parents who let their children wander out into the world alone and unprotected. In her worldview, if you love your children, you keep them home, where they are safe and protected.

Negwa laughed, "I tell my children, if they love me, they will never leave me."

Americans tend to raise their kids to be independent and self-sufficient, allowing them to make their own decisions—and mistakes—and deal with the consequences. In contrast, Arabs tend to raise their kids to depend on family for their basic needs and in discerning choices, because the family, not the individual, is held responsible for the outcome. In a time of crisis, the family is obligated to help.

Though these are two different ways of guiding children to adulthood, at the heart of both is parental love.

Negwa nodded her head in agreement, "Yes. Americans and Arabs. We have different habits, that's all."

"Is this why you dropped by today?" I asked. It was unusual for her to visit during work hours.

"No, I came to say goodbye, because I am going with my father on the pilgrimage to Mecca." I was delighted for her good fortune. She had never made a pilgrimage, and I was flattered that she came to tell me before leaving.

"*Hagg mabroor!*" I called to her. "May your pilgrimage be pleasing to God."

The pilgrimage took on added significance two months later when her father died.

ع

As Negwa left our house, Brad returned from a meeting with Sister Heba and announced with great annoyance, "She wants to put a twelve-year-old boy in my adult English class! His grandfather came to the school and asked her. She can't tell him no, so she wants me to evaluate him and make a decision." He let out a deep sigh of frustration. "I don't see why we can't have policies and guidelines and just tell people these are our rules."

We learned to our frustration that in situations like this, Egyptians would not give a direct no, nor would they express an American-style regret with an answer like, "We understand but our policy forbids it." No one directly refuses a person's request, because you never know when a return favor might be needed later.

Because of this, Egyptians spend a lot of time and energy cultivating relationships. While we agreed in theory that people are more important than rules and institutions, the reality meant that students were constantly asking Brad to change the days or time of classes to suit their own individual schedules. While this frustrated Brad, it unknowingly worked to our advantage one time. The kids wanted to take drawing lessons, but it conflicted with basketball practice. I explained that to the art instructor, expressing our regrets. The next day, he showed up at our house, saying he had rearranged the art schedule to accommodate our kids.

We sat down to eat our midday meal and, in what had become a family ritual, told our "adventures of the day." Brad began by telling us his latest story with the bishop. They had been meeting daily for more than a year, and while the bishop's English had improved greatly, we also benefited in learning more about the Coptic Orthodox Church directly from the top.

"A few days ago," Brad began, "I had asked him why he always travels in a car with tinted windows. You remember when he visited us when we lived in the school apartment?"

We remembered indeed. The school was right around the corner, and we had naïvely assumed the bishop would walk over. Instead he was driven by a chauffeur in a car with tinted windows and accompanied by two guards. When the kids asked about this, he replied, "I cannot walk anywhere in Beni Suef or Egypt for that matter. Too many people stop me to kiss my hand and ask for a blessing." The kids were relieved to meet someone who got more attention than we did.

Brad continued his story. "So the bishop explained he had tinted windows for security reasons. He paused and looked at the ceiling, struggling to find the right word, and finally said, 'There could be bad Muslims trying to hurt me.'" Brad knew there had been violence in the past from Muslim extremists on the police and authority figures.

"So today, we were practicing pronunciation and the bishop asked the meaning of the strange-looking symbols above the words.

You know, the schwa A and the long O. I explained that these symbols were phonetics."

"The bishop's face lit up, 'Yes, that's what I was talking about yesterday. The Muslim phonetics.'"

Brad let out a great belly laugh. "He had confused the word phonetics with fanatics!"

15

Smelling the Breeze

It was Friday. The weekend. So Nicholas called his friend Jonathan to come over and play. "Mom, he's in church today from one to six o'clock," Nicholas reported to me. "How boring can you get? There's no way I would go to church for that long." Nicholas had lost sight of the fact that today was not just any Friday. With Easter only two days away, it was Good Friday. Egyptian Christians call it Great Friday.

"Nicholas," I implored, "please, this is the time to call your Muslim friends to play. You know, we think we came here to set an example of Christian living, but how does it look to call friends to play on Good Friday?"

The discipline and devotion of Egyptian Christians was impressive, and we often fell short, causing me to sometimes wonder what they really thought of our Christian witness.

As it turned out, Jonathan was late for church. Good Friday prayers began at nine a.m., and it was standing room only at five o'clock when we showed up. Most folks were still going strong, even though they had been fasting all day—a no-food, no-drink fast. The kids naturally were restless, and I couldn't help but hope that there were extra blessings for any mother who would bring her kids to a nine-hour church service.

Everyone left at six-thirty and went home to break their fast with *tamaya* (fried bean patties) and bean sprouts. "It's poor food," a friend explained, "and the idea is to identify with the suffering of Christ. The monks eat only bread."

However, the night wasn't done. Christians returned to church at nine for all-night prayers. I showed up at one a.m. to a packed church, kids included. I visualized for a moment how it would work if a church in the United States held a nine-hour prayer vigil.

Would people sign up for one-hour shifts? Would they come to the church or remain in the comfort of their own home? Who would prepare the food and coffee for the snack breaks? Who would prepare the program for nine hours of singing and praying? And who would come?

In the Coptic Orthodox Church, it's really not that complicated. People show up because it's their tradition in celebrating Easter. Food: none. Hot tea: none. Water: none. The program is their prayer book. We read the book of Revelation. We sang only one song: "Oh Jerusalem," a rousing hymn accompanied by the lighting of candles. It was not a social event; there wasn't even a welcome by the bishop, who led the service. People were there simply to pray and sing, and that's what we did all night long.

My Arabic teacher once explained: "Easter is a great time for us because we can spend so much time in the church. We don't feel tired or hungry, because we are praising God and we are so happy to do that. For a short while we have just a little imagination of what heaven will be like."

I surveyed the crowd of several hundred people singing joyfully; I could see it was true.

Prayers ended at dawn, and I walked home on the almost deserted streets. A man and a woman pushed their colorful sandwich cart down the street, eager to claim their spot and prepare bean sandwiches before the breakfast crowd arrived. Through an open mosque door, a muezzin was standing in front of a microphone, giving the sunrise call to prayer: "Come to prayer! Come to goodness! Prayer is better than sleep!" Millions of Muslims were getting out of bed and gathering their prayer rugs for dawn prayers. Thousands of Christians were making their way home from churches after praying all night. It was an image to capture and hold. What if this scene was the headline on the morning news? Most of the world sees only the violence and political chaos in the Middle East, but in Egypt, I saw a stronger force: Muslims and Christians faithful to God.

"You really should take better care of yourself. Make up your hair and your face. Your husband will love you more." That was the unsolicited advice from Maggie who, while not understanding my approach to simple living, wanted to make sure I understood that image and appearance do matter.

Maggie and I entered a popular hairdresser's shop; it wasn't much bigger than a large bathroom. Blow dryers whirred; old-fashioned curling irons were heated over open gas flames; large bridal portraits smiled down on us. Looking at the packed room, I concluded that on Easter weekend, Christian women were in one of two places: the church or the hairdresser's. Maggie and I settled comfortably into the chairs, and while people seemed to keep coming in, no one was leaving.

Maggie's family used to be rich, she explained. "My family had a lot of property, so we had high status and wealth until we were forced to sell it during the time of President Nasser. And even though that has been more than fifty years ago, we still must give the appearance of wealth so that people will not look down on us."

Gamel Abdul Nasser was the first president of modern Egypt. He came to power in a 1952 coup, cozied up to the Soviets, and enacted land reform as a way to help struggling, landless peasants. Maggie's family and thousands of others had land confiscated. They were reimbursed, it didn't compensate completely for their loss. Fifty years later and with no land or money to show for it, it was still important to keep up the image of wealth and status.

Image. Appearance. Reputation. So much of daily life focused around this trio, and its importance can be seen in a story Brad told me. Once he and a male friend from Beni Suef were sitting at a beachside café. His companion drew Brad's attention to a nearby table and whispered conspiratorially, "Do you see that woman?" Brad looked over at the four young people, three male and one female, innocently drinking tea. Brad's friend stated matter-of-factly and with a vulgarity that the four, whom he did not know, were in a sexual relationship. Brad was flabbergasted at such an outrageous statement. "What!? How can you say that?" But for his companion, there was no other explanation for a woman sitting with three men, for that was the image he saw.

We started to refer to the image-appearance-reputation trio as "the globe theory" after Sister Heba purchased a beautiful and expensive globe for the school. It was too heavy for teachers to lug to their classrooms and too expensive to leave it in one. The solution: build a glass case and mount it seven feet high in the corner of a room, rendering it inaccessible. There the globe sat, gathering dust and serving no practical use as an educational aid. But it did serve a greater purpose: it showed guests that the school was financially secure enough to purchase expensive educational equipment. I wondered how many maps could have been bought for the same price and permanently mounted in each classroom?

"*Salaam aleikum.*" A Muslim woman, wearing a niqab entered the hairdresser's and greeted us all. Silence. The owner turned off the blow dryer to tend to her. I chided myself for not responding back, embarrassed by my accent, which would cause curious heads to turn my way. The woman sat down and removed her face veil to get her face "threaded," that is, have facial hair removed by using thread, not scissors or cream. I had always thought one benefit of veiling was that one could look unkempt beneath—gray hair, hairy legs— but Muslims spent just as much time and money on their appearance as Christians did to look beautiful for their husbands.

"Salaam aleikum," (peace be with you) is in all the Arabic phrase books and is one of the first expressions tourists learn when setting foot in the Middle East. What these books neglect to mention is that in Egypt, Muslims greet each other this way but not Christians. I thought it was a wonderful way to begin a conversation, especially among people you do not know, but it was not appreciated among Christians. Some smiled at my naïveté and ignorance; others got upset and would chastise me, "That's for Muslims!"

My Arabic teacher gave a more in-depth explanation. "'Salaam aleikum' literally means peace depends on you; 'salaam likum' is peace be upon you, as Christ greeted his disciples."

It was acceptable for me to use the later phrase but not the former one. Yet every Muslim I asked always translated *salaam aleikum* to mean wishing the other person peace. It was one instance when I thought the semantics of religion were just too picky. But I compromised easily by greeting all with peace, salaam.

Maggie looked at her watch. We had been waiting for almost two hours, with little progress in sight. Knowing she had a lot more important things to do than sit there with me, I suggested she could leave. But the process of parting was no easy task, because Egyptians feel so responsible for their guests. It took some convincing that, yes, I was capable of getting my hair done by myself; yes, I did know my way home; and no, I wouldn't pay more than the agreed-upon price.

Once Maggie left, I kept eyeing the Muslim woman, who was calmly sitting in the chair, tilting her face left and right, as the hairdresser glided a red thread across it. The urge to have a new cultural experience took over, and before I knew it, I was sitting in the chair. The hairdresser unwound a piece of thread and held both ends taut in her hands with the middle section in her mouth. She moved the thread—together, apart, together, apart—so rapidly that it made a whirring sound just like an electrical razor.

Ahhh! I almost jumped out of my chair! Pain seared through my cheeks as she scraped them with what was no longer an innocent thread but a lethal weapon in her hands. That thread took out hair by the roots! My eyes stung with tears and my face burned. I gripped the chair as if I were at the dentist getting a filling.

"That's all for today," I said meekly.

"But I have only done half your face!"

"Thank you," I whimpered, willing to suffer through life with a half-hairy face. Oh, the foolish things one does in the name of cultural experiences!

My turn with the hairdresser finally came and I selected light-brown highlights which, two hours later, looked red, as though I had collided with a donkey cart piled high with tomatoes. Ironically I would discover that red-highlighted hair made me look more Egyptian and reduced the comments on the streets from the *shabaab* (young men).

Having fulfilled my religious obligations of a new hairstyle and clothes, we spent Easter day in much the same way as Christmas—greeting the bishop and visiting at the girl's orphanage. Palm Sunday, Holy Thursday, and Easter Sunday are holidays for Christians but not Muslims, a generous allowance, I thought, from a government that many Christians claimed persecuted them. Easter in Egypt lacked the secular, commercial trappings found in the United States. There were no chocolate bunnies or marshmallow chicks, and definitely no honey-baked ham. People spent a pleasant day visiting family and friends, hanging out at the gardens and clubs, and walking along the Nile River or riding on *feluccas* (sailboats).

A Palm Sunday celebration with other workers from Mennonite Central Committee.

"Would you like to spend *Sham Naseem* with our family? We always travel to my husband's village and spend the day hanging out." Sandy, another friend I had met through my daughters, was talking about a holiday, the name of which literally means "smelling the breeze." It falls on the day after Easter and is one of the few holidays celebrated by both Christians and Muslims. Originating from the times of the pharaohs and continuously celebrated for four thousand years, it centers around a tradition of being outdoors all day "smelling" the greenness of spring and the beginnings of new life. Even eggs are decorated, a custom that trickled over to Christianity and became part of our Easter celebrations.

"Do you think we should mention something to her about our security situation?" Brad asked as we were discussing the invitation. Going to this village would involve traveling south of Beni Suef, deeper into Upper Egypt, a region known for its violent past with militant Islam. Generally foreigners could only travel south with a tour group or a police escort. But I knew a few people who traveled independently without any problems, so I rationalized that maybe we would be lucky too. That turned out to be a naïve assumption that did not take into account how seriously our security situation had recently changed.

A month earlier, in April 2005, a motorcyclist driving through a popular tourist area in Cairo had thrown a homemade bomb into a crowd, killing four people, all foreigners. A couple of weeks later, another young man had thrown a small bomb and killed only himself. A short distance away, two women completely covered in niqab shot up a tourist bus before shooting each other in a suicide pact. It was rumored that the two women had been engaged to the other two bombers. According to the government, it was a bizarre event explained as dysfunctional behavior of one family, not a resurgence of terrorism.

But we felt the impact immediately. The next day, our three grandfatherly guards, who had been with us for a year and a half, were reassigned and replaced by younger, stronger guards with bigger guns and walkie-talkies.

"You'll need to tell us where you are going so we can provide an escort for you, not to school and work, but anyplace else," one of them said to us. Sure enough, as we walked to the nadi the next day, a big, blue police truck followed us, with six armed guards sitting in the back.

"How long do you think you will be in the club?" the plainclothes agent responsible for this "covert" activity asked me. Since when were Egyptians concerned about time? The police patiently waited in the police truck until we finished our visiting. Much to our astonishment, as we jumped into the microbus to go home, one guard with his big gun slung across his front, got in with us. As if we didn't manage to get enough attention on our own! Sure enough, this aroused lots of curiosity and comments from some other passengers, always eager to show off to foreigners, with our own guard joining in the antics.

After a couple of weeks, the guards, realizing they could not keep up with the comings and goings of our family of five, began to relax. They even started taking their chairs over to the fruit and vegetable stand across the street, hanging out with Um and Abu Amzat. It baffled us that, while the bombing incidents happened in Cairo, none of the foreigners living in Cairo got extra protection, but our family, two hours away, did. For the rest of our time in Egypt, we would continue to have six guards—two per shift, one in uniform and one plainclothes—to protect us.

As per the guards' instructions, I informed them of our trip to the village with Sandy's family, and they arranged for a police truck to escort us to the train station. How was it that we could walk alone to the train station to buy tickets, yet when it came to actually catching the train, we needed a police escort? Nicholas, always one to see the silver lining in the dark cloud, took advantage of another opportunity for adventure and hopped in the back of the police truck with the solders, while the rest of us took a taxi to the train station.

It wasn't long before the tourist police spotted us. Located at every train station, they kept an eye on the comings and goings of foreign travelers, all under the guise of security.

"Where are you going?"

"To Maghaghrah"

"Where are you from?"

"America."

"When will you return?"

"This evening."

The questioning continued: train number, car, seats, time of departure, time of arrival. It was routine now, but in the beginning we struggled to understand; ironically the tourist police speak little English.

Inevitably the attention would turn to Nicholas. "What are you doing here? Leave these people alone."

"I'm with them."

"What do you mean, you are with them? You're Egyptian."

"I'm American. This is my family."

"No! You are Egyptian. What? Really? You are American?"

"He's my son," I would say, letting them ponder the genetic probability of that. How could a boy have brown skin, dark hair, and speak Arabic but not be Egyptian? It just did not make sense to them. But soon they were patting Nicholas on the back, talking and joking with him. Egyptians aren't strangers for long.

We disembarked an hour later, only to be met by a "welcoming committee" of fourteen guards. We were stunned. I had expected two or three at the most, but fourteen? Sandy's cousin was there to meet us, and with a look of bewilderment, asked, "How many foreigners are coming today?"

"Only five. Don't you know we are famous and important people?" I joked. It was an attempt at humor, but my heart was sinking at the thought of spending the day under these circumstances. We piled into his car and caravanned with two armed vehicles in front and one behind through the small town, causing all the kids on the roadside to stop and gape at the "government officials" passing by.

We turned on a rutted dirt road leading to the village, passing through fields of ripening wheat, where farmers straightened up from their labor to stare at the caravan. If anyone wanted to take a shot at us, we were sitting ducks. This was the irony of the "security." If we had just gone by ourselves in a car, no one would have paid any attention to us.

Sandy stood on the porch when we arrived, mouth dropped open in surprise. "Do you always have to travel like this?" I began to apologize, something I continued to do throughout the day. All fourteen policemen piled out and began to make their acquaintances with the family. When the chief asked to search the house, the male elders put their collective feet down. One came forward to explain. "My cousin was mayor of this village for the past ten years, before him my father was mayor for fifty years and before him, my grandfather. We have been mayors of this village since 1882. We are good, honorable people."

I was naïvely hoping that declaration, plus the fact that the village was majority Christian, would send the guards home to enjoy the holiday with their families. But no such luck. Though they didn't search the house, they settled into the huts that had once been used by other guards when the family had ruled the village.

We set out determined to enjoy our day, first gathering with Sandy's family on the porch of the big house to eat the traditional breakfast: salted fish, white cheese, green onions, bread, and *fiteer*— very thin, flaky, buttery layers of dough baked like a pizza.

"Check this out," said Brad, browsing through an Arabic newspaper. "Here's an advertisement in English for the fish we are eating: 'Vacuum Rotten Fish.' Well, doesn't that sound yummy?" We knew the fish was salty but didn't realize it wasn't cooked.

"The salt cooks it," explained Sandy's husband.

Uh huh. It tasted, well, kind of salty and rotten.

ج

Muslims usually have Arabic names; Christians are generally named after saints or have western names like Sandy, Mark, and Heidi. Sandy was lively and vivacious with bouncing brown hair and worked as a news reporter for a local TV station. She handled all the foreign interviews in English, a language perfected by a year's stay in California with relatives. While in the United States, she had made learning to drive a goal. When her relatives objected, a determined Sandy simply took the car herself and headed to the freeway. No disaster occurred, but besides learning to drive, Sandy gained more confidence in attempting daring goals.

Being a strong woman of such achievement might seem contrary or threatening in a conservative, male-dominated society, but Sandy's life demonstrated compatibility with the surrounding culture. Happily married with two girls, she juggled her job around her kid's and her husband's schedules. Before she left for work, dinner was all prepared for her family. Sandy's husband, like most men, was not capable of much more than putting on water for tea. But such inequities weren't an issue for her. In fact, Sandy wouldn't call it inequity, but merely his culturally assigned gender role. She wasn't frustrated by her husband's helplessness, because she didn't expect more of him. When Sandy started her career in TV, she accepted that the job was in addition to her responsibilities in the home. Being successful and independent in her work wasn't a threat to her marriage because she and her husband maintained their traditional roles.

Once we were talking about activities for women, when Sandy became defensive. "I was watching *Oprah* the other day and there were some women on the show talking about women in the Middle East, saying how oppressed we are. This kind of stuff makes me so angry. I just got up and turned the TV off. We do not see ourselves as oppressed. This is simply our life, and we are happy with it. Things like swimming and women riding bicycles, these things aren't part of our culture, so it doesn't bother us not to do them."

By then I had seen that women in Egypt have many rights and freedoms. They can study at universities, drive cars, own businesses, stroll the streets window shopping, vote and hold government positions, wear suggestive clothing, work among men just as women in the west do. But these freedoms do not depend on what is written in the country's constitution and laws. Rather, independence for

Women selling inflated goat skins used for making butter.

women here depends on three people: father, husband, and brother. This trio determines how a female will spend her life. If she is blessed with a modern, educated, and trusting father, she could have endless privileges and opportunities. But if her father is suspicious and a hardcore traditionalist, her life could be filled with barriers erected by him.

One of my male acquaintances summarized it this way. "I help out my wife with the kids because we have love in our marriage. In the west, your marriages are equal, but here in the east, the husband is in control of the family. That's what the Bible says, and that is our culture for Christians and for Muslims." Sandy would be in perfect agreement with this statement.

We spent the day outdoors. Though the guards confined us to the compound, it was large and had something rare for Egypt: green grass. The kids played and rode a horse brought over by a neighboring cousin. I walked up the stairs to the roof, eager to get a view of village life. On the next roof over, a woman sat beside a huge, mud-brick oven, baking bread. Her daughter, who looked about seven years old, fed the flames with branches and pulled an oversized dress up to cover her slim shoulders. She briefly looked at me and gave a hesitant wave. On another roof a woman sat shaking an inflated goatskin hanging from a tripod; after an hour or so, rich cream would yield a solid hunk of butter. But twenty-first-century technology also made an appearance: dusty, white satellite dishes perched on a few rooftops.

I stumbled on some rubble and found buried underneath it a metal hand with blue stones dangling from it. This symbol, often found in houses and cars, protects one from the "evil eye" of harm and jealousy. It's an Arab tradition that neither Islam nor Christianity can wipe out, putting it in a class of religious folklore.

The sun was beginning to set, and the guards wanted us out of the village before nightfall. The family had been lovely to us and to the "extra baggage" we brought along. Throughout the day, fourteen guards needed at various times to use the bathroom or the telephone, to drink tea, and to eat meals. The family wasn't obligated to accommodate them but graciously followed traditional rules of Egyptian hospitality to the uninvited. Of course they would not think of accepting payment from us to reimburse for what they had spent on the police. After eighteen months in Egypt, it was the first time I felt a visit with friends was a burden on them. But there was also a lesson in how to be gracious under difficult circumstances.

Return train tickets were all sold out, so we hired a private taxi to take us to Beni Suef. It was the most dilapidated car in which we had ever ridden, and I thought that if the police were really concerned about our security, they would have insisted on a decent vehicle for us to travel in. The car reeked of gasoline fumes, but we didn't blow up when the driver lit a cigarette. A missing dashboard panel exposed a host of assorted colored wires.

We wanting to breathe air other than gas fumes, so we tried rolling down the windows but none of them had handles. Nicholas found a screwdriver stuck in his window slot, but it fell apart in his hands when he tried to use it. Fortunately the kids were exhausted and, stretching out on the wiry seats, bounced their way to sleep. The driver picked up the rearview mirror and stuck it to the windshield. Hanging from it was a metal hand with blue stones. On the dashboard wires lay a Qur'an.

"Egypt needs all the religion it can get," I thought, "as surely there are no safety standards to rely on."

Neither could we rely on the police for safety. They insisted on providing an escort all the way back home, flashing their lights and sirens so they could easily overtake slower drivers. The little, two-lane road had all the usual traffic of people, food vendors, and big transport trucks, interspersed with an occasional herd of buffalo or goats coming in from the fields. Maneuvering through this was tricky enough, but at night drivers generally didn't use headlights until, coming upon an oncoming car, they suddenly flashed their lights, temporarily blinding the other driver. I distracted myself from the dangers by reading the Arabic signs we passed: "Quiet the speed." "Remember God." "Bebe town, 15 kilometers." "Praise God." It would be hard to find any place in Egypt where you would not see at least one reference to God.

I finally spotted the English sign that let us know we had arrived: "Welcome in the Regional Authority for the Promotion of Tourism. Beni Suef, the Pearl of Upper Egypt." We felt more like oysters than pearls. The normal one-hour trip had lasted two hours because we had to wait an hour at a checkpoint for the police to switch security vehicles. All of this gave us plenty of time to concoct schemes of how we could avoid security next time: stay home and "smell the breezes" of Beni Suef.

16
Dressing for Others

"Maybe I should just walk away, that would get his attention," I thought. My arms were growing tired from holding two plastic bags full of groceries. It was a small store, the kind found on every block, selling all the basics: food, drinks, chips, and cleaning supplies. It was my last errand of the day, but the clerk had dropped me to do the bidding of a louder, more demanding customer. The squeaky wheel gets the grease; the timid get ignored. Corner grocery stores didn't have any sense of orderliness, just a handful of folks yelling out orders to the harried but talented clerk who could retrieve goods, put them in a bag, add up the amount in his head, and listen to the next person's demands, all while carefully inspecting the money handed to him.

"Two eggs!"

"One packet of shampoo!"

"One diaper!"

One diaper? Wouldn't you need another one just a few hours later? In most places it was cheaper to buy in large quantities; in Beni Suef, you bought what you could afford at that moment. I had more food in my bags than he was likely to sell all day long, but that didn't make me a preferred customer. Finally he tore off a piece of cardboard from a yogurt container and added up my purchases, offering a tired smile.

I knew the wait was my own fault. If you wanted attention, you needed to be loud and repetitive, throwing in a couple of hand gestures for good measure. But I often stood waiting patiently, as if I'd be rewarded for my good manners. Fortunately I had the right amount of change and did not have to send the clerk—or likely myself—off in the elusive search for change.

I entered our doorway, where the guard sat leaning back in a

Sharing a Ramadan meal with the family's guards in the stairwell of their apartment building.

plastic chair against the wall. With the Qur'an in hand, he recited out loud as his head moved rhythmically back and forth. His machine gun stood in the corner. Sometimes I enjoyed listening to the Qur'an for its melodious rhythms, which can be mesmerizing and consoling. Other times, it was just loud noise blared in taxis and stores. Once when a friend and I traveled on a bus to Cairo, the Muslim man across the aisle asked the driver to turn the sound down, as he had a headache. "It's the Holy Qur'an!" bellowed the driver and, just to prove that people can be more religious than courteous, cranked the volume louder.

"Madame Gigi, you light up our place!" cried out the guard.

"No, your presence does!" I responded in the normal greeting fashion. I used to reply "thank you," until I caught on that compliments were a way for me to either compliment the person back or simply give thanks to God.

"Madame Gigi, why are you here in Beni Suef?" The new guards had settled in and were becoming acquaintances. They also eagerly accepted any cakes and snacks I brought their way.

"I teach English at St. Anthony's." It was the easiest way to reply.

How could I say I was there to build friendships with Christians and Muslims? That I was there to see how God was working in their lives?

"Does the school pay you?"

"No, we get money from a church in the United States."

"How much money?"

"It's enough. We are volunteers, so not enough for a car and a satellite dish but enough to have the basics in life."

Volunteers. The word sounded so hallowed and sacred in the States sounded so hollow there. As volunteers, we had traveled in Egypt more places than any of our acquaintances would in their entire lifetime. As volunteers, help in any crisis we encountered, any healthcare we sought, any money we needed was merely a phone call away. As much as we sympathized with others' plights, the reality was we had passports, we had connections. We had more security and wealth as volunteers than any of the guards would ever have as employees.

"Madame Gigi, I want to get a visa to the U.S. How can I do that?"

"Why do you want to go to the U.S.?"

"I want freedom."

"Freedom to do what?"

"Freedom to work. I have a wife and two small children, and I want to give them a good life." And since he made only fifty dollars a month, who could blame him?

By then the other guard had finished making tea and joined in our conversation, nodding his head to indicate that it was his goal too. It seemed to be everybody's goal. No matter how angry they were at the United States for siding with Israel in another atrocity, no matter how angry they were at Iraq being turned into a battlefield for suicide bombers and civil war, no matter how shocked they were at the moral decay, shallow values, and materialistic greed of our society, all that could somehow be forgiven with the promise of being able to make a decent living and support a family. America, with all its faults and warts, still embodied that dream of opportunity. It was a dream I could relate to because both of my grandfathers thirsted for the same things a hundred years earlier when they left Sicily as poor shepherds for the sugarcane fields of Louisiana. A century later, America is still that dream for people seeking a better life.

I walked into the apartment and Nicholas greeted me. "Nadir

is beating Fatma again. I can't believe you didn't hear it downstairs. It's been going on for at least an hour."

All was quiet by then.

"Should I go over and do something?" I asked, mainly to myself.

"Yes, Mama," said Rebecca, looking up from her schoolwork.

I took a deep breath and knocked on the door, no real plan in my head. Nadir opened it, his hair a mess, his white galabaya stained with blood.

"Is Fatma there? I need some eggs."

"She's not here." The door slammed in my face.

I expected no less. We had learned that there is nothing we could do while the beatings were going on. We could only wait until he finished, then pick up the pieces and clean up the mess. So we waited. We busied ourselves, pretending we were concentrating on whatever we were doing, but we were all distracted by whatever we imagined happening next door. Suddenly we heard a loud retching noise coming from their bathroom.

I raced for the door, landing only to see three men coming out of their apartment.

"Nothing is happening," one man stated. "This isn't important."

"I think this is important," I replied as if I had power to do something.

Mumtez and Medo came to the doorway. Medo's eyes were watery with tears and fear, and he immediately walked over to me. I was giving him a hug and welcoming him into the house when Mumtez, ever in the role of big brother, came over to get him. Likely he feared further angering his father for not being in the house. The door closed, and we waited.

About a half-hour later, Fatma shuffled over, looking terrible. Her hair was completely disheveled, and marks and bruises were already starting to form on her face. Blood dripped from her hand and was smeared on her feet.

"Rebecca, get something from the freezer for her head. Emily, get me a wet washcloth," I called out. The girls sprang into action. Rebecca held a package of frozen peas on a big knot forming at the back of Fatma's head; I gently wiped her hand as she yelped and whimpered in pain.

"I need to go to the hospital, Gigi." I was glad she wasn't resisting that idea. Nicholas offered to play with Mumtez and Medo while Fatma went and got her headscarf. She wound it around her head, despite the pain of doing so; walking outside without it would have felt to her like walking around naked.

We slowly meandered down the stairs, Fatma leaning heavily on me. Um Amzat saw us on the street and lifted up her hands, crying out in anguish, "May God forgive him! May God make it easy on you! God be with you, my daughters!" The guard flagged down a taxi for us and we set off for the hospital.

The taxi driver took one look at her face, asked what happened, and Fatma, with a sudden burst of energy, launched into the whole story. The driver, intrigued by the story, kept his eyes on her through the rearview mirror and, much to my irritation, slowed down, wanting to hear it all before we arrived at the hospital. Fearing she would faint, I was getting impatient.

The taxi driver wanted to take her to the police to file a complaint. "What he did was wrong," he said. While I was heartened to hear of his support for justice, we needed a hospital first; plus, it just got Fatma more excited as she argued with him. When we finally arrived at the hospital, he refused to take my payment.

It was my first time in an Egyptian hospital. I was prepared for the worst, having heard stories about hygiene and the treatment of poor people in the underfunded government hospitals. I expected to see mobs of people waiting in long, disorderly lines. But the place was deserted. It was also in the throes of renovation; the main hallway was littered with broken glass, concrete chunks, and piles of sand and gravel.

We meandered our way through the mess to an open window. Fatma gave her name, and we were instructed to go down the hall. That was the extent of the paperwork. Fatma placed all her weight on me as we walked. While a wheelchair would have been useful, it could not have made it over the piles of rubble.

The doctor instructed Fatma to go in the restroom and wash her hand. It was a typical public restroom, swarming with flies and smelling terrible. No hot water; no soap; no towel. The doctor put one stitch in her hand as she squeezed mine to endure the pain. "So, what happened to your hand?" the doctor asked.

"I cut myself while cutting vegetables."

Why was she so eager to tell all to a taxi driver but nothing to a doctor? For his part, the doctor accepted her lame answer, not inquiring why her face was bruised and puffy. She was given a prescription, and ten minutes after we walked into the hospital, we walked out. We did not pay anything for the visit, and I suppose we got what we paid for.

A taxi let us out in front of the apartment building, and Fatma finally collapsed. The guard got up just in time to give her his plastic chair, and I sent him to the store for orange juice. But Fatma, ever aware of proper public behavior, didn't sit for long. I helped her to her feet, and we slowly made our way up the stairs.

"Come into my apartment and rest," I suggested.

"No, Gigi, I can't do that." She opened her apartment door and collapsed again at my feet. I surveyed the scene in the dark room. Nadir was asleep on the sofa, three male friends were next to him, watching TV. A pool of blood was drying in front of them. One friend nudged Nadir awake. He walked over to Fatma, lovingly helped her to her feet, gently wrapping his arms around her, and walked her to the bedroom, carefully sidestepping another puddle of her blood.

I stood silent and furious. Furious at those three men for sitting and pretending that this was a normal, acceptable thing. Furious at myself for delivering her right back into the hands of her abuser. I wanted nothing more than to shake off all my training and theories of nonviolence and slap each one of them. Had I had more confidence in my Arabic, I would have at least given them a good yelling at. Every social-work-trained bone in my body called out for justice, but I could only stand in silence.

The guard who had just arrived with the orange juice was furiously waving at me to get out of the room. "Madame Gigi, these are bad people! We are here to protect you. Stay away from them."

A half-hour later, Mumtez came over. "Mama wants you, Aunt Gigi."

Nadir had left. I unwrapped Fatma's headscarf and wiped her head with a wet washcloth. She took two aspirins, a swallow of juice, then laid her head back on the pillow and went to sleep. I went home for our mop bucket and yellow rubber gloves. The room looked like a murder scene. There were three more puddles of blood on the bedroom floor, and blood was splattered on the walls. Her yellow blouse, now orange with bloodstains, lay crumpled in the middle of the room. A bloody handprint was smeared on the doorframe. She told me later how he had dragged her across the floor by her hair. How could she have lost so much blood yet only need one stitch for her hand?

There are times in your life when what is happening before you seems so unreal, so out of the ordinary, that it doesn't seem to be your own life but a movie you are watching of someone else's life. That was how I felt as I called out to the air, "Am I really in a Muslim woman's bedroom with a bucket of water, scrubbing her blood off the floor? Is this what I am doing in Egypt?" It was a far cry from my assignment as "English teacher resource." But it wasn't that far off from other vague but equally important MCC ideals: to share another person's pain, to reflect the love of Christ to those who are suffering, to bring comfort and hope to those in despair.

I turned to Fatma, sleeping soundly on the bed. "Heal her wounds, God, and comfort her with your presence." I turned out the lights, went home, and found comfort from the prayer on my wall: "May God bless you with tears to shed for those who suffer, so you will reach out your hand to comfort them and change their pain into joy."

The next morning we walked to her parents' house, and though it was only a few blocks away, it took longer than usual as the full effect of the beating seeped into her muscles and joints, making each step slow and painful. She found a rag to make a sling; her face was now black and blue with bruises, which were made more prominent by the framing of her scarf. It was my first time to meet her parents, who lived in a small but tidy and comfortable apartment.

"What did he do to you now?" her mother loudly demanded as we sat down. "What did you do to make him angry?" Fatma responded in kind, and they were soon embroiled in a shouting match. Her father was in the kitchen, making tea and occasionally yelling out his contribution.

I wondered if perhaps she had come home looking like this so often that she no longer elicited sympathy from them. How could a mother see her daughter in this condition and not get out of her chair, hug her, and cry with her? For me the lack of compassion was the hardest part of the whole sad affair, and I was grateful that they were so busy arguing among themselves that no one noticed the tear that slid down my face.

From what I could piece together, her mother did not want her to leave Nadir, because there was no place for her and the two boys in the parents' small apartment. Her father was more sympathetic but had nothing better to offer her.

"The cat loves the one who is strangling it," her mother emphatically stated, implying that in spite of Nadir's abuse of her, Fatma still loved him.

Fatma didn't dispute that, but it did make her angrier. "Let's go, Gigi. You see! My mother wants to send me back. She wants to see me die."

What had happened to trigger Nadir's anger so viciously? Fatma later told me she had been on the balcony with Medo when "a friend of Nadir's came by looking for him. I told him Nadir was asleep, because he had just come home and I knew he was tired. Nadir heard me and accused me of lying." Nadir found her on the balcony, "wearing my short-sleeve blouse and without a headscarf, and said, 'Hey, why are you dressed like that?'" It's permissible to dress like that in the privacy of one's house, but on the balcony, it's tantamount to standing naked in public. That was too much for Nadir. "He grabbed me by the hair and began punching and hitting me, calling me names and insults, and accusing me of untrue things." In the midst of the fighting, he had grabbed a kitchen knife and cut her hand.

While Fatma was relaying all this to me, one of our guards and another plainclothes detective came and talked with Fatma. Nadir was arrested later in the week, not for his abuse of her—she never filed a police complaint—but for some crime he had committed years earlier.

Was that just a pretext to put this guy away? Was that brought about by our guards and thus done more to protect us than Fatma? I never knew, but was grateful that he was out of the picture for a while.

Fatma now had another serious concern. During the beating Nadir had declared "I divorce you" for the second time. For Muslims, three declarations ends the marriage. Fatma wasn't taking any chances on being discarded. She consulted a sheikh to inquire if the divorce threat was valid if declared while Nadir was under the influence of marijuana. The sheikh said no, the second divorce declaration didn't count.

Temporarily freed of her abusive husband, Fatma was not joyful. "Who will take care of us now, Gigi? Where will I get money and food from?" Those were real concerns, but the reality also was that Nadir never provided for those things when he was home. Each afternoon, Fatma and the boys would trudge over to her parents for their one meal of the day. When she did not go there, she would come to our house, often having the good timing of arriving just as we were about to eat. But pride would not allow Fatma to take things directly from us, so while we sat and ate with her boys, she sat on the sofa, whining and moaning about her fate in life. It was culturally appropriate for me to beg her to eat, but I became weary of those pretensions.

Then I had an idea. Fatma had said she could not get a job because the pay would be so low that most of it would only pay for Medo's childcare while she was at work. "If you find a job, I know a church (meaning me) that will pay for childcare," I proposed to her one day. She made some efforts to ask around for work, but the odds were stacked against her because she had no skills and no previous employment. Plus, unemployment was high and most jobs were obtained through family connections, which Fatma did not have.

Throughout the summer, the girls and I were beading necklaces, cross-stitching table coverings, and making pillows. Fatma showed some interest, and we tried to teach her and show her that she could make them at home and sell them on the streets. But it was not to be. Fatma's depression was much greater than her self-confidence. And it was beginning to take its toll on our family. We were starting to dread the afternoon ringing of the doorbell and the disruptions that would ensue as we endured one crisis after another.

"I have nothing more to offer her," I complained to Brad one evening. "I get weary listening to her complaints, because there are no solutions for her."

"Look, if you don't like the kind of relationship you have with her, change it. This seems to be too much. It's too stressful. Set some limits with her."

That was easy advice to offer in the calmness of our bedroom; it was harder to figure out while the drama was unfolding.

Because we had traveled during the school year, we needed to do school work during the summertime. We decided to get back on a school schedule and had all our books spread out on the dining room table, when we heard, not the ringing of the school bell, but the doorbell. The kids let out a collective groan, "Not now!"

"Nicholas, go tell her we are busy. We are studying." Because of the emphasis on private lessons, it was an easy excuse all Egyptians understood.

Nicholas stuck his head out the door. "She says she wants you, Mama."

"Tell her I will come over when we finish."

"She says she needs you now," relayed Nicholas, getting weary of being the message boy.

Wham! We heard a loud noise.

"She fell down!" Nicholas cried out.

We leapt from the table to find Fatma collapsed in a heap by their metal door, her body twitching spasmodically. Fatma had "extra electricity on the brain," also known as epilepsy, and was having a seizure. We dragged her to her living room, which had a mattress in the center. The family slept under the ceiling fan on these hot summer nights.

"Nicholas, take Mumtez on your bike and go get her brother." Rebecca brought over a wet washcloth that she held on Fatma's forehead. I held her hand throughout the seizures; usually they lasted about fifteen seconds, coming every minute or so. She had medicine for the seizures but her stressful life, the beatings, and poor nutrition all exacerbate the frequency and severity of them.

It was hard to concentrate on studies after that.

For unexplained reasons, Nadir was released from jail after only one month. Fatma's despondency grew as her marital life continued to disintegrate before her eyes. Every day a man on a donkey cart rode down our street, hollering through a microphone to buy used goods. Nadir, in one of his rages, grabbed all of Fatma's clothing—dresses, scarves, undergarments—and tossed them over the balcony to the passing donkey cart. Since Fatma was my size, I gave her a couple of outfits—no easy task, as Muslim dress is quite different from Christian clothing. But it did little to lift her despairing spirits.

"What do you want to drink, Fatma?" I asked during our afternoon teatime.

"*Ashrab sim.* I want to drink poison."

One of the ways she manifested her depression was with physical complaints. Whether they were real or imaginary didn't matter anymore, and I rationalized that taking her to a doctor would at least provide some psychological, if not physical, release. Fatma insisted that the Coptic Orthodox medical clinic would not treat Muslims, but I knew that wasn't true and offered to pay for the visit and accompany her. But feeling and fearing her increasing dependency on me, I drew the line at paying for the prescription.

"Ask Nadir or your parents to get it for you." She took my advice and came back to show me the black eye she received for an answer. Damned if I do and damned if I don't.

𝒆

One day I heard loud, wailing moans of despair that sent goose bumps up and down my arms. I rushed into Fatma's apartment to find her on the floor, slapping her face spasmodically, pulling at her hair, and tearing her clothes. It was as though a wild spirit had taken possession of her.

She calmed down enough to recount a conversation with a friend of Nadir's who had just called out to her from the street.

"Where's Nadir?" the friend asked.

"I don't know; he isn't here."

"Is he at his other wife's house?"

"What other wife?"

"Oh, uh, sorry, uh, nothing."

It was what she had always feared: Nadir taking another wife.

Polygamy, though legal in Islamic religion, was not very common, largely due to the poor economy and the financial difficulties of supporting two families. It was permissible under Egyptian law, but the husband was required to obtain the permission of his first wife. Women could also have it written in their marriage contract that they would be granted a divorce if their husband took another wife.

Why would Egypt modernize polygamy instead of just doing away with it? Basically because it is permitted in the Qur'an, the government cannot do away with it. During Muhammad's life in the seventh century, tribal wars were common and many women were left widowed with no one to care for them. Polygamy was a legitimate way to care for lots of war widows and their children. It wasn't unusual for men to have ten or fifteen wives. Muhammad saw the benefits and abuses of this system and, knowing he could not abolish it altogether, limited the number of wives to four, admonishing that if the husband could not treat them all equally, it was best to marry only one.

But the ideals of Islam and the reality of daily life didn't always match up. And for men like Nadir, it mattered not what the laws were.

ت

I was not alone in my quest to help Fatma, and her situation provided a good topic of conversation with my friends. I headed over to Um Abdullah's, who was home caring for her eight children. I could always count on her for a delicious meal and some frank advice.

"Her situation is just terrible, Um Abdullah. What can she do?" I asked.

Um Abdullah's advice sounded like a marriage manual from the early twentieth century. "She should be quiet and speak in a low voice. Make her home nice and quiet. Don't yell, as that makes a man nervous. She needs to keep her house clean. Keep herself pretty, neat, and clean. Smile at him and ask what he needs. And always she should pray, because on the last day God will open the Book of Judgment and see all that she did—the good and the bad. And God will ask her, do you go to the paradise or to the fire?"

"Is this the counsel girls receive before marrying?" I wondered. It was definitely not advice for dealing with an abusive husband.

I sought the opinion of a Christian friend as we walked along the Nile River one summer evening. "The problem is that she does not respect Nadir's anger or his jealousy," my friend told me. "Her behavior disrespects him. What man can tolerate that humiliation from his wife?"

"In the U.S.," I explained, "spousal abuse works something like this: the husband beats his wife and one of them, usually the husband, will leave for a while. Then the husband feels guilty and returns with apologies and promises never to do it again. That will last for a while, and then it starts all over again. But with Fatma, it's different. She never gets apologies."

"Oh no," my friend remarked. "An Arab man never apologizes. He has too much self-respect and would not want to lose power over her." Power and control are the center of all abusive relationships, regardless of country, culture, or religion.

Fatma's situation regularly came up with Suad, who asked, "Why is she still with him?"

"Because her family's house is too small."

Suad shook her head. "My family was eleven people in a one-room house. She is with him because she loves him. She doesn't want to be without a husband."

An acquaintance with whom I sat at the nadi while our daughters played basketball gave the most common response. "I can assure you that most women are not like her. I fear you will leave Egypt with a bad impression of marriages after seeing hers. Believe me, I have never heard of these things before."

But I was beginning to have my doubts. Was Fatma's situation truly that unusual, or was I getting an inside look at the skeletons that most people, concerned about reputation and image, took great care to cover up? Egyptian society is strictly divided along class levels, and people don't know much about how others live. As a foreigner who could wiggle between the classes, I'd seen that where a person lives, with whom they associate, and what they choose to see all influenced how they judge their own society. "Eat as you like but dress for others" is an Egyptian proverb, and many people only wanted me to see the elegantly dressed part.

What was most troubling about all my conversations was that Nadir, the husband, never came into the discussions. While my friends would shake their heads when I described his actions, no one condemned him, no one suggested she call the police, no one expressed any anger toward him. Some expressed understanding and even sympathy for him; most just rendered him completely irrelevant. The responsibility fell on Fatma's shoulders, and the reactions focused on her behavior. Ironically, while all this advice came from women, they all complained that it was women who were always held responsible for the break-up of a marriage. Were they not also perpetuating this belief?

Our summer was not all gloom and despair. I finally hit on an idea that allowed me to help her in a concrete way. I gave Fatma money to buy all the ingredients to make an Egyptian dish. We cooked it together—she was a very good cook—then we split the dish and each took home half. It was not charity, because we benefited as much as she did. Sometimes we would put on music and dance together. I tried to imitate the way she swiveled her hips and seductively moved her hands. Fatma looked so beautiful and carefree when she was dancing, as if something else possessed her soul and set her troubled spirit free.

17

Fly in the Teacup

"Daddy, what are they doing?"

"I have no idea. All I can see is a mob of shabaab (young men), in front of the Internet cafe."

It was three-thirty in the morning. Hearing the commotion, Brad had sprung from his bed and run out onto the balcony, surprised that Rebecca had beat him to it. At first, it sounded like fans celebrating a victorious soccer game. But then there would be wailing as if mourning the death of a loved one. Perplexed about it all, Brad and Rebecca shrugged their shoulders and went back to sleep.

We discovered the reason the next morning when I saw Girgis on the street. "Congratulate me, Gigi!" he said, beaming. "My son got his high-school exam results and scored ninety-seven. That's exactly what he needs for pharmacy school!"

So that was why the streets had been filled with young men. The ever-dreaded high-school exit exam results had been posted on the Internet. The exam results determined what college, if any, a person could attend and for what field of study she or he qualified. The ones with high marks were shouting joyfully; others mourned sorrowfully as their dreams and hopes flittered away.

That same week, an ocean away, young people across America mobbed bookstores as they waited to buy the latest Harry Potter thriller. It was a coincidence that both events occurred only a few days apart, but I couldn't help making a comparison between the two educational systems. With all the faults of the American schools, there is something impressive about young people waiting in line to buy a 607-page book.

It would be a rare Egyptian child who picked up a book in the summer to read for pleasure; for most, their only books were textbooks. We lived in a city of a quarter-million people, but there were no bookstores. Tiny shops sold either religious books or school supplies.

I once visited with an English teacher and his wife, a librarian, in their home. He proudly told me how they had only one book in the house—a Bible, which they read each evening. While that was admirable, it was also puzzling: how could an English teacher and a librarian not love books?

Two weeks later, we were having a pleasant dinner on our rooftop with a Muslim family. It was a warm evening under a bright moon with a steady desert breeze keeping the mosquitoes away. We were barbequing hamburgers and swapping stories from the Bible and the Qur'an. The Qur'an recognizes eighteen of the Old Testament prophets, though with different characteristics. These include Adam, Abraham, Jacob, and Moses. Four New Testament figures are recognized in the Qur'an: Zachariah, John the Baptist, Mary, and Jesus. Our guests told us the story of Joseph from the Qur'an, and we found it to be almost identical to the biblical version. It was one of those moments when I wished a satellite camera were above us, beaming this meeting of Islam and Christianity to the world.

But that was not the image we and the world saw the next day. A triple bomb exploded in the tourist resort city of Sharm El Sheik, killing eighty-eight people, most of them Egyptians. It was Egypt's worst terrorist attack and a shock to many of our friends.

"We don't know who did all these terrible acts," one said. "It can't be Egyptians. It's not our nature to be suicide bombers."

But denials couldn't change the facts: four Egyptian perpetrators died from their own explosions. They were not considered martyrs.

Our family had vacationed in Sharm El Sheikh just one month before. I watched the television news, and my heart sank as I saw piles of concrete rubble, twisted rebar, hollowed-out car shells, and a steady stream of ambulances carrying away the dead and the injured. I saw a China House restaurant sign bent in half, dangling grotesquely over the destroyed restaurant. We had eaten at that very restaurant and had our picture taken by a funny waiter named Mohammad. Was he at work when the bombers struck?

Two weeks later, disaster struck Beni Suef. We were entertaining a priest and his family for dinner. Rebecca and Nicholas were at the nadi, playing basketball. Just before eleven p.m., Rebecca burst in the door.

"Hug me, Mama, just hug me!" She was too shaken to say any more, so Nicholas described what had happened. "Tons of smoke was billowing out of the Cultural Palace across from the nadi. So naturally everyone left the club to see what was happening. Hundreds of people were out in the street and, oh man, there was all sorts of chaos. We saw a man running by us. His body was glowing red and his skin was, like, melting off of him. It was really gross. That frightened Rebecca, and she wanted to go, so she got on the back of my bike and we came home. But I really wanted to stay and watch. It must be a fire or something."

We woke the next morning to news that made international headlines: a fire in the Cultural Palace had killed fifty people (eight more would eventually die), with an equal number injured. The small room held only a hundred people, so few survived unscathed. A play was being performed and the set, covered with paper and wood, caught on fire from candles that surrounded the stage. Of the two exit doors, one was locked and used as part of the set. I could imagine the panic, horror, and chaos as the audience tried to escape the engulfing flames and smoke through the one remaining door, a door blocked by chairs knocked over in the stampede. We decided to go see the site.

It was Friday, the Muslim holy day. The mosque at the end of our street always had an overflow crowd. Men filled the street, sitting on green plastic mats, listening to the noontime sermon. Even though it was the shortest route for us, it would have been disrespectful to walk through the crowd. Instead we took the long way, passing one mosque after another, each with its own overflow crowd taking up the whole street, each broadcasting a sermon from a loudspeaker, drowning out the next mosque's sermon. Though each mosque had a different speaker, the tone of voice was the same: strident, harsh, angry.

We arrived at the Cultural Palace and looked in the charred room. It was completely black and empty. All the chairs and props had burned down to a thick pile of ash with wisps of smoke still drifting from it. Looking about, we were surprised by what we did not see. There were no flowers or wreaths, no candles, no yellow tape marking a disaster area to keep out curious spectators like us. In fact, there weren't many curious spectators at all, just a few men standing around in the yard, smoking cigarettes. We expected to see the site commemorated as a public testimony to the disaster, with people expressing their grief and anguish over this senseless tragedy. But people were not grieving publicly. Weren't they shocked and angry when they woke up that morning to find that a largely manmade disaster had ended so many lives?

When I read in a Cairo English paper how the local emergency personnel responded, I felt worse. One fire truck showed up an hour after the blaze had started, with only two firemen. How could this be when the fire department was less than a mile away? Ambulances did not arrive for at least two hours. How could this be when one hospital, where I had taken Fatma to get her hand stitched, was only one block away? The hospitals could not manage the burn injuries; many were sent to Cairo by taxis and died along the way. I further read that a young man, a microbus driver, stopped his vehicle when he saw the flames and helped out. He now lay in a local hospital with burns over 70 percent of his body. In my opinion, he was a local hero, but nobody seemed to know about him.

The pathetic response from the fire department and hospitals, and the lack of fire safety equipment at the Cultural Palace raised the ire of the arts community in Cairo. But not a sound was heard from those who had the most to lose—the residents of Beni Suef. No one expressed outrage. No one asked how such a tragedy could be prevented in the future. No one asked why the emergency services were so slow in responding. No one seemed to care. Worse—no one seemed to expect any better.

No person, no organization, no church, and no mosque demanded any better for the citizens of Beni Suef. The paper quoted a Cairo writer's association: "An ambulance and a fire engine should be placed outside such venues; such measures are especially necessary in the light of Beni Suef being a hotbed for Islamic fundamentalism, which makes terrorist strikes quite likely." But it appeared that even our local terrorist organization, if it existed (we never saw evidence of it) took an apathetic attitude. No one was going to shake things up.

I was bewildered. Surely others felt as angry as I did. I made some tea and brought it over to Um Amzat. Though I could not understand all she said, I got a better gauge from her about the thoughts and feelings of local folks.

"*Umra Rabbina*, the order of God has happened," she cried

out, her anguished face pinched up. "They are all martyrs and will go to heaven!"

Martyrs? How could that be? I associated martyrs with defending their faith. How did people attending a play fit in this category? My friend Sandy later clued me in that *martyr*, a term used by both Christians and Muslims, can also mean a person who dies in war defending country or dies at work while making a valuable contribution. Being designated as a martyr meant more financial compensation for the surviving family members as well as greater honor bestowed upon them. The fire victims could be considered martyrs of Egyptian culture. But the Sharm El Sheikh suicide bombers were not martyrs; they attacked their own country and were not defending it from outside aggressors.

Did "the order of God" really cause the tragedy? Did people truly believe burned and disfigured bodies were God's will and not human irresponsibility? Sandy confidently nodded her head and explained, "I know some people were responsible for the fire and should be held accountable. But I also believe that the people who died—it was their time to go. Perhaps there could have been a kinder way. But I believe that God is in control of all, and people die because God wants them to."

I believe that too—well, kind of. But I had a hard time with the theology that God wanted all those people to die on that fateful night. If they weren't at the play, would they have all died in separate car accidents?

She added, "You know, after something terrible like this happens we say, '*Qada wa qadr.*' This means 'God has willed something and it happened.' It is predestination. That's why the Minister of Culture didn't resign and even said, 'No one can imagine my grief . . . but such is fate and destiny.'"

If all is "fate and destiny," what is the point in investigating the fire department, the hospital, the Cultural Palace? Perhaps "fate and destiny" was the explanation for why no one seemed outraged and why no one was looking at how it could be prevented again. All is determined by God, not by people. Does an attitude of "fate and destiny" testify to faith in God as the controller and power of all things at the expense of individual and government responsibility?

On the lighter side, I could simply say God was having a busy week. Just before the Beni Suef fire, half a world away, my hometown in Louisiana was swamped by Hurricane Katrina's high winds, heavy rains, burst levees, and evacuated "refugees." A rich, educated, modern, secular, and democratic nation could not escape nature's—or was it God's?—wrath, which, according to some of American religious and political leaders, was wrought because of abortion, homosexuality, same-sex marriages, and the withdrawal of the Israeli settlers from the Gaza Strip. My own take was that Hurricane Katrina was sent to give my sister and her two daughters time to visit us in Egypt. Why else would God have closed their school down for a whole month? Unfortunately my sister was not of the same theology and didn't come visit.

č

We were beginning our third year, long enough to notice a new trend in Beni Suef: an increase in the number of young girls veiling, some as young as five (traditionally girls don't veil until puberty).

One summer evening at the nadi, I was watching the kids play basketball when Dina, one of Emily's friends, showed up for training with a green scarf wrapped around her little face. She looked like a girl playing dress-up.

"Oh no. That is too young. Ten-year-old girls should not be veiling," commented the Muslim woman sitting next to me. She called Dina over to ask why she was wearing a veil.

"Because I have been going to Qur'anic lessons at the mosque and our teacher says we should veil." Her face, always cheerful and smiling, looked even happier. "She says we will get more points in heaven." My neighbor just shook her head sadly.

A minority of women dressed in either extremes: completely covered in black with niqab or dressed in tight jeans and shirts. Their dress styles reflected a splintering society. The women in niqab represented those who wanted to abandon modern developments and adopt more conservative values. The other side wanted to disregard traditions and embrace a western lifestyle regardless of its pros and cons. But we found the vast majority of people were in the middle, wanting a modern, progressive nation but not a westernized one and a corresponding loss of values, culture, and morals. Most important, I thought, was that Muslims and Christians were looking to their respective religious leaders to lead the way and keep their

Home schooling on the roof of the apartment.

young people from being attracted to the extremes of either side.

We were beginning our third year at the school and feeling more confident in our roles. I finally had come to accept that while working with the least competent teachers had been my original goal, that could be achieved only if they saw themselves as needing my assistance. And they didn't. Instead I was teaching two classes and working with two of the best teachers. Our children were taking some classes in the school. Nicholas and Rebecca were also each assisting a teacher. Brad's adult English classes had more students than ever, with sessions added on.

It seemed as if overnight our lives suddenly had gotten easier. Brad could drive an MCC car when in Cairo, which had the dents to prove it. Nicholas could handle all our affairs in Arabic and knew every businessman's name within a mile of our apartment. Rebecca and Emily could shop for all our food and bicycle all over the town. The heat, noise, dust, and chaotic streets no longer seemed so overpowering. We could handle it.

I had read that the stages of settling into a new culture could be described in a parable. First year, fly falls in the tea: toss out the tea. Second year, fly falls in the tea: take out the fly and drink the tea. Third year, fly falls in the tea: drink the tea, fly and all. We were right on schedule; when the butcher, with a cigarette dangling from his lips, fed a hunk of meat into the grinding machine, I no longer kept a vigilante eye on where those cigarette ashes might fall. While we didn't expect to change the culture, I was surprised how fast the culture had changed us. Having one drinking glass for four people made dish washing easier. I no longer winced when I saw Emily toss a piece of trash on the sidewalk. My instructions to visiting guests from the United States were, "Put your elbows out and shove your way though the crowd. This is no time to be nice!" We regularly showed up at appointments a half-hour late, sometimes being humorously chastised by friends who expected punctuality from Americans. I calmly waved to the kids one night as all three, sans helmets, piled on a motorcycle behind a friend and drove off through the maze of traffic.

But there was one aspect of the culture to which we could not accommodate ourselves: harassment from shabaab, young men who hung in clusters on street corners. We estimated that if we had an Egyptian pound for every comment we received, we'd have enough money to outfit Beni Suef in traffic lights, should they ever desire such a thing. Usually Rebecca and I endured the harassment together—a mother's presence deters nothing—and we were sometimes amused by the creativity. One night we heard a young man yell out "012-422- . . . " just after he passed us—his mobile phone number.

Rebecca, tall with blond hair, was always in the spotlight; yet she continued to go out and engage the culture. I was proud of her creative problem-solving skills when she discovered, "If I ride a bike, by the time I pass the boys, I can't hear their comments!"

Harassment by giggling, curious girls and boys could be tolerated and, at times, ignored. Once, after a particularly hard day that included a group of young boys throwing rocks at us, I went to Um Abdullah in frustration. "Look those boys in the eyes and say, 'I am a mother. I live here. I know lots of Egyptians and they are good people. What about you? Are you good or what?' Gigi, you have to shame them." I tried it once, and, surprisingly, it did work. But that was with children.

I did not have the courage to do that with young adults. The harassment by the shabaab was another level completely. I knew we weren't alone in this predicament: sexual harassment occasionally happens to all females in Egypt, Christians and Muslims, but for foreigners, it is a constant menace. Part of this is due to American films, which portray western women as promiscuous, and frankly, some is due to western women who come to the Middle East looking for this exact type of action.

Before I could seek out my network of friends to discuss this issue, Doctor Negwa came to me. "Rebecca shouldn't be out by herself," she said. "Either you, Mr. Brad, or Nicholas should accompany her."

"Oh," I said, a little startled. "Why is that? Is there some crime wave happening?"

"No. No. We don't have crime here like in your country, but when girls become teenagers, they need to have their family's protection. In our culture, females don't walk alone, especially at night. It gives the impression that nobody cares about her."

Rebecca was twelve. She was maturing and would hear compliments like, "You have grown like a bride!" Having no male relative present with her made her vulnerable. I appreciated the advice but didn't want to unnecessarily stifle Rebecca's independence and adventuresome spirit. Wouldn't it be better to give her the tools and self-confidence to handle uncomfortable situations? Still, Egyptians would interpret her being alone as obviously indicating her parents weren't much concerned about her, which would make her fair game.

During a visit to Um Abdullah's, I asked her fifteen-year-old daughter, "Imani, what about you? Do boys bother you on the street?"

"I always dress like this, so no."

"Like this" meant only her face and fingertips exposed, which was not so practical for us. "But my father doesn't let us go out because of the shabaab. We can only go to school and come home."

One look at her sister's eyes confirmed what she said: they were puffy and red from crying because her father would not let her go with her university group on an outing to Cairo.

Um Abdullah explained, "We say, 'the shadow of a man is better than the shadow of a wall.' That means men can protect us even better than a house can."

"Well, okay, but is anyone teaching these boys not to say these things to women?"

"I tell my son all the time, but it goes in one ear and out the other." Yet no one kept the son from going out.

The girls at the orphanage had recently told Rebecca she was too old to ride a bike "because the boys are bad." The response to sexual harassment was to guard the girl or keep her home. Educating the girl about ways to be safe and seek help didn't seem to be an option.

The general consensus was we should ignore the shabaab and look straight ahead; anything we said would only encourage them more. Sometimes I did that, but I also got tired of being passive and powerless. Once I turned around and angrily clapped my hands at a group of heckling boys and received a greater shock: they immediately jumped up and ran off before I got two words out! Other times I would seek refuge in a store and tell the nearby clerk, who would usually go out with a raised fist and yell some words at the offending group. I remember in our early days my reluctance to ask shopkeepers for assistance, fearing they would use violence. But by then, I didn't care, rationalizing that the young men deserved it.

Women gave me advice, but they didn't show much sympathy. Every single one smiled and said a version of, "It's because you are foreigners and so beautiful. All the shabaab want to be with foreigners." Somehow we should feel flattered. The seriousness of the harassment was also minimized by the comment, "Yes, but its words only; they won't hurt you. The shabaab don't touch." Perhaps not the locals, but that was not true for foreigners. While I wasn't fearful, that still didn't make the harassment acceptable.

Strangely, over time I began to sympathize with the shabaab. Anyone saying "Hey, beautiful one" to a forty-three-year-old woman dressed in a long skirt and elbow-length sleeves in summer, with kids in tow, is obviously desperate. The truth is, these young men had no appropriate ways to socialize with females. Dating does not exist; males and females don't hangout together or sit and talk casually. Gender segregation begins in grade school, where boys sit on one side of the room and girls on the other. It continues into adulthood. Many visits and meetings are constantly interrupted with the playing of musical chairs as new people entering a room cause a regrouping of the sexes. Just as I was instructed on our arrival to view men as "males"—not friends or acquaintances— so were these young men instructed from childhood to view girls as "females."

Christians, through church gatherings and monastery trips, have more opportunities to interact with the opposite sex. A minority of Muslims and Christians take the view that gender segregation degrades women and reduces them to figures of sex and temptation. But for the majority, that is exactly how they see women—in terms of sex and temptation. For them, it's better to prevent disaster by segregating than suffer the severe consequences of a ruined reputation.

Discussing this with Sandy, I stated, "Don't you think that if boys and girls had the chance to be together—"

"They would have sex," she interrupted me, "and you know they will. There are horrible consequences for that in our society, so we must keep them apart."

Though Sandy is a Christian, she would agree with the prophet Muhammad's comments, "When a man and a woman are together, a third person is present and that is Satan." His seventh-century observation about human nature is still valid today in Arab society.

Males and females often live completely separate lives, only knowing the opposite sex through siblings or cousins until they are engaged. More than one woman said something like this to me, "I got married when I was twenty-three years old and had no brain in my head about men and love." Age wasn't the issue; it was the complete lack of interaction—positive or negative—with the opposite sex.

Even the economy plays a role in the harassment. If the shabaab were working, they would have enough money to marry and become fathers, thus making them respectable men in society. But most men cannot meet the financial requirements of marriage before age thirty, making for a long adolescence. But I also began to wonder: if I rationalized Egyptian men's sexual harassment due to the lack of sexual opportunities, what does that say about western men who have unlimited sexual freedom but also similarly harass women?

Meanwhile the restless shabaab continued to hang out on street corners. I supposed it was our fate to endure them.

18

At the Mercy Table

At our last Ramadan in Egypt, my goal was to participate in one of the "mercy tables"—feeding areas sponsored by mosques for poor people to break their fast.

Just the week before in the cosmopolitan city of Alexandria, six hours north of us, there had been a week of violence and rioting between Muslims and Christians. A DVD of a play performed two years previously in an Orthodox church found its way into the wrong hands. After listening to a Friday sermon denouncing the play as insulting to Islam, thousands of angry Muslim men surrounded the church, trying to set it on fire. Buildings were destroyed, Christian businesses ruined, cars overturned and torched. More tragically, a nun was seriously stabbed and police killed three Muslim protestors. The tension of the riot rippled throughout the country. We MCCers were warned by our country representatives to avoid areas, especially poor ones, where violence between Christians and Muslims could easily erupt.

That warning echoed loudly in my head as Brad and I walked to a mosque in one of the poor areas of Beni Suef. We separated— he sat with the men at their tables and I was further down the alley with the women and children. One quick look at my dress confirmed that I was conspicuously out of place: appropriately enough, it had long sleeves and was long enough to be sweeping the street, but it was gold-colored while every other woman was dressed in solid black, head to toe. I took a seat at an old, rough plywood table and looked into the smiling face of a young woman sitting across from me.

"Where have you been? I haven't seen you in so long! I miss you!" I looked at the pretty girl with big swinging gold earrings and registered a complete blank.

"I met you at Um Abdullah's house. I clean her house. You were there with your three children. How are they doing?"

We had probably met briefly in the kitchen over a year earlier, yet she remembered us. Foreigners, no matter how brief the acquaintance, do make lasting impressions, causing me to frequently remind my children that all we said and did was not only noticed but remembered and talked about.

"I know this woman too," said a young man as he tossed a stack of pita bread onto the table. Another unfamiliar face, but I listened in astonishment as this young man gave exact directions to my apartment, right down to the number on our door.

"And how do you know me?" I curiously inquired.

"I know Nadir, your neighbor. I was at his apartment the day he was beating his wife and you came over and saved her." He turned and went through the whole story with the women sitting at the table, but I was too stunned by that revelation to hear any of his words. That had been six months before.

"How do you know Nadir?" was the only question I could ask, although I really wanted to know how he could have sat there and watched him hurt Fatma.

"From school. He used to be a real nice guy but he has changed a lot. That was my first time seeing him since a couple of years. His problem is that he takes drugs. He had been smoking a lot of *bango* (marijuana) that day." (Marijuana is illegal, but we occasionally smelled it while sitting in the outdoor gardens or walking through the alleyways.)

BOOM! A cannon signaled the end of the fast; we could begin eating. The meal was a bowl of beans in a tomato sauce, simple yet spicy and delicious. Afterward someone passed around pieces of chicken that were scooped from the greasy pan and placed in our hands. Tea was supposed to be served, but my abrupt departure prevented me from experiencing that part of the meal.

"Would you like to wash your hands?" said a young girl who had brought me over to the mosque sinks. Afterward I started talking with one of the organizers of the "mercy tables." Kids, hearing my accent, pushed in around me, rubbing their hands on my arms and patting my purse, which in hindsight I should have left at home. The gathering crowd made me anxious and distracted my conversation; it was time to exit. But I didn't want to leave without making a donation; obviously I didn't need the free meal.

"Is there somewhere private we can go? I want to give some money to help pay for the food," I said to the young man in charge. Privacy? In Egypt? What was I thinking? He apparently didn't know either, as he pulled me over into another corner a few feet away. I fumbled through my purse for some money, handed it to him, and turned around to leave, only to find a sea of black garbed women with outstretched hands. They had just seen me giving money to this one man; where was their fair share?

As they pressed around me, their hands caressed my hair and my face. They were not boisterous and demanding; they simply surrounded me with pleading, desperate eyes holding all sorts of life's pitiful stories. I could feel their breath on my face and could see their lips forming pleading, wailing sounds. The heat and smells and suffocating feelings were making my knees weaken. I was drowning in this black sea of sorrow when I felt a hand on my arm lift me up and call out, "This is a good woman! She saved a woman from her husband's beatings. Let her pass!"

It was the young man who had witnessed Fatma's beating. "This is a kind woman. God has mercy on her because she has shown mercy to one of our own!" His words rang out as he maneuvered me through the parting women, down the street, and away from the crowd that could have turned into an excitable mob.

The streets were still quiet as everyone was home eating, giving me some time to reflect as I walked home and chastised myself. "Why hadn't I left and gone back the next day to donate?" I'd had noble intentions but my timing was terribly wrong.

I thought back to that day of seeing three men sitting in Fatma's house near her pools of blood on the floor. I could not recall any of their faces, but one easily recalled mine. We never know the kind of impact our actions—or lack of actions—will have on another person. What if I had given in to my impulse to slap each man sitting in that room? What would that young man have remembered of me then? If I ever needed any confirmation of the power of nonviolence, this was it. That young man remembered me for my helpfulness, not for any outbursts.

The prayer on my wall concludes, "And may God bless you with foolishness to think that you can make a difference in the world, so you will do the things which others say cannot be done."

19

The Trouble Foreigners Cause

"Who are you going to vote for in the presidential elections?" I asked a teacher during the morning break. Egypt was having its first multiparty presidential elections. For almost fifty years, people had voted by referendum—yes or no—for the president already in office. But President Bush had been pressuring Egypt to put other candidates and political parties on the ballot. Though Egypt resented the outside interference, President Mubarak, after twenty-four years in office, would now have some democratic competition.

"I will vote for Mubarak, of course," said the teacher matter-of-factly.

His remark surprised me. For the first time he actually had a choice to vote for someone else, and yet, he was going to vote for the same person. If Mubarak couldn't achieve something in twenty-four years, why did he need another six-year term? Why not have voted for someone with new ideas and, maybe, a different way to do things?

There was a collective response that went roughly like this: "Mubarak has the most experience and wisdom. He has good relations with all our neighbors—Jordan, Israel, Syria. This is an unstable time with Iran, Iraq, and Palestine. You don't change the captain of the ship in the middle of sailing. Besides, we don't know the other candidates and we don't trust them. You know our proverb 'The one you know is better than the one you don't know.'"

Though overall turnout was expectedly low, 88 percent of voters chose the man who made them feel most secure. If Mubarak completes his term, he will have served thirty years, longer than many pharaohs.

What about the runner-up? He received 6 percent of the vote and a five-year prison sentence for voter registration fraud, plus a future ban on running for political office. The message was clear: dabbling in democracy and challenging the status quo is risky and dangerous.

۲

Elections were over, winter break arrived, and we took Suad up on her offer to visit her village again.

"We're going to visit with some friends," I said to the guard.

"Okay, see you later, Madame Gigi."

Whew! Lucky for us, it was one of the quieter guards on duty, who didn't ask any questions, and we were free to go. Had the guards known our true destination, they would never have let us go without a police escort.

Hamdy, Suad's son, met us at the microbus station—a mad-house swarming with villagers steadying bundles of vegetables or crates of live ducks on their heads, all bound for sale at the market. Horns honked sharply, barkers loudly called out their destinations, smells wafted up from food stalls, goats and dogs competed for scraps in a pile of rotting trash, a donkey's loud bray echoed like a wheezing accordion. My senses were swimming. I watched a peasant woman with a huge head of cauliflower sitting solidly atop her head; she was completely unaware of the horse standing behind her, nibbling on her soon-to-be-cooked dinner.

Microbuses traveling out of Beni Suef didn't leave until all the seats were filled, so the drivers could make the maximum amount of money. Our family (minus Brad who, according to proper village protocol, could not visit a widowed woman such as Suad) and Hamdy were the only ones in the microbus. But we were not alone; a gaggle of curious boys was hanging onto the window frames and door, their faces pressed against the glass, calling out friendly (to them, obnoxious to us) greetings. To avoid further waiting, we quickly negotiated a deal with the driver for roughly a dollar, and were on our way.

It was a Friday, and as with every Friday morning in Beni Suef, the men were preparing to go to the mosque, and women were on the balconies hanging just-washed sheets and blankets on the clotheslines. Village girls were scrubbing dishes and huge, metal cooking pots in the polluted canals. It wasn't unusual for farmers to "bury" their dead animals in these same canals, and we occasionally spotted bloated buffaloes or donkeys floating along. Rebecca had once struck up a conversation with village girls, inquiring if they had running water in their houses. "Yes," one girl replied, "but we enjoy washing things here (in the canal). I get to visit with my friends that way." For some women, it was the traditional and acceptable way for them to socialize; for others, it was a necessity because not all villages had indoor plumbing.

After a half-hour, the microbus driver drove through the winding, rutted village streets, scattering playing children, sleeping dogs, and romping goats until he screeched to a halt at a narrow alleyway. No trees, no flowers—the only greenery was the fields that surround the dirt-brown village. The main street was a mess of potholes, litter, and animal droppings. But the labyrinth of alleyways, where the villagers lived, looked tidy and swept clean of dirt and debris.

We had visited Suad five months earlier and now, on our second visit, I could see changes in her rough, little brick house. Before she had a rickety, wooden ladder on which she dangerously trudged up to the roof while balancing a plastic tub of wet laundry on her head. Now there were sturdy concrete steps leading to the roof.

The other improvement was her kitchen, which now had a real sink and faucet. Previously she had one water spigot near the doorway. Under this tap, she would set a tub and squat to wash dishes, taking care that water didn't drip on the dirt floor. Now, in the kitchen, running water flowed into a sink so she could stand while washing dishes. Scanning the unfinished brick wall, I saw a new, white dish rack. Our MCC group had once visited a village, and the leader of a church-based health program commented that he knew they were making progress in hygiene with a family when the mother acquired a dish rack. A simple dish rack allows wet dishes to dry in the air rather than sit on the dirt floor, where they are more exposed to germs and diseases.

I saw the third improvement when I went to the two-by-two-foot "bathroom" and squatted over a hole in the ground. I looked up and saw yet another water spigot directly over me; they could now shower with running water. Of course, it was all cold water, but Suad now had water in two different rooms. Having a house-keeper didn't just benefit us: Suad had put the extra money to good use in improving her simple home.

After our arrival, Suad heated a pot of water on the one-burner stove and poured it into a metal tub to bathe Rehab, her six-year-old daughter. Rehab sat on the small stool, shivering and whining, while her mother scrubbed her clean with a loofah sponge, taking care not to get her arm cast wet. The day before, Rehab had fallen off a decrepit children's ride and broken her wrist. Many of these rides, resembling carnival relics from the late 1800s, were set up during festivals. Likely, a western country had donated it after it failed to meet safety standards.

It was January, and though not a cold day, cool drafts seeped through cracks in the wall and roof. A gust of wind blew in, sending a shower of debris spewing down from the roof. Rehab was now wailing.

"Stand still!" Suad chastised. She then lowered her voice and soothingly asked, "Do you love Kareem? Do you love your aunt's son?"

Rehab nodded, wiping her nose with her other arm as her cries subsided. Suad's children, Rehab and Hamdy, were conveniently matched in age and sex with Suad's sister's children. "They will marry each other, in sha'allah."

Rehab dried off, got dressed, and sat on the stool while her mother tried to comb through a mass of black, wiry hair. Girls are proud of their long, thick hair, shiny with grease and woven into a tight braid that flows down their backs. But such wasn't the case for Rehab. She looked like she had just returned from the beach after a sand fight. But it wasn't sand, and while I would have liked to have been optimistic and think "dandruff," I knew it was lice.

Suad tediously combed through the mass of hair. She picked up a dented can, poured the liquid in her palm, and rubbed it into Rehab's head. It was kerosene—the poor person's lice control medicine. I wondered if years of kerosene build-up might seep through the skull and into the brain.

I made a mental note to show Suad the lice shampoo we had. Suad, who had never been to school, was curious about many things I had in my house. She often picked up a bottle or tube and, holding it only an inch from her face, for her eyesight was very poor, tried to decipher the product by looking at the picture. These weren't imported fancy goods but local products that I bought from the pharmacy around the corner from us. Yet for a village woman who lived a sheltered life, shopping in Beni Suef could be as intimidating as shopping in a city.

I always thought illiteracy meant not reading words, but Suad could not recognize numbers either. One day she brought me a telephone number and wanted me to make a call for her. I looked at the scribbled handwriting on the crumpled paper. "Suad, this isn't a phone number," I told her. "These are the prices of something you bought in a store. All phone numbers in Beni Suef have seven digits and begin with the number two." The irony was not lost on me that a foreigner was explaining the phone system to a native. But for Suad, the telephone was indeed a foreign instrument.

Bath accomplished, Rehab ran up on the roof to play with Nicholas, Rebecca, Emily, and her brother, Hamdy. Suad and I carried up a mat and a low-legged, round, wooden table and set it amid a pile of drying corn ears that would be ground into flour to make crisp, cracker-thin bread. We tore off pieces of bread and scooped up beans and chicken cooked in tomato sauce. Most villagers raised chickens on their rooftops, as it was a cheap source of protein and often was their only meat. But because of her housecleaning jobs in Beni Suef, Suad didn't have any hens roaming around. After eating, we distributed the gifts we had brought, which include a plastic bottle of green, apple-scented dishwashing liquid. Suad was pleased.

The kids spent the afternoon wheeling each other down winding alleys on a wooden window shutter fashioned into a skateboard of sorts. Suad and I sat on the doorstep and talked with all the neighboring women who dropped by. Word had gotten out that foreigners were in the village, and our trustworthy "fan club" had arrived. Of course, we were just as curious about them, and when Nicholas brought out his camera, the boys hammed it up with delight while the girls cowered behind their mothers' skirts.

"The kids would be cute if they didn't look so dirty," observed Nicholas. I looked at the assembled lot in front of us: runny noses; swarming flies on the face; dirty, bare feet; dry, wiry hair sticking up; torn, holey, ripped, stained clothing that was too big. Listless, vacant eyes peered out from dirty faces. Unfortunately there was some truth in the stereotypes I'd read from authors who'd described children in deprived or undeveloped villages around the world.

Evening came with the sun falling behind the fields, casting a golden glow over rows of corn. Suad's sister and her family took us riding in their donkey wagon through the fields. We piled in the back and huddled under blankets to protect us from the chilly night air. Emily sat up front with Hamdy holding the donkey reigns and guiding us into the star-filled night. We sang whatever pop songs we could think of, laughing and munching on freshly picked corn. Suad tilted her head and trilled in jubilation.

Only a few years younger than me, Suad had one of those lives that I had only read about in books. One of nine siblings, she grew up in this village in a two-room, mud-brick house. Come nightfall, her mother spread out a plastic mat on the floor, and the whole family lay down to sleep sardine-style. The other room held the family's prized possessions: sheep, a few goats, a couple of cows, and a water buffalo.

We rode past an old school, likely the one Suad had told me she could not attend because it was too far away. "But that wasn't the only reason," she confided one day over tea. "I was a girl. My mother did not like girls and would beat us hard when we were young. I don't really know why; she was just devilish."

In traditional families, boys are valued for helping the family with manual labor, carrying on the family name, inheriting the money and the land, and taking care of the parents and sisters. Her mother didn't have much use for seven daughters.

Suad's father arranged her marriage when she was nineteen, to a man who was sixty-five, older than her own father.

"Couldn't you say no, that you didn't want to marry an old man?"

"At that time, no, girls could not say anything. But today, there is freedom and a girl can say yes or no to her father."

Her husband was a sick, old man who needed someone to take care of him; Suad was a poor, plain-looking village girl without any options in life. Besides, a wife is cheaper than a nurse. They had fifteen years together before he died, and she was thankful when he did. Her hope was never to marry again. "Madame Gigi, I am free now. I can go to the market and buy or sell food, I can work outside the house and make money, I can buy what I want for myself and my children. Ilhamdulilah."

Once our donkey ride ended, Suad's sister invited us to her little hovel for tea. That sounded fine to us, but Suad wanted us to return to her house. I braced myself for a "fight over the foreigners." People, usually relatives, would get into arguments over who would entertain us at their house. Suad's sister had me by one arm, tugging me toward her house, while Suad insisted we go back to her place. Neither would ask me what I wanted to do, which was a relief, as any response I gave would only betray the other. In the end, our loyalties lay with our host, and we went off to Suad's house, leaving her sister pouting in the street.

We sat in the "summer room" and ate our supper: hot-dog buns that we dip in warm, sweet milk. This room had two wooden benches with mats and a table that held a small black-and-white TV. Why do old TVs that can only crank out two channels of "snow" and static always have perfectly working volume dials? The room was soon filled with an Egyptian actress's loud, sultry voice belting out a tune from the 1950s. A naked light bulb dangled by a wire from the ceiling. There was nothing else in the room, and I pointed out to Rebecca and Emily that they had more stuff on the floor of their bedroom than Suad had in her entire house.

There was only one bed in the house and, of course, it was offered to us. Mindful of Rehab's nit-filled hair, I spread our scarves and jackets over the pillows and mattresses, and Nicholas, Rebecca, Emily, and I lay sideways in the bed with our feet dangling over the edge. Where were our hosts? On the floor. They spread a plastic mat on the hard-packed dirt floor—with no pillows—and fell asleep instantly. For us, it was impossible to get comfortable. The mattresses and pillows, stuffed solid with cotton, felt like concrete. But we were in good spirits and laughed our way to sleep.

When we woke up, fourteen-year-old Hamdy was already at work. During the school winter break, he was a barker on a microbus calling for passengers from seven in the morning till late in the evening. For ten hours of work, he earned roughly fifty cents. "In two years, he will finish school and can work," Suad said. "Then I won't have to clean so many houses." She was looking forward to that day. Boys may be desirable, I thought, but nobody said their life was easy.

Though most of my interactions in Egypt had been with females, there was no doubt that men had a lot of responsibility and pressure. Their value and necessity is expressed in the proverb, "A house without a man is like a body with a soul." Boys are groomed from childhood to take care of their sisters, even if the boy is younger. One day he may have to support his unemployed or divorced sisters. The role of the husband is to provide money for his wife and children and for the household to function. Men are also financially responsible for their parents. Since men are the parents' insurance and pension plan, families, particularly villagers, prefer to have sons. In today's poor economy with so many financial demands, it is understandable why so many men seek to go abroad, particularly to the Arab oil kingdoms, to make a decent living.

After breakfast, Suad handed me a headscarf to wear ("so you will look like the rest of us"), and we set out for a walk through the village. Her ten-year-old niece, Seham, bounced alongside us, talkative and energetic, readily flashing a confident smile, reminding me of an Egyptian version of the character Heidi.

Our first stop was at the home of another niece who, over tea, asked me about my travels in Egypt. I awkwardly recited my long list, aware that for most villagers, a trip to Cairo, a mere two hours away, was a once-in-a-lifetime experience. Surprisingly the niece had been far from her village: she had once visited her husband, who worked in a swank tourist resort on the Red Sea.

"Most women in our village never leave their house without their husband's permission. If he sees her buying sugar at the store without asking him—whop!" Suad said, snapping her fingers in the way Egyptians do when referring to beatings.

Her niece smiled and nodded in agreement, saying, "This is a Muslim village, and the men here are very strong. They take care of their wives, want them to stay by the house, take care of the children. Things like that."

Suad turned to me with a broad smile showing a row of tea-stained teeth. "What does a man want but someone to cook for him, clean his house, and"—she wrapped her arms around herself—"give some love? I have no use for a man. Ilhamdulilah."

Suad began to tell the niece about my neighbor, Fatma, and they were off into a discussion about "disciplining" wives. What a privilege it was to sit with women and just get glimpses and stories of their lives! The many hours and hard work put into learning Arabic paid off in moments like that. Tea finished, her niece, with a baby on her hip and several children scampering around her legs, walked with us to her family's fields, which stretch along the edge of the village. The kids picked bright green alfalfa to feed the buffaloes and donkeys while we nibbled on fresh sugarcane. Suad didn't own any land "because the small field we had went to my husband's partner when he died." This was a serious disadvantage for Hamdy, who, having no land to inherit, would have to find another way to make a living in a village that didn't have much else to offer.

We continued our village walk, which Rebecca later described in a home-school assignment. Here are her words:

> As we were walking through an unfamiliar part of the village, children stopped their games to stare and shout "*aganib oho* [hey, foreigners]." Some decided to follow us at a distance nudging their friends and whispering. Some of the young men started shouting out marriage proposals to my sister and me; a few hopped on bicycles to follow. When we arrived at a store I realized it was quite different from the ones in Beni Suef. This one was a small wooden shack with a few boxes of potato chips inside. Outside was a tin tray stacked up on palm-tree crates; on the tray were a few boxes of gum and wafers all covered in dust.
>
> Suad asked the woman who owned the shop if we could sit down and drink tea. Smiling widely, she gestured to the shack; we all sat down on the cardboard floor trying not to be too squished. Outside gathered about thirty wide-eyed children, all covered in dirt and grime, completely oblivious to the flies buzzing all around them. They were staring at us foreigners. The woman brought out a little gas burner and set on it a fire-blackened tea pot to boil water.
>
> As we were sitting down eating chips, the shack suddenly felt very hot and crowded. Kids, and now adults, surrounded the little shack. In their enthusiasm to see the foreigners, it wouldn't take much force to knock the flimsy shack over. With a gas-burner inches away, my mother was afraid that the whole shack would burst into flames.

My mother said, "Let's go stand outside." Then we heard crying and yelling. Naturally, we all rushed out. Sure enough there was Seham sobbing into her hands while Suad shouted at her. Apparently, Seham had been trying to shoo the children away from us when one boy hit her. When Seham lowered her hands we saw bloody scratches around her eyes. She quickly pointed the boy out and everyone pounced on him.

The woman who owned the shop started shaking him and yelled, "What's wrong with you? Don't you know better than that? Shame on you!" The boy wiggled out of her grasp, ran toward a nearby house, picked up a brick and threatened to throw it. The people who had been rushing at him stopped, and started backing away warily.

The boy turned and dashed straight at us. For a fleeting moment I thought "Oh no, he's going to throw that brick right at us." Luckily, he dropped it and ran right past me and my mother, pushing over the tin tray and spilling its contents all over the ground. As he made a mad dash to escape, a man caught him and dragged him off.

The woman who owned the shop went into hysterics saying her business was ruined. Turning to Seham, she started blaming everything on her, which, of course, made her cry harder. While we were picking up the spilled gum and wafers, I realized that it was *our* fault, not Seham's. If we had never come, none of this would have happened.

Suad quickly hurried us away from there, saying they would get the police.

My mother asked "Why? What will they do?"

Suad replied, "They will hit him."

This was just a small part of daily life in an Egyptian village. The next week Fatma told us that the police made the boy's family pay twenty pounds, four dollars or four-days wages, to the woman whose candy had been knocked over.

While we were eager to leave the area, Seham refused to budge. In the melee, the boy had grabbed her headscarf and Seham would not walk through the village without her head covering, for that would have brought more shame on an already humiliated ten-year-old girl. Finally, someone retrieved her scarf.

After this incident, it was time to leave the village.

Suad did not want to parade us through the village again, so we left through the fields and alongside the canal. We walked and walked, making another discovery about social class: when middle-class people say it's too far to walk, everyone piles in a car and rides three blocks; when poor folks say it's not too far, they can easily walk two miles. We were all somber about ending our visit on a sour note. I was concerned the police would get involved, and knowing that there were foreigners in the village who didn't have permission to be there, there could be problems for Suad and our own guards as well. We had simply wanted to have a fun village experience, but not at our guards' expense.

Suad, however, was not concerned about the police. She was humiliated by her villagers' behavior around us. "All the things they yell out to you, and wanting to see you and be close to you. No, this is not right. Shame!"

I kept reassuring her that it was nothing unique to her village but something we endured everywhere we went. And I thought, "Had you not known us, you too would have joined in with the others." Suad was experiencing her village in a way that had never been possible before—through the eyes of foreigners.

Likewise, we experienced authentic village life the way most foreigners never get to, through the eyes of a person who lives there. We did not have a middle-class Egyptian guide interpreting village life for us and telling us not to drink from this glass or touch that child's head. We did not have a police guard and ten armed soldiers trailing behind us, keeping a horde of curious kids and adults at a distance.

After an hour of walking, a microbus finally appeared and drove us into Beni Suef. Suad rejected all my protests that we could get home by ourselves and insisted on accompanying us. Once we reached town, she and Rehab hopped on another microbus and began their long journey home. Not only had Suad devoted two whole days to feeding and entertaining us, but our visit also caused

Seham paints Rebecca's fingernails before a morning walk.

her to cancel her Saturday work day—and pay. And through it all she insisted she was honored by our visit.

Village life is often defined in terms of poverty, filth, aggression, and ignorance, and there was plenty of that. But there was also dignity, generosity, and beauty. People were poor, but we did not see any beggars. Family and neighbors helped each other. When Suad baked bread in her neighbor's enormous mud oven, she made enough to share with her neighbor. Another neighbor let her keep water in her refrigerator so we would have cold water to drink when we visited. Women sat on doorsteps, surrounded by children, talking and laughing with one another. People found joy in each other.

I left feeling hopeful, as I was continually amazed at people's resilience and ability to carry on with daily life, a life that would be too hard for us to endure for more than a weekend. Suad and her fellow villagers were never too burdened by life to welcome strangers, to sit, chat, and laugh a bit.

20

Suzanne

"We sacrifice ourselves for the prophet!" chanted a group of teenage boys who had just finished school for the day. I stopped and watched about twenty boys marching down the street, their arms pumping placards into the air. A blue police truck was parked nearby; six armed soldiers kept a distant but mindful watch on them. It looked like a harmless demonstration, but I wondered if the fury over the Danish newspaper cartoons of the Prophet Muhammad had come to our town.

Every morning for that week in February 2006, the lead news story was not the carnage and violence in Iraq but reports about thousands of furious Muslims, waving signs and Qur'ans, protesting throughout the Islamic world. The Danish embassy in Iran was set ablaze; Danish consulate offices in Syria and Lebanon were trashed; demonstrators were killed in Pakistan and Nigeria. Egyptians were demanding President Mubarak to register his protest by recalling the Egyptian ambassador to Denmark, an action he had so far rejected.

The boys continued down the street. I glanced at the passers-by, students and workers all on their way home, and noticed that no one was paying them any attention. No one joined their march; no one shouted any words in solidarity. Perhaps they were all just thinking about what they were going to have for dinner. Perhaps the group soldiers discouraged any involvement.

That was the only public demonstration we witnessed but, meager as it was, it did express the anger, humiliation, and frustration that many of our Muslim friends were feeling. This was just another volley of scorn heaped on their religion from the west. I breathed a sigh of relief that at least this time the volley hadn't come from an American newspaper.

There were rumors of Danish products being boycotted, so I

decided to test it. "Do you have any butter?" I asked the shopkeeper. He shook his head no and pointed to the poster on the wall of Danish products—butter, cheese, and cookies —right down to their barcode numbers.

"Denmark people don't like Muslims," the shopkeeper flatly stated. "They are bad people! Look what they have done to our prophet."

"You know, some people were here last year from Denmark helping out in the school I work at," I commented. "They were young people, good people who—"

"If they don't respect my religion," he interrupted, "then I don't need to sell their products! This is a religious duty."

A few days later, Doctor Negwa and I were sitting in my living room watching demonstrators in Cairo burn Danish flags on TV. She was perplexed by her own people's violent reactions and the western mindset that provoked it.

"We respect Jesus. Why can't westerners respect our prophet? We would never insult Jesus and neither would you."

I thought of the American artist who at an exhibition displayed a cross soaking in urine. I thought of the singer who insulted Pope John Paul II and ripped up his photo on TV.

"Actually Negwa," I began, but then I just closed my mouth. How could I explain to someone who didn't even crumple paper that has Qur'anic verses on it, that, well, yes, in the west we do insult our religious figures and symbols all under the glorious name of freedom of speech? Oh sure, some Americans had protested these actions, but the impact was not the same. Religion does not stir our passions the same way it does in the Middle East, where it is woven into the fabric of daily life.

Negwa continued, "You cannot be a religious person—a Muslim, a Christian, or a Jew—and make such pictures of Muhammad, Jesus, Moses, or any saint. Regular people, yes. But them? No. They are high above us. They can make no mistakes. We can only respect them. This is not freedom of the press or free speech. It is against politeness and respect."

That, of course, was the dividing line. For Muslims, it was respect for religion and faith; for westerners, it was freedom of expression. Both sides were claiming the same thing: the right to defend their values. I have long since stopped believing the cliché "people are the same everywhere." We aren't. We are different. We come from different cultures. We see things differently, and we get offended by different things.

Our problem is that we are so busy defending our own values that we fail to respect, or even acknowledge, the values of "the other."

Negwa had her own ideas. "We must educate people about Islam. We can protest and say we are angry but all this fighting and burning things—no, this is wrong. But I fear something is very wrong and frightening in our world. We must continue to pray for God's forgiveness and mercy."

ع

Suzanne spoke in flawless, unaccented English. "I refuse to live my life as a blind person. I want to do everything that people with eyesight can do. My father wanted me to learn so much and stressed education very strongly. He died thirteen years ago, and though he was very protective of me, I miss him so much."

She and I were sitting in a coffee shop. Yes, a coffee shop! I was a bit nervous and feared the loss of my good reputation, for coffee shops in Egypt are strictly a man's world. I hesitated to enter, but Suzanne kept reassuring me it was all right. Being blind gave her a special status: who would bother a blind woman and her foreign companion?

We had met Suzanne through the school for the disabled where she had worked. I had never been acquainted with a blind person before, and our relationship started out awkwardly. Was it offensive to say, "See you later"? I learned that words referring to eyesight didn't offend her. And because she was outside the ordinary rules that govern female protocol, she was able to expose me to places in Beni Suef where women wouldn't dare to venture, like this coffee shop.

The shop was tastefully decorated with big sofas where men sat, smoking and drinking tea, discussing everything from marital problems to world issues. The room was a bit smoky but, fortunately, alcohol was absent. Due to the Islamic prohibition on drinking, alcoholism is one social problem with which Egypt does not have to deal. I wistfully thought how many more lives could be saved if there was a prohibition in the Qur'an about tobacco!

Suzanne was born blind because of anti-depressant medication her mother took while pregnant; the doctors didn't know the medicine would be harmful. "What I really want to have is eyes," Suzanne told me. "Not so I can see, but so I would look normal. Our society puts a lot of emphasis on how people look. If I had eyes, I would look more pleasing to them. That's it."

I glanced at one of the big TV screens showing sexy music video clips. Banned on regular TV, the videos came via satellite dishes from neighboring Arabic countries. It smacked of hypocrisy to me that Arabs criticized the west for its degenerate morality, but Arabic music videos featured the same bump and grind degradation of scantily clad women.

"In our society," Suzanne said, "it's important to keep up the appearance of being rich and avoid the pity of people and relatives. Many people see blind people wearing dark clothes or unkempt. I want to show you can be blind and respectable."

Her black curly hair, streaked with blond highlights, was pulled back into a tight ponytail, drawing full attention to her small but pretty face, accented with high cheekbones and a ready smile that showed off perfectly white teeth. Suzanne always looked elegant in fashionable pantsuits, perfectly coiffed hair, and carefully applied makeup.

What Suzanne lacked in eyesight, she made up for in intellect: with a degree in English from a Cairo university, she was fluent in English, French, German, and in Braille—both Arabic and English versions. She was musically talented and played the recorder, flute, keyboard organ, and numerous old Arabic instruments.

And like all other females, Suzanne had marriage goals. "I want to marry, and there is no question of giving birth to a blind baby because my blindness is not hereditary. But the man's family would question why he could not get a perfect wife. It makes me sad because how culturally refined and intelligent a woman is isn't so important. Only appearances count. At least here in Beni Suef."

Her coffee arrived and I stirred in the sugar for her.

"I know God made me blind for a purpose, and I don't know what it is. I want to be of some use to someone. I fear if I stay as I am, my brain will atrophy. What does it matter if I speak languages and travel to other countries? How does it benefit me?"

Ever aware that, in her early thirties, life was moving on, Suzanne was always searching for her place in the universe. Her daily life was a routine one starting out with tea and arguments with her nervous mother; tutoring her nieces in English, French, and Arabic; and participating in church activities when she could find an escort to accompany her. She practiced music and took care of her loyal dog. One highlight for Suzanne was translating for the British woman who led "female issues" group sessions at the orphanage.

"Suzanne, can you go back to school?" I asked, not really sure how another degree would benefit her.

"I tried at the university here in Beni Suef to get a master's in linguistics, and they were interested in me too. Then the interviewer asked me what my religion was. After I said Christian, his tone suddenly changed, and he told me because my undergraduate degree was from a university in Cairo, I must continue my studies there. That's it."

She said it matter-of-factly but clearly was burdened by the disappointments and frustrations in her life. But her boredom also sparked a dream inside her. "It would be an honor to be a martyr, because I would go to heaven without any doubt. It could be in the name of Jesus or for the homeland, Egypt. Jesus gave himself for the sake of the community; it is good if one sheds his own blood and saves all the community."

In a passionate and earnest voice, she continued, "I would love to go to Palestine and be with the Palestinian children, for their sake. People tell me I have a comforting face. If anything happened to the children, I wouldn't run away but I would die bravely, like Rachel Corrie. That's it." (Rachel Corrie was a young American woman who protested the Israeli government policy of demolishing the homes of Palestinians. On March 16, 2003, she guarded the home of a Palestinian pharmacist by standing bravely in front of an Israeli bulldozer. The giant machine crushed and killed her, and her death made her a hero in this part of the world.)

Suzanne had no desire to end her life; she simply wanted to feel useful. I could just envision her with an international accompaniment team, standing confidently in a bright, fashionable outfit, complimented by matching high heels and purse, with a big smile of accomplishment on her face as she struck a blow for the freedom of the oppressed. Oh, how I wished I could make that dream come true!

The hour was nearing seven in the evening, and more men were coming into the coffee house, adding more smoke and noise. It was time to leave. We walked out and hadn't gone far when a woman, elderly and shriveled-looking in a worn-out, black dress, called out. "Hey, lady!" She lifted a shaking hand from her wheelchair arm-rest and grabbed my hand. "I just want to touch her!"

"What? You want what?" I was confused.

"Oh," said Suzanne, taking it all in stride, "she wants to touch my arm." She stuck her arm out in the air, where the woman's gnarled and shaking hands grabbed hold.

"Pray for me, my lady. Ask God to help me," the old one said. Some people, especially poor Muslims like this woman, see blind people as holy and having special connections to God.

Ǝ

Every fall or spring—seasons more observable on the calendar than noticeable outdoors—Suzanne and I would head to a mall in Cairo for her biannual shopping spree. Ever conscious of looking good, this was where it all began.

"I want an outfit I can wear to weddings this summer. Perhaps a mauve or soft pink color. Something shiny or sparkly that makes people say, 'Oh, wow!'"

Soft pink? Sparkles? Hardly words I imagined coming from a visually impaired person. Yet I could tell from the way she said them that she knew how she wanted to look.

After exhausting all of her allowance, which came from her father's pension, we treated ourselves at Pizza Hut. From our corner view, I could watch a world entirely different from provincial Beni Suef stroll by: teenage girls in tight, hip-hugging jeans and shirts; young couples holding hands.

Suzanne wanted to live as normal a life as possible, which meant she preferred to walk rather than take the convenience and safety of a taxi. It was a recurring dilemma for me: did I encourage and support her independence or use common sense and take the safe route? I enjoyed describing the street sights to her, but negotiating through the traffic was challenging enough for sighted people. One time I had just released Suzanne from my arm when a taxi drove close enough to clip my elbow on the window frame.

We would often stand at an intersection and, overwhelmed by all the noise and traffic coming from every direction, I would quip, "Do you want to get hit on the right side today or the left?"

"No, I don't want to die here. I'm saving it for Palestine, remember?" It helped to have a sense of humor.

Suzanne had all a person could wish for: talents, skills, intellect, beauty, faith, and humor, but her blindness overpowered them all. Had she been born elsewhere, she might have more possibilities to realize her dreams. Even Cairo had some progressive programs for disabled people, but in lowly Beni Suef, two hours away, it was out of her reach. Suzanne could identify with the Palestinians' despair and hopelessness, not because she had no desires to die, but like them, she was seeking her own liberation.

A bumper-sticker slogan came to mind: "Dream globally, act locally." Then another idea clicked with me: Suzanne wanted to be needed, and who was needier than my neighbor, Fatma?

ت

After learning her husband had taken a second wife, Fatma began to realize that it was all over for her. Every day she continued clearing out her apartment, one plastic bag at a time. The previous day she had locked her keys in the apartment and gone to find Nadir to get another key. She found him at the coffee shop around the corner. When she kissed Nadir's hand and said, "I'm sorry," he grabbed her by the neck and started choking her. Then he threw her down on the street and kicked her.

But what bothered Fatma the most was all the men who were sitting in the coffee shop. Some looked up to watch, but most did not even do that.

For Fatma, this was the proverbial straw that broke the camel's back. The beatings in her private apartment she could endure and suffer, but she could not tolerate the public humiliation of a beating in the street. She and her boys went to live with her parents, finally realizing that her eight-year-old marriage had ended.

Fatma and her boys were a few blocks away, and truth be told, it was a relief for us and a welcome break from the daily chaos they inevitably brought. Now they would come over about once a week, not daily. The kids would play ball on the balcony or computer

Suzanne and Fatma.

games, while she and I talked over tea or cooked some food together. Sometimes we would crank up the music loud and have our own belly-dancing sessions; other times we went shopping or to a relative's engagement or wedding party.

It was during one of these visits that it clicked with me that Fatma and I had become neighbors. We weren't equally yoked, and she still depended on me for trivial things, but we shared as much as possible for two very different people.

When I introduced Suzanne to Fatma, it was also bringing two different worlds together. Suzanne was soft-spoken and sophisticated, whereas Fatma was boisterous and sometimes crude; Suzanne was a thinker who articulated her thoughts and feelings carefully, while Fatma expressed herself in a rapid-fire volley punctuated with swear words, finger snaps, and slaps. Suzanne was middle class and highly educated; Fatma was lower class with a high school diploma. Surprisingly the one area they had in common was religion: Suzanne was Christian and Fatma Muslim, and they both tried to live faithful and obedient lives.

I had mixed feelings about bringing Suzanne and Fatma together, because sometimes the conversation was troubling. In one visit, I walked into the living room just in time to hear Suzanne's advice, "The problem, Fatma, is that you don't respect Nadir's jealousy or his anger. I see how you talk to men that you don't know, and he sees that too. If you would take better care to meet his needs and not to provoke his anger, well, he might not be so harsh with you."

"Suzanne," I interrupted, "what does it matter? He has another wife. This marriage is finished."

"But I want her to see the error of her ways so she can change her behavior around men. If she marries again, the same thing will happen."

I knew I should have just kept my mouth shut. This was their culture and, though I did not agree with the advice, it made sense to them. While I thought Suzanne was blaming Fatma for Nadir's abuse of her, Suzanne just wanted Fatma to recognize her responsibility in the marriage. Suzanne was echoing what many acquaintances said to me about Fatma: "Anyone who behaves as she does, deserves what she gets."

Actually I was amazed that Suzanne wanted to keep meeting with Fatma, because it was a huge step out of her comfort zone. Then Suzanne had an idea. "Valentine's Day is coming up soon, and even though we don't celebrate it in Beni Suef, it's one of my favorite holidays."

It was just a week away, so we agreed to have some kind of get-together with my kids, Fatma, and her boys.

21

Valentine's Day

On Valentine's Day I stopped at the flower seller on my way home. While the gardener was arranging a mixture of roses and other flowers, he launched into his favorite subject with me, the politics of George Bush.

"So, now that Iraq is completely messed up, he is turning to Iran. Your president is going to invade Iran, and then who is next? Egypt? America will go country by country until it controls the whole Middle East and has all the oil." This is a common sentiment and fear among many Egyptians.

His assistant didn't need as many words to express his views: "Beel Clintoon" and his thumb went up; "George Buush" and his thumb went down.

Hoda, one of Brad's students, stepped up behind me with her order and to invite us to visit her family. "I live with my mother because I am now divorced and that is very shameful in our society. My husband works at a tourist resort on the Red Sea. He prefers to be there with the Italian women than home with his family."

"Oh, I am sure that was a great shock to you."

"You know, in our religion, he could have taken another wife. But no, he says he does not want to be married at all. I cannot understand this. It is not our culture. Everyone wants to get married, but he gets strange ideas from working with so many foreigners. What are you if you are not married?"

Hoda would have never accepted being second wife, but it was a concept she could understand. Choosing to be single wasn't within her realm of thinking. I was familiar with Hoda's distressing divorce through a paper she had written in Brad's class describing a "turning point" in her life:

In Egypt they believe that divorced women are guilty and do not have the right to a complete life. . . . But I have always an inner feeling that I can depend on myself, succeed and go on to overcome my sadness. I thought, "Why don't I convey my love to all the people around me—my parents, my son, my friends?" Also, I decided to be closer to God and depend more on Him. There is nothing impossible when we say, "I will succeed!"

We chatted some more until I paid for my bouquet.

"I stayed here until he finished," confided Hoda. "If not, he would have charged you double." I just smiled to myself. We could live here ten years and people would still assume we were always being taken advantage of.

I turned the corner to our block when I saw Um Amzat waving at me from her produce stall. Trying to wiggle a rose free, I walked over to her.

"Here you are." I handed the rose to her, reaching over the basket of cantaloupe and peaches.

"*Asal.* Honey. You are honey!" She beamed with delight. "Um Nicholas, when did you say you are leaving?"

"End of June, in sha'allah."

"Oh God! Oh my Lord! Why? God help us! Are you angry?"

"No! No! Nothing like that! We said we would come for three years and now, unfortunately, three years is finished," I explained.

"Tell the church you want to stay longer." She lifted her hands to heaven; her anguished face had tears running down it. "Jesus, do something! Um Nicholas, I can't make it without you." She grabbed a rag and dabbed at her eyes. "I can't! I can't! I miss you already. The guards don't want you to go either." Comforting herself, she murmured, "God is present. God is present."

"I know. It's hard for us too," I said sympathetically. "The other day Nicholas was saying that he doesn't want to leave, because everyone is so hospitable and kind." That was after he had gotten lost and had seven different people give him rides and money to get back home!

"Um Nicholas, you remember your blanket I borrowed that day when we went to my village? Can I have that for a gift?" Her

Jennifer, the family's guards, and Um and Abu Amzat at their fruit and vegetable stand.

eyes got larger, and she moved so close I could feel her breath on my face as she whispered conspiratorially, "And what about that big basket you have? I could set it here on the table and put fruit in it. You're not going to bring it with you, are you?"

Ahhh, she could probably find some comfort to replace me! I bought some strawberries then headed to our doorway.

"Hey, what's that?" called out the guard pointing to my bag.

"Strawberries."

"I know. But your husband just bought some this morning." Everything we did was everyone else's business.

Fatma called with news that Medo was sick and since it was raining, could we come to her mother's house? Rain? In the sunshine land of Egypt? Oh, how we would welcome a good, hard rain that would wash all the dirt and dust away! But no. Rain, as we have experienced it three times, is a daylong drizzle that causes all the dust and dirt to turn to mud. Since the streets have no drainage, the mud sits until the sun dried it up the next day.

But it was funny how people reacted to rain. All the shops in Beni Suef closed, and folks barricaded themselves indoors in preparation for "winter," when the temperature usually dropped some.

Indeed, as I walked to Suzanne's apartment to get her, the streets were practically empty; even the taxis and microbuses remained parked. Perhaps there was some standard of safety; people recognizing the dangers of "driving while drizzling"!

℮

Suzanne and I settled on the sofa at Fatma's mother's house. The first time I had met Fatma's family was after her severe beating, and I remembered feeling that her family was cold and indifferent to her situation. But after a few more visits with them, it was clear they did love and care for her and her kids; they just had no idea how to handle a rebellious daughter who continued to fight the culture rather than submit to it. During a previous visit at our house, Fatma had pulled down her jeans and showed me her thigh. Right next to a tattoo spelling NADIR were several bruises given to her by her father and his belt during an argument.

The tension between Fatma and her mother hung like a heavy cloud of pollution in Cairo's sky, darkening what was to be a fun evening. We sat around drinking tea and exchanging polite greetings, the superficiality of it grating on Fatma's nerves before she sharply cut in, spewing her fury at her parents upon Suzanne.

"They won't let me work," Fatma complained. "They won't let me leave the house. I can't talk on the telephone without them asking who it is. They don't give me any money; I had to call Gigi yesterday to bring me tissues for Medo because he was sick. They don't trust my morality."

"Fatma is too friendly with men on the streets," the mother complained. "She should say 'hello' and 'how are you,' and that is all in a public place. People will question our reputation and what kind of daughter I have raised. She can't work now, because the children need her. God will solve our problems."

It was a typical mother-daughter conversation, but it was about ten years too late. I had to remind myself that Fatma was twenty-seven, not a fifteen-year-old begging her mother for more freedom and independence. I had seen her friendliness—it was borderline flirtation—when we were in a taxi once, and it surprised me because she was completely out of line with the normal protocols of behavior between unmarried strangers. If Fatma were living in the west, no one would have raised an eyebrow. But in Beni Suef, she was providing the neighbors with all sorts of juicy tidbits for the gossip mill.

Her immature behavior was worrisome to me; she believed nothing was her fault. She blamed her mother for all things wrong. She took no responsibility for her decision to marry Nadir, saying, "It was my fate." And she was desperately seeking to fall in love again.

"Today I saw a couple on the street," Fatma recounted by way of continuing her complaining. "He looked into her eyes and I could see that they love each other, and I want that love too. I want to get divorced so I can marry again. So I can have the rights of a wife."

"Rights of a wife" meant sexual relations.

"Suzanne, if she asks Nadir for a divorce, it will provoke his anger," the mother countered. "If Fatma marries again, Nadir will take the children from her."

Her voice was calm and reasonable while Fatma ranted and raved in the background. No doubt the mother has traveled this territory many times before. "No one loves my daughter like I do. She is a precious jewel to me, and I am the only one looking out for her rights. God sent us angels who are not sexual to show us that we can be celibate too. She should look to the angels."

On and on it went as I silently questioned why we ever went there to spend a fun and frivolous holiday talking about divorce! My head was starting to pound.

Fatma's mother wanted her to remain married to Nadir, though not necessarily live with him, as he was on his third wife. While the mother feared Nadir would claim custody of the boys, the greater fear was Fatma's, and the family's, reputation. If Fatma were divorced, she would be viewed as just a step above a prostitute. Divorce, regardless of circumstances, always reflected badly on the wife. The common thinking was that a husband would seek a divorce only if his wife had low morals.

Divorce in Islam can be a relatively easy affair. The husband says, "I divorce you," three times, and it is finished. The wife returns to her family and both are free to remarry. All that had been written in the marriage contract as belonging to the wife, right down to the dishes, is returned to her. Children usually stay with the mother unless she remarries, then custody reverts to the father. I sometimes wonder if the threat of hearing "I divorce you" occupies women's thoughts and fears, and thus compels them to serve and please their spouse.

If the wife seeks the divorce, however, it gets a little more compli-cated. Though the Qur'an gave women the right to initiate divorce, it is a fairly recent law in Egypt. Since the wife is breaking the marriage contract against the husband's desires, she forfeits all her rights, including the apartment, dowry, and household articles. The wife can have the "right to divorce" written into her marriage contract, but it needs to be agreed on by the would-be husband, "and few men would give up their self-respect to allow their wives this option," I'd been told. Plus, any bride contemplating divorce options on the eve of her wedding, when the contract is being prepared, would be looked upon as shrewd and devious. Neither of these ways of divorcing appeared to truly favor women, but all my Muslim female friends defended these terms for divorce as fair and just. It was one of those issues I could not come to terms with.

"I can't take it anymore," Fatma said. "I want to put my kids in an orphanage and go to a mental hospital." Her loud voice sud-denly dropped to a whisper as tears slid down her checks and her lips quivered, "I want to pour gasoline over myself and set myself on fire."

"Ask God to forgive you for saying that!" Suzanne urged. "For the sake of the children!"

The social worker in me couldn't stay quiet any longer. "Is it possible to see a psychiatrist and get some medicine for depression? You know, medicine could help you think and feel better." I wasn't so convinced of that myself, as her choices in life still wouldn't change, but Fatma liked the idea. Money for the visit and prescrip-tion seemed to be the barrier. "I'll pay for it," I said, recalling the black eye she had received last time when asking her husband for money to fill a prescription. Suzanne would find out if a psychia-trist was available.

As it turned out, a few days later she went for an EKG brain scan—it was free—and was told she didn't need any anti-depressant medication. I didn't see the connection between the papers showing her brain waves and her depression, but there was nothing more I could do.

$\tilde{\mathfrak{e}}$

The rain stopped. We were in need of a little fresh air, so we said our farewells to Fatma and family and walked to Suzanne's home.

We were silent. The roads were practically empty as I guided Suzanne around puddles and mud without fear of stepping in front of an impatient driver. I was troubled by the options for divorce allowed to Fatma under Islam. And I was curious how the Coptic Orthodox Church would respond, knowing the church permits divorce only under conditions of adultery or conversion.

"Suzanne," I said, guiding her past some wandering goats drinking from a puddle, "if Fatma were a Christian and her husband beat her, could she then divorce him?"

"The correct thing to do would be to discuss the issue with the priest responsible for their area. He could help them to either resolve the problem or learn how to bear and tolerate each other. If it is impossible to resolve, the children are put in an orphanage until the family is better able to cope."

Bear and tolerate? Remove the kids, not the abuser, from the home? "But the parents cannot divorce?"

"In the church? No. They could get a civil divorce by the court, but the church doesn't recognize it and they cannot remarry. Sometimes people leave the Orthodox Church." Her voice dropped to a whisper. "Or convert to Islam."

Hmmm. Not too many good options there either, I noticed. "So is it better to commit adultery?"

"Well, if you want to anger God—the church allows divorce for adulterers, but they cannot remarry. The one who made the adultery cannot remarry and neither can the wife because of the children."

"Not even the wife? Why is that? Don't you think it would be better for the children if the wife remarried?

"I remember my father telling me, 'Parents must love their children more than themselves so they will pass love on to their children.' Remember, Jennifer, how Fatma's mother told her, 'You must sacrifice for the children and accept your fate.' In our culture, parents have a great responsibility to their children and the children to the parents."

"True, but don't you think the mother's life would be easier if she had a husband and the kids a father?"

"Not in our culture. She should not marry again because of the children. Once she has a baby by her new husband, he will be jealous and favor that child over her own. It will be a catastrophe for the other children."

Suzanne continued, "That's why the best thing for Fatma is to get back with Nadir, so the mother and father can raise the children. If someone could explain to him Fatma's irritating behaviors and be more sympathetic to him, I think he would be kinder. She should agree to obey him. That's it."

Suzanne had a completely different view of marriage than Fatma. For Suzanne and all Coptic Orthodox Christians, marriage was a sacrament "until death do us part." For Fatma and Muslims, marriage was a sacred covenant with a specific set of agreements, which, if it failed after family mediation, could lead to divorce. While divorce is permissible for Muslims, Muhammad stated, "Of all things God permits, divorce is the most hateful thing."

We had covered this territory before, and I just couldn't agree that the boys and Fatma were better off with such a violent man. We walked in silence for a few moments.

"I think there are a lot of unhappy marriages," I said.

Suzanne nodded her head, "Yes. We call them 'silent divorces.' Couples who live separate lives without actually ever getting divorced."

When we reached her door, Suzanne fumbled in her purse for her keys. "Here take some money and buy some treats for Fatma and the boys," she said, handing me part of the money she tithed each month.

I walked alone past the church and guards, past piles of sand and gravel that almost blocked the whole street. But I paid no attention to it as I was completely lost, deep in my own troubled thoughts. Muslims suddenly seemed the winner in the "rights" department: they could divorce, though the consequences are high. A Christian woman did not have that right even if her spouse was abusive.

I recalled one of our MCC visits to a village to learn about programs organized by a Protestant church. One Protestant minister summed up the frustrations rather well: "It is extremely difficult to change cultural attitudes and beliefs, and it is almost impossible to change the religious ones. In Islam, it could be the treatment of the wife; in Christianity, women speaking in the church. Many men simply want someone to cook and clean for them and be in bed with them. They do not know how to treat a woman—that she has a mind."

Christian denominations in the United States are less concerned about maintaining tradition. Because of our materialistic, fast-paced, and independent lifestyle, American churches continuously engage the culture. Issues that Americans endlessly debate are not issues for the Coptic Orthodox Church, because the Bible defines its policies. Women's participation in the liturgy? Not possible, according to the Coptic Church, as there is no recorded history of that in the early church. While the church supports equal rights in society, like the right of women to work outside the home, it remains unapologetically patriarchal and male-dominated. Homosexuality? The Bible clearly condemns it; no discussion necessary. Divorce? It's condemned in four different biblical books. Abortion? That's not so clear cut as there are no specific biblical directions. The culture of honor and shame generally prevents pregnancies outside of marriage. As for unwanted pregnancies within a marriage, abortion is legal, and it is a decision for the spouses to make.

In Egypt, Muslims marry in the mosque and Christians marry in the church. There are no civil marriages. But the courts can grant divorce for both religions. A recent court ruling forced the Coptic Church to let followers remarry after a civil divorce. Pope Shenouda was quite clear in his response: "No power on earth can force on the church anything against the teachings of the gospel or the church. The church will never wed divorcees, regardless of the court ruling." Because of this uncompromising stand, Christians must decide between loyalty to the church and the desire to terminate a marriage. For those divorced Coptic Christians who want to remarry, often the only option is converting to another religion.

The Bible was written two millennia ago and the Qur'an thirteen hundred years ago. Today these ancient books are used to both liberate women and oppress women, depending on who does the interpreting. Western Christians have largely dismissed those parts of the Bible that we find too inconvenient to live with. But most Coptic Christians accept even the difficult parts, like no divorce options and wives submitting to husbands, and live within those limitations.

The wet streets were now returning to normal chaos as people, animals, and cars were drifting back. I felt overwhelmed and distracted from all the heavy conversations; a throbbing pain echoed in my head. Pool tables had recently sprung up in the alleyways, like green, fuzzy mushrooms after a rain, giving the shabaab something to do with their idle time. They gathered around them, catcalling and "welcoming" me again to Beni Suef. I turned a corner and cocked my head toward a peculiar smell. Was that marijuana coming from an open apartment window?

"*Ya abla! Ya madam!*" A girl shouted out for me. I ignored her, eager to just get home.

In some ways, the Coptic Orthodox Church and Islam are the mirror images of each other. Muslims are taught to submit to God and the Qur'an; the Coptic Church teaches submission to the Bible and the authority of the pope. Both religions affirm that biblical and Qur'anic laws must supersede secular laws in a democracy. Both religions have strong, male, authoritarian clerics and a history of submitting to them rather than questioning them. Both faiths seem to emphasize rules and rituals rather than spirituality. Even the clergy in both faiths wear beards! And of course, both Islam and Coptic Orthodox are convinced that they alone possess the absolute truth about God.

"*Ya madam!*" That same voice! She sounded like one of the girls I had once bought tissues from and then expected me to buy them whenever I saw her. I didn't even turn around, though I could hear her catching up with me.

"*Ya abla!*" The girl, huffing and panting, grabbed my elbow.

"What?" I called out, turning around to face her. "Why can't anyone just leave me alone?" It was more a demand than a question, and it mattered not whether I spoke in Arabic or English, for my loud voice and flying arms were a language by themselves. In response, she lifted her cupped hand to my face, and there in her palm lay my favorite earring. I instinctively raised my hands to my ears and, sure enough, one had fallen out onto the wet, muddy alleyway.

I barely had time to stammer out a thank-you before she turned and ran away. "Forgive me, God, and keep her heart generous." Usually I make an effort to respond to friendly gestures on the street if they are from females. Just a short conversation in Arabic about being from America and living in Beni Suef goes a long way in dispelling stereotypes about Americans. But that night I felt empty inside; I had no more to give. The stress of the day had finally gotten to me.

☙

The next day Fatma and her boys, carrying two plastic bags, came back to their apartment. Her marriage may be over, but she still had the key. We walked over to see the apartment, as it had been sitting empty for four months. It looked like a windstorm had just blown through, furiously spewing clothes, plastic bags, keys, glass bottles, and trash from one end of the house to the other. Dust and dirt layered all. There was no furniture, no bed, no stove, no refrigerator. Everything had been sold to a recycling vendor. There was no water and no electricity.

Fatma looked wearily at me, and said, "We're staying here. I told you yesterday I couldn't take it anymore."

My kids were all excited about them moving back, but I squashed their eagerness to make her place livable. "I gave her some candles, sandwiches, and a blanket. We will do no more. She is fighting against her culture and she will lose."

Lose again, I thought sadly. We watched Fatma close her metal gate and padlock herself in, locking herself in her own prison. She was running away from home like a fifteen-year-old girl. I wanted to admire and maybe even encourage her determination to be her own person, but I knew it was self-defeating. Sure enough, the next day she returned to her family, her other prison.

The prayer on my wall gave a boost to my sagging spirit: "May God bless you with anger at injustice, oppression, exploitation of people and the earth, so that you will work for justice, equality, and peace."

22

Honor Is Like a Match

"Would you be willing to teach reproduction to the class? It's our first year to have an eighth-grade class, so my first time to teach it. And, well . . . I . . . I don't think I can teach it. But you! You are a woman; you are from the west; these things come easier for you."

I tried to keep a straight face. But watching a grown man—a science teacher, at that—stutter with face turning red at just the mention of "reproduction" told me he was in serious trouble. If he could barely utter those words to me in the privacy of his office, what would he say to a classroom full of fourteen-year-olds? I didn't readily agree to teach the section, as I first wanted the director to approve it. If any complaints came from parents, I would need her support. I also wanted to check with a few reliable friends about what the boundaries were, as I anticipated I would be tiptoeing in a minefield.

First, I went to Doctor Negwa; I knew she could speak without blushing. She confirmed that my anxieties weren't unreasonable. "You need to be very careful about what you say, making sure that you only say what is in the science book. Some parents speak to their children about these matters but most don't. The problem is that you are from the west, so if you say something bad, people will immediately say it's because you are from America."

I had run across this before: the word for "west" and "strange" are similar, prompting my Arabic teacher to explain, "If it is from the west, it is strange; if it is something strange, then it must be from the west."

Thanks to having had our children in the school, I had already encountered some issues that I would have never thought of as a problem, such as benign boy/girl notes of the "do you like me? I like you" variety. At least to me they were benign. But for the girl's parents, they were cancerous and needed to be cut out. Torn up, in this case. This happened early in our arrival, when Nicholas, innocently ignorant about girl-boy relationships in this new culture, sent a note to a girl who passed it on to her friend.

The note found its way to the mother of one of the girls, who immediately paid me a visit. She asked if there were any more notes because "I don't know this girl's father. If he finds the note, he could beat her or something. I cannot say because I don't know them well, but we do not want to cause any problems. And we don't know about the principal. She could 'fire' the children from the school for writing these notes."

This was a Muslim woman, concerned about her daughter's Christian friend. I was grateful for her honesty. It all seemed so harmless to me, but in a culture where the relationships between the sexes is "a sensitive issue," as one politely stated, this could be a serious offense.

Having to limit what I said in the science class to what was in the textbook did not seem like such a difficult task; the chapter was only four pages long. The male and female reproductive systems were briefly and conveniently described as "a complicated process." While it extolled the virtues of sperm and egg, the chapter made no reference as to how they get together, a fact that was not lost on my sharp-eared students, who suddenly showed that they could be curious about a subject.

But they could not formulate a question. The girls (boys were taught separately) went around and around among themselves over how to ask me *the question*. But because no one had the courage to actually voice it, they finally decided to write me a note: "In what way can the sperm go and find this egg?" It was so cute and so innocent, and I tried not to smile. I also tried to figure out how to answer it, because I remembered well the instructions not to say any more than what was written, and the term "sexual intercourse" was not explained anywhere.

"Why don't you take this paper home and show your mothers and ask them?" was the best that I could do.

One whole page in the textbook went into great detail about symptoms, complications, and treatment of syphilis and gonorrhea, two diseases I had almost forgotten about in this age of AIDS. The chapter had only one sentence to say about that: "It is one of the diseases which are transferred by forbidden sexual intercourses." It was hardly worth mentioning.

The last page, ominously titled "venereal health," had another garbled English sentence: "From the habits which is inherited through the generations is the female circumcision, it exposes her to dangerous physical and psychological harm and affects her family life."

A Muslim student, who had lived her whole life in Italy and had only recently arrived in Beni Suef, immediately raised her hand and had a host of questions: "What is circumcision? What physical and psychological harm? What are you talking about?"

I was beginning to wonder myself. Why put it in a sentence like that, a sentence that could only cause fear and confusion, and not give any explanation at all? I did what most teachers do when they don't know how to answer a question and turned it over to the class: "Can anyone explain this to her?" Most girls kept their heads down, pretending they were intently studying the paper.

Feeling that an answer had to be given, I stepped out of my self-imposed boundaries. "Some parts of a girl's sexual parts are cut off." The answer undoubtedly put more fear in her! There were no pictures, no diagrams, and no words for any part of the external sexual organs. Of course, my vague, awkward answer could only beget another question. While I was familiar with female circumcision, I didn't know much about its practice in Egypt. And I wondered if any girls in the class had been circumcised and were only just now hearing about "physical and psychological harm."

The science teacher and I taught this chapter together twice. During my third year, I'm happy to report, he stood on his own two feet, teaching boys and girls together. But teaching the course got me thinking about circumcision, what it involves and how much it was practiced.

౿

Female circumcision is a four-thousand-year-old tradition that began among the countries that border the Nile River and over the years spread to other African countries and pockets of the Middle East. The types of circumcision range from cutting off the clitoris to cutting off all external parts, so that the whole vaginal area is left smooth. The latter part is more common in Somalia, Sudan, and other African countries, which was a cause for bragging among some Egyptians. "We only cut off a small part, but other countries really do horrible things to their women." I suppose it is human nature to find another group with worse behavior than our own to somehow justify our own actions.

The first news that took me by surprise was hearing from some women that female circumcision didn't exist anymore. One commented, "Why is that even written in the science book? That was an old Egyptian problem that finished in the last generation. That is why no one in your class knew what it was." I was not convinced.

Female circumcision is not divided among religions but among social classes. It is more commonly practiced among poor, rural villagers and moderately educated, lower-class folks like my neighbor Fatma. So naturally I directed my first inquiry to her, as we sat around one evening, sipping tea. I no longer worried about how to phrase questions gently, for most Egyptians were blunt and to the point, so I just jumped right in and asked if she had ever been circumcised.

"Of course, you must be. Every girl must be." Fatma was nine years old when she and two cousins were brought to a local clinic and under anesthesia had their clitorises removed.

"Why did you get circumcised?" I asked.

"I didn't want to look like a boy when I get married, Gigi!" She laughed. Many women believe that as the girl grows and develops, so does her clitoris, thus comparing it to a penis.

"Is it a part of your religion? Required in Islam?" Fatma shrugged her shoulders; she didn't know.

"If you had daughters, would you circumcise them?"

"Of course I would, Gigi." She looked at me with surprise and smiled. "I am a good mother. This is necessary for girls."

On my next visit to Um Abdullah, I decided to work this topic into the conversation. Because she was always talking about her strict husband and Islamic laws, circumcision should fall right in line.

"We don't do that in my family." It was not the answer I expected. "It's not nice for the girl when she wants to be with her husband. I had this done when I was a girl and now I don't enjoy my time with my husband. The Qur'an says we cannot refuse our husbands when they want sex, or else he will look for another woman. Then we both go to the fire—you know what that is? Hell—because I made him go and look somewhere else." She smiled and waved the spatula in her hand at me, "So it is easier for the girl if she enjoys being with her husband."

"And your husband? Is he okay with that, or does he want them circumcised?" I asked, always mindful of who makes the decisions in this family.

"He says never mind if they are not circumcised; they will enjoy their husbands more, ilhamdulilah."

Suad's niece, Seham, was ten years old, a common age for circumcising girls. After cleaning our apartment one day, while having our tea break, I asked if Seham would be "purified," the word most commonly used.

"Of course. She will go this summer because you heal better in warm weather. Madam Gigi," she said proudly, "all girls in our village are purified."

"Why is that necessary?"

"We must do this to the girls because we want them to be pretty for their husbands." She gave a chuckle, as if amused she had to explain something so obvious to an educated foreigner.

She ticked off a list of attributes on her fingers. "We want them to be calm, to be quiet, to be polite and sensible. So they will get a husband and get married." Her face turned serious, and she frowned while wagging her finger in my face. "You cannot have a hot girl! Shame!"

Girls were described as "hot" or "cool." A girl was considered sexually "hot" if she had a clitoris; therefore, circumcision was needed to "cool" her down. Controlling the sexual urges of women was the main justification of female circumcision. Honor and respectability of a family depended on the behavior of its females, specifically the virginity of their unmarried daughters.

Suad was silently peeling an apple, then looked up with a worried expression on her face, and said, "You will circumcise your daughters, won't you?"

"You know, Suad, we don't do this in my country." I could just see the wheels churning around in her head, for she now understood why America was such a moral wasteland.

"Why?" she asked, with a half-smile on her face, as if this was the most ridiculous thing she had ever heard of.

"Because it hurts the girl," I said, using Um Abdullah's line. "It causes a lot of problems and pain."

That hardly satisfied, because in her world that wasn't a real issue. She shook her head unbelievingly. "If we don't do this, the girls will want to run with the boys all the time. How do you keep girls safe?" *Safe* meant virgin and marriageable.

"I try to teach my children what is right and what is wrong so they will have good behavior."

How to explain that in my culture virginity is a private, personal thing, not a family or societal issue? How to explain that virginity is a goal and a noble virtue to bring to a marriage but not a matter of life and death? But what I said didn't matter, because Suad deeply believed that something so valuable as virginity could not be left up to parents' flimsy teaching or hopeful wishes for obedient daughters.

Girls are seen as seducers and tempters. No one even fools themselves that men are capable of resisting temptation; thus, the onus is entirely on the female to remove any thought, hint, or suggestion of sexuality. A woman wearing tight clothes is criticized for "not respecting a man's weakness." I had my answer as to why young men aren't taught about not sexually harassing women. In the eyes of their society, the problem did not lie with them.

This is not to say that young men are encouraged to "sow their wild oats" while they are young. They are not, and both Muslim and Christian men are expected to be virgins at marriage. Sexual relations outside marriage are strongly forbidden by the Qur'an and the Bible and, unlike many western Christians, Christians in Egypt seriously adhere to that prohibition. Nevertheless, sexual relationships outside marriage occasionally form in discrete places.

I had heard of Muslim men divorcing their wives six months after marriage because it was found that the wife was not a virgin. Why wait six months when it was obvious on the wedding night that the wife wasn't a virgin? One young man explained, "Because the husband does not want to give the appearance to others that he married someone who was not a virgin. If he divorces her the next day, everyone would know why. If he waits a little longer, it's not so humiliating for him."

Blood from a ruptured hymen on the wedding night proves the family is reputable, respectable, and trustworthy. Much is done to protect the female and her virginal status because, as the saying goes, "a girl's honor (virginity) is like a match—you only strike it once." There are no second chances. Well, almost none.

"Hymen reconstruction surgery" is available in Cairo among the elite. But for the masses, the consequences are serious. Without proof of virginity, an engagement or marriage would end, dooming the girl to life as a single person. That may not seem so devastating to westerners, who can live freely and happily as single people. But it can be a lonely and shameful existence for Egyptians.

My friend Sandy once told me about a Christian girl who was engaged to a boy that her parents selected. But she then eloped with someone else. "The father and brothers were so shamed they could not even lift their heads. It was terrible, Gigi. The girl came back and they completely disowned her."

I gave a look of surprise; it seemed so drastic to me.

"No, they had to, Gigi. For days the father and sons went around with their heads hanging down. No one can allow a daughter to bring that sort of shame on the family. What about this girl's other sisters? Now they cannot marry. No one wants to marry into a family with that kind of reputation. What that girl did to her family is horrible. The mother now dresses completely in black as though her daughter died."

The other women sitting in the room all nodded their head in agreement.

In some extreme cases, the family can kill the girl. "Honor killing," done by the family to restore their honorable reputation, is illegal in Egypt and, according to everyone I asked, was something that happened in the past but rarely occurred anymore. But I did come across this in one newspaper: "A farmer in Beni Suef confessed to stabbing his seventeen-year-old unmarried daughter to death after discovering she was three months pregnant. . . . The farmer was referred to the prosecutor's office for questioning."

Sandy agreed he would likely use "defense of honor" as his reason. "Everyone understands he had to do this, because what she did was terrible to the family's honor and reputation."

"But, you have two daughters. Could you do this to them?" I asked.

"Well, we raise our daughters properly and even now at age eleven and nine, tell them they cannot wear spaghetti-strap shirts.

And my husband is very protective of them, sometimes too much, I think, and the girls don't have much self-confidence. I don't think we will circumcise them, but it means we will always be near them. You know, it's not just our culture that demands virginity at marriage, but the Bible too."

All parents want their daughters to marry into good situations, and to avoid these terrible consequences, so much time and energy is spent on the prevention part. In fact, all of society is structured around prevention. Preserving honor and virginity explains why girls dress conservatively; why girls don't swim around males; why some girls remain in the home; why girls are accompanied by someone when outside the home; why girls don't ride bicycles; why engaged couples don't kiss before marriage. The main task of parents in raising a daughter revolves around the issue of maintaining her virginal status and an intact hymen until marriage.

ॡ

Female circumcision has no religious origins, though some ignorant clergy, both Christian and Muslim, continue to perpetuate that myth. Some Christians, particularly poor, uneducated villagers, believe they have a religious obligation to circumcise girls just as boys are circumcised. Other Christians circumcise because of religious prohibitions on sexual activity before marriage.

Some Muslim sheikhs claim it as part of a "woman's duty" in Islam, though it is not practiced in many Islamic countries, including Saudi Arabia, the birthplace of Islam. I knew from my previous work with Afghani refugee women in the United States that circumcision was not practiced in their country, even during the misogynistic rule of the Taliban. "Why would we hurt our daughters like that?" I recall one Afghani asking me.

For years, educators in Egypt have worked to dispel myths—such as, a girl would not sexually develop unless she is circumcised—and give medical information about infections and difficulties during childbirth caused by circumcisions.

But I learned from Suad that circumcision can't be treated as a personal, private decision.

She cut an apple in half. "See this?" she said pointing to the core. "It's ugly. Like a girl down there. You cut it like this" and she sliced off the core. "Now it looks pretty and smooth. Clean. If you are not like this, no husband would want you. He will be very angry and blame the mother. It would be a terrible thing not to do this to girls. They would never marry."

It does "takes a village" to end circumcision, and there are some innovative approaches of getting a whole village to agree to discontinue the practice. Families need reassurance that if they do not circumcise their daughters, sons from other families will still marry them.

Female circumcision is largely regulated and enforced by women. Mothers insist on their daughter's circumcision; mothers take them to the clinic; and women, either midwives or female doctors, perform the surgery. But men also play a peripheral role, particularly if they refuse to marry uncircumcised girls. Surprisingly, most of the education being done today addresses women only, completely neglecting the role of men in the family and the culture. This is a serious omission in a country where, according to a local newspaper, 90 percent of females are circumcised.

Once I was visiting with Doctor Negwa and another gynecologist when the subject of circumcision came up. Her colleague reported, "When I was about thirteen years old my mother took me to the doctor. He told her that my clitoris was too large and would likely cause some infections as I got older and that I should have it removed for medical reasons. My sisters did not have this problem, so they did not have the surgery." Clitoris too large? According to what standards? And who is looking and measuring? Was this a new excuse to justify circumcisions by wrapping it in medical terminology? Why had I never heard of this type of surgery in the United States?

"But doesn't that interfere with enjoying sex with your husband?" I asked.

"I think that sex begins in your mind, with your brain. I love my husband, so for us it is nice." She added, "Sometimes women come to me after giving birth and they want to be circumcised because they were not circumcised as teenagers. Why? They want to look beautiful for their husbands, just like women in the west want to have breast surgery or facelifts. Really, this is no different."

In our home schooling, I read to my kids about the practice of foot binding in China. Before the age of two, girls' feet were broken by their mothers and wrapped in cloth to prevent their feet from growing beyond three inches. This had the effect of confining the girl to the house, and she needed to be carried to go any distance longer than a block. But it was also a sexual stimulant for men who would not marry women with "big feet." It seems that women throughout the ages have suffered and disfigured themselves to be desirable to men. Foot binding was a thousand-year-old tradition but just recently the last shoe store in China selling miniature shoes closed down due to lack of customers, which gives us all hope that attitudes and traditions can change.

❦

"Hi, girls! What are you doing?" I was in the school playground, talking to a group of girls holding small pieces of paper in their hands.

"We're going to visit the fire station, so we are learning our questions."

"Uh huh. And who wrote the questions?"

"He did!" They chorused, pointing at their male teacher. Field trips to question the firemen, or to visit the governor or the bishop, were rehearsed ahead of time. The school never missed an opportunity to stifle creative thinking.

I found Weam, who was waiting with her children near the slides. "Look at how old and rusty this is." she said. "You see why I don't allow my children to play here." Sounding like a lawyer, she ticked off a list of the dangers. All true, but to my accustomed eyes, it didn't look so bad. We gathered our children and went to her apartment.

Weam and her four children had lived in New York for thirteen years but recently moved back to her hometown, Beni Suef. Rebecca and Emily immediately connected with her two daughters and were helping them with the cultural and educational challenges, which were much like the ones they had faced two years before.

Rebecca observed, "They are foreigners in the school like us, but no one gloats over them, because they look Egyptian; the students just ignore them."

At first, Weam told me they returned so her children could learn more Arabic and about Islam. But as our relationship developed, I discovered another reason—concern about her daughter, now at the vulnerable age of twelve, being exposed to all the dangers and temptations teenagers encounter in American schools. But moving back home to Beni Suef brought its own set of anxieties, causing Weam to confine herself to her home, children's school, and her family's home, which were all within a six-block radius. "The kids are young; the people drive too crazy. It's easier to stay home," she explained.

Her days were filled with cooking and house cleaning and complaining about weight gain. It was perplexing and sad to see how she could have the courage and self-confidence to live in New York, then to leave it, but she could not muster the confidence to take her kids to the Nile River a mere mile away. In an odd twist, I, the foreigner, was reassuring her of Beni Suef's safety and encouraging her to get out more with her children. But Weam, as a "daughter of Beni Suef," had a lot of new cultural issues to deal with that were unique to her situation.

"My husband and I had decided when we lived in the U.S. that we would not circumcise our daughters. We were educated that it was not necessary and that it can cause problems, like infections." She got a far-away look in her eye and stared out into space. "I remember my circumcision and my God, that was too painful."

"What do you remember?" I asked.

"I was fifteen years old and all my cousins were doing it. We are raised knowing this is going to happen, like you know your period is going to happen. Everyone is all excited, telling you, 'You will be a woman; you will be like one of us.'"

She sipped some tea and passed me a box of Russell Stover chocolates, a gift from her husband, who still lived in New York. "We were brought into the living room with a midwife and her assistant. I was on the sofa, held down by the assistant while the midwife took a razor and whack!—I don't know the English word—cut it off. Oh my God, the pain. Fire. Like fire."

Weam was circumcised the old-fashioned way—midwife and razor. Today it is usually done in a clinic with anesthesia and sterilized surgical tools. I couldn't help but make the comparison to drug addicts in the United States getting sterilized needles from clinics to stop the spread of AIDS. Was there a concession acknowledging that if women insist on being circumcised, it's better to be under medical supervision?

"Is there some kind of celebration afterward?"

She looked at me as if I were crazy, "Are you kidding? There's too much pain for a celebration. After boys are circumcised, they kill a goat and it's a big celebration. But for girls? No."

"So where does this leave Samaha?" I asked, referring to her oldest daughter, who was twelve.

"Circumcising her became a big issue soon after we arrived. I was quite surprised by that," she said while busying herself with the teacups on the tray. "I argued back and forth with my family and my husband's family. You know, we are cousins so I am really talking about one family. They kept saying, 'But we want her to be a part of the family. To look and act like us.'"

Conforming to the family tradition of circumcising females was a way that Samaha, who was deemed "too American," could fit in with her cousins.

"It was very difficult for me without my husband here, because they would have listened to him better than me. But I stayed strong, and we agreed to let a surgeon look at her and decide."

Weam took her to a doctor, who said Samaha's clitoris would not grow any more.

"That was a great relief. If the doctor had said otherwise, oh my God, what would we do?" She silently shook her head, contemplating it. She had won a battle over family tradition, but she'd have to fight again over her other daughter. Weam may not have much influence on her extended family, but if she could raise her own daughters intact, then she would help her society change, one family at a time.

Female circumcision might never run its course in Egypt, but many families are learning that it is a tradition they can do without. Fatma and Suad hadn't yet seen how it is possible to maintain a girl's virginity without circumcision. But many families, like Um Abdullah's and Weam's, were proving that discarding the tradition is not creating a generation of promiscuous females. It is one example where challenging a tradition, instead of passively acquiescing to it, has not caused the moral fabric of society to unravel.

ت

While Weam shared with me her frustrations of settling back into her old culture, I could also confide in her my anxieties about returning to life in America, which was now only a few months away. When we had left the country, our children were just that—children. But now, at fifteen, thirteen, and eleven, they were at different stages in their lives. The anxieties I was feeling weren't anything unique to me, and I knew I had a lot of company among American parents of teenagers concerned about peer pressure, dating, driving, and alcohol. But we had spent three years living in a society where these concerns were minimal or nonexistent. My Egyptian friends' most pressing problem with their teenagers was passing school exams. That would be such a welcome worry!

Whenever my women friends and I gathered and discussed raising children in the United States and in Egypt, Egypt definitely won as the easier place. Traditional values, like rules regarding male-female interactions, aren't written down and don't need to be discussed and debated; people are socialized to learn them from childhood. All of society is set up to reinforce these values, leaving little room for error. No parent fears that boys will be present at a birthday party for a fifteen-year-old girl. Everyone knows that is taboo and trusts that only girls will dance with each other at the party. It's not difficult to raise children to be modest and chaste when parents share these goal and concerns.

We had learned that there was much to enjoy, appreciate, and admire about Egyptian family relationships. Children are included in all activities from mundane errands to celebrations and gatherings. Adults tolerate a lot of noise and chaos from children. They aren't shooed away and told to leave the adults alone, though sometimes we wished for that. Children grow up with lots of aunts, uncles, and grandparents, who not only help out parents, but also ensure that family values and loyalty are passed on to the next generation. Teenagers are not their own subculture with their own music, language, and way of dressing. They hang out a lot with friends but also are fully incorporated into the family. Parents' advice and wisdom is sought and valued. Adult children often spend their free time visiting or taking care of their parents. God, family, work—in that order—are the three values reflected in the daily life of Egyptians.

Egyptian families have their disagreements; kids get angry and frustrated. But at the end of the day, everyone knows peace will be made or a truce tolerated, because family is the core of their lives. In a fast-changing world, family and faith remain as the only security and refuge they can rely on for emotional and material support.

If Rebecca and Emily were to experience their teenage years in Beni Suef, they would gradually have more doors closed to them, merely because they are female. I could already see this in Rebecca. She used to walk comfortably on the streets but now received too much attention from males. She was now deemed "too old" to ride a bike. She was no longer comfortable riding the microbuses but preferred the privacy of taxis. It took a lot of mental energy for her to go out. I wanted her to be self-confident and for a not-quite thirteen-year-old, she was doing a marvelous job. But I knew the day would come when she would simply choose to stay home. I had seen the same passive acceptance by women who recognized these inequities and complained about them, but lacked the motivation to challenge the status quo.

I came to realize that girls and women in Egypt did not have less freedom; they had different freedom. A door may close, but that doesn't mean they are sitting on the other side of it feeling sorry for themselves. Females don't hang out in coffee shops, but they do socialize in outdoor gardens and clubs. Girls may not ride bikes, but they can practice karate and basketball. Restrictions on swimming or bicycling bothered us, but I never heard much complaining from other girls. The restrictions were my issues, not theirs. They do not question these cultural practices any more than I question my cultural practice of not marrying cousins. It is simply how one is raised, and people everywhere are basically raised to do as everyone else in their culture is doing, even in individualistic North America.

We were living in a conservative community with strong traditional and religious values. There "it takes a village to raise a child" and "family values" weren't just empty clichés or convenient political slogans. We experienced its strengths, such as parents taking care of their children well into adulthood, and its drawbacks, such as adult children conforming to parents' wishes over their own desires. There are some values, such as respect for adults and modest dressing, that we would take with us and continue to teach to our children. But other values, such as delaying interest in the opposite sex, will remain a continual struggle in the United States, where the social structure to back it up is lacking. Unfortunately values aren't so easy to pack up and take home; some things I would simply need to carry in my heart.

23

A Miracle for Maria

As our time in Egypt drew to a close, we needed to wrap up a few last projects. One of them was getting a ramp built for a disabled girl, Maria. It had seemed like such a simple idea a year before, but with only a month left in our term, I was having doubts about pulling it off.

For the past two years, every Wednesday morning, the children and I had boarded a school bus that took us to the outskirts of Beni Suef. The Coptic Orthodox Church ran a sheltered workshop, a fancy term for a collection of old, crumbling buildings next to a cemetery on the edge of the desert. It was at this dreary facility, alive with the joyful chatting and singing of disabled children and adults, where we first met Suzanne.

Each day started on the school bus with a staff person telling a story of a Coptic saint. Another person led prayers and lifted each person's name to God for healing. The dedication and kindness of the teachers, and the resulting encouragement of the students, was amazing to watch. Salaries were about twenty-five dollars monthly and didn't stretch far enough, and unlike school teachers, the teachers there could not offer private lessons to supplement their income. When I commented to one teacher about this, she nodded her head in agreement and stated simply, "We are doing the work of God."

The last one to board the school bus was the little girl who had become Emily's friend. This is how Emily described her:

> Maria is nine years old with long black hair in a braid.
> She was born with cerebral palsy so she can't walk.
> She is in a wheelchair, wears diapers, but doesn't wear
> shoes. She can feed herself and has a very short neck.
> Her mother pushes her in a wheelchair up a dirt road

> then picks her up and puts her on the bus. A worker
> puts her wheelchair under the bus. I like to push her in
> the wheelchair, but it's very hard to push over the sand
> because the school is in the desert. We sing songs like
> 'The Wheels on the Bus' and 'Head and Shoulders.' I
> help her with the motions.

Once the bus arrived at the school, we spread out into different areas. Rebecca helped with cross-stitching; Emily dipped candles; Nicholas sanded wood for icons in the carpenter's shop; and I usually went in the Montessori room. At break time one day, I peeked out the office and saw Nicholas with about fifteen students in a circle on the sand, kicking a soccer ball.

"Yea, Mona! That was a great kick!" hollered Nicholas.

"I know, but look at my shoe!" Mona yelled back.

She held up her shoe, which was in two pieces, but the big grin on her face showed she was quite proud of her achievement. It was great to see my kids' ease and confidence with disabled students, confidence that had been painfully built over many months, for it had certainly taken a while to get used to the students who drooled, grabbed at clothes, soiled themselves, or asked repetitive questions.

One Wednesday morning we were in the office of the director, Sister Dimiana, for the tea break when Emily asked why Maria didn't come to school that day. "She fell down and broke her hip. May God heal her," Sister replied. "We can stop at her house on the way back to Beni Suef if you would like to see her."

We decided to visit the following week, as we wanted to bring Maria some gifts. After our visit, Emily wrote,

> When I saw the 'steps' leading to her house, we under-
> stood how she—or the person carrying her—fell. The
> 'steps' are cement blocks all jumbled together with no
> ramp or railings. It was hard for me to climb up.
> Maria was lying in the bed and lays there all day long.
> The doctors will put a pin in her hip and plaster on her
> leg. I hope she comes back soon to the school because
> I miss wheeling her around. Remember her when you
> pray.

An idea came to us: why not get a concrete ramp built for Maria so she could be safely pushed in and out of the house in her wheelchair? Each week we gave our kids an allowance and, from that, they put aside a small part for charity. We agreed to reserve that money for a ramp. I would talk with the director, who took to the idea right away and promised to get an engineer to look into it.

We took a break from the sheltered workshop in the summer—just thinking of being out in the desert exhausted us. Once school started, we returned to the workshop but discovered that Maria had not yet returned to school. Neither had any work been done on a ramp. Sister had liked the idea, so it was puzzling as to why no action had been taken.

But first we wanted to find out why Maria hadn't returned to school; it had been six months since the accident.

Sister shook her head sharply. "Her father was angry at her for 'making the toilet' in the bed. I don't know what he did to her, but her other leg is now broken. He's bad, bad, bad! May God have mercy on his soul." Our hearts broke as we heard of this agony for a helpless, innocent child.

"I don't know what the doctors will do for her now," Sister continued. "She is fragile. She just lies in bed all day long now. *Rabbina maaha.* (God be with her.)"

"Sister, we still want to build this ramp. Someday she will get out of the house again, in sha'allah. I think it will make their life a little easier. Or do you have another idea that we could do?" I pressed.

"Her mother is working now and is never at home, so Maria is in bed all day by herself. It would be better for the mother to stop her work and be home with her. If you could pay her salary, about twenty dollars a month, that would be best for them. If her mother was home, Maria could also come back to school, but now who can get her ready and out of the house?"

"Does her father work?"

"No, he spends his day at his mother's house. He is useless, a useless man."

"But don't you think that the father will just take the money and use it for himself?"

"No," Sister said shaking her head, "he just eats and sleeps at home."

I wasn't so easily convinced. An unemployed father described as "bad, bad, bad" just couldn't be trusted in my book. I should have never asked for another idea. I could understand Sister's logic that it was better for the mother to be home, but encouraging a mother to quit her job and become dependent on me was completely contrary to the goals both we and MCC have. I decided to keep prodding Sister on the ramp.

Many more months dragged on without anything being done. I rationalized that Sister was busy with her own construction project, as they were building a large new school closer to town. Perhaps she just needed to accomplish that first. Time passed. Maria was still not back at school.

Finally! The new school was completed. They moved all the workshops and equipment and settled into a brand-new, three-story building. Nothing happened with the ramp, and we were in the countdown stage of our departure. Was my desire to build a ramp unreasonable? At what point should a foreign volunteer realize that a project that seems so wonderful and simple is her own issue and not the desire of the local program being assisted? When should she just give it up? It was tempting to take the project on ourselves— to find Maria's house, ask the mother for permission, and if she agreed, find a builder and get the ramp built in a mere few hours. But we reminded ourselves that we were here to work *with* people and existing projects, not to create our own. Plus, we wanted to stay on good relations with Sister Dimiana, though by this time we were quite frustrated with all the foot dragging.

That's when I went to our MCC contacts, Linda and James. We sat around their kitchen table and tossed out ideas about why such a simple project couldn't get off the ground, or on the ground, in this case.

"Maybe Sister cannot do something special for one student and not for the others. . . . Building a ramp is so public. Everyone will see it, but giving a monthly salary doesn't attract so much attention and gossip. . . . Maybe Sister can be responsible only for students while they are in the school and Maria is no longer attending school. . . . Perhaps the parish priest where Maria lives is responsible for her family and it's out of Sister's territory."

We realized that we were hampered by language and culture and would never completely understand all the politics that went on in a church parish. We decided to contact a priest, who was a friend of MCC's in Beni Suef and could probably cut through the invisible barriers much easier than we could.

A few phone calls later, it was all taken care of, and in a better way than I'd ever imagined. The priest paid a visit to the new school and not only met with Sister Dimiana but also found that Maria and her mother were actually there. Only a few days before, Sister had convinced Maria's mother to quit working at the hotel and come to work at the new school as a cleaner. It was less pay, but it meant that Maria could conveniently attend school once again. The mother also wanted a ramp to be built. The priest arranged for an engineer to do the work and promised to call us about the bill. We would give the money to the church without telling the mother it came from us.

"Make sure the engineer does a good job," I told the priest. "We want the ramp to look nice and be useful for the family." We had seen plenty of shoddy work and wanted this to be a nice gift for Maria's family. In short order, the priest called back to say that the engineer had already completed the work and absolutely refused any payment.

☙

"Can we put Maria in the wheelchair and get a picture of her going down the ramp?" I asked her mother, Um Mina. We were standing outside her concrete house looking at the ramp, eager to get a picture before the sun set.

"No," Um Mina replied, shaking her head so that her gold hoops jiggled. "She isn't dressed. But Emily can sit in the chair and go down the ramp."

Emily vigorously shook her head no. "I'm terrified of that thing!" She didn't mean the wheelchair but the ramp, which did look intimidating. There was very limited space for a ramp: the distance from the steps of the house to the end of the property line was six feet. The house was four feet off the ground, so the ramp had to be short and steep. The engineer cleverly inserted "speed bumps" to slow down a vehicle on the ramp, but it looked like one would go soaring wildly.

Emily finally relented. Um Mina held the wheelchair handles; I held Emily's hand and whoosh!—the wheelchair flew down the ramp. Emily screamed and Um Mina laughed as the wheelchair landed.

Emily and Maria's mom try out the newly built wheelchair ramp.

I had to convince myself that though the ramp wasn't perfect, it was better than what they had before. Plus, there were now concrete steps going into the house and not just a jumble of concrete blocks. It wasn't the ideal I had visualized for Maria, but it was good enough, and sometimes that is what we have to settle for.

Once inside the small house, we greeted Maria, who was dressed only in a T-shirt and was sitting on the floor, wedged between her bed and a sofa. She gave a big smile, waved at us, and shook our hands. Emily sat on the floor with Maria and played hand games while the rest of us squeezed in, sitting either on Maria's bed or on the sofa.

During the day at school, Maria was in the wheelchair. Once home from school at two p.m. Maria's mother took off Maria's clothes and diaper and set her on the floor on a red plastic potty. Her legs, useless and limp, were wrapped in a plastic sack, resting on a pillow. Unable to sit up straight, Maria's torso hunched forward. She stayed in that position until about eleven p.m., when her mother put her to bed.

"Some people tell me that if I had brought her to America, my daughter would not be like this today. She could have been cured."

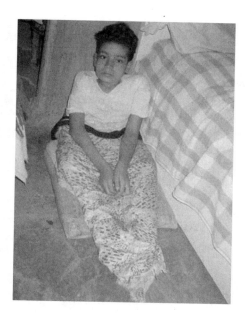

Maria. She sits on a potty, covered here by the sack on her legs, from the time she arrives home after school until late into the night.

Her voice cracked and became higher as tears welled up in her eyes.

Oh, America! The land of magical medicines and miracle doctors! I tried to explain that there are children like Maria in the United States and that there aren't any miracle cures. But these words were little comfort to a mother who daily watched her daughter suffer. Maria was lucky to have the sheltered workshop, but it didn't provide her with physical therapy or the family with social services. Um Mina relied on what she had. "But God is with us. God will heal her."

"Look at this," Um Mina said, raising Maria's T-shirt and pointing to her lower back, where her spine twisted and protruded, a mass of bruises and ulcers. "Look at her feet." Through the sack we could see her toes covered with red marks—ant bites. Um Mina looked at me with her large brown eyes. "If I had tile on the cement floor, we would not have ants. The ants crawl on Maria, and she has bite marks all over her legs. Can you help me with this? I want to have a floor in every room so Maria can sit in all the rooms, not just here in one spot."

I didn't quite know how to respond. Fortunately she went in the kitchen to make us some tea, leaving us to discuss her request. It wasn't so obvious to us that covering a cement floor would solve her ant problem; our apartment had both tile and ants. While Maria's house was sturdily made of concrete, cracks abounded for all sorts of critters to crawl through. Throughout our visit, we were constantly slapping the mosquitoes off our legs and scratching new bites.

How to convince Um Mina that tile would not solve her ant problem? The solution to us was to get Maria off the floor and into a chair. She would need a special chair equipped with a potty seat and with sides to hold up her torso so she would not fall over. We discussed the chair idea but didn't make much progress. While I could describe the chair and its benefits, I didn't have the language or cultural skills to convince an uneducated and stubborn mother about her daughter's needs. Someone from the school would have to do that. I ended up telling Um Mina I would discuss the issue with Sister.

Um Mina's son, Mina, worked at a barbershop in the village, and both Brad and Nicholas needed haircuts before we left Egypt the next week. Maria's mother took them to the barbershop while we stayed and played with Maria. We had brought a ball, along with some other gifts, and played a tossing game with Maria. I was glad we had come to visit but also felt sad and powerless that we couldn't just pull out a magic wand and make it all better. Maria was obviously delighted with our visit and loved directing orders to Rebecca and Emily about how to catch the ball.

"Close your eyes! Throw with one hand!"

At ten p.m., our taxi arrived as planned. Brad and Nicholas had returned from the barbershop looking sharp and clean and smelling of hairspray. We began the difficult process of saying farewell, as Um Mina, not completely satisfied with my indefinite answer, clearly wanted us to stay, as if letting us go was to let go of hope also.

In the taxi cruising down the desert highway, Nicholas commented, "I am glad we did that. It meant something to the family and it was fun for us."

We all silently nodded in agreement.

24

Go and Return in Peace

"If you live here three years, you will see how Christians suffer."

I remember those words spoken by the first priest we met when we temporarily lived in the girls orphanage. During our three years in Egypt, we worked hard to engage both Coptic Christians and Muslims. Sometimes it felt like we were walking on a balance beam between them, trying to listen and understand their beliefs and frustrations while exercising caution not to lean too much to one side. I must confess it was easier to write about Muslims and Christians three months into our stay, because I thought I knew everything. I thought that by the end of our three years, I definitely would have had Christian-Muslim relationships all figured out, all neat, tidy, and organized like the bags and boxes now in our living room. But as time passed, all my ideas, conclusions, and solutions slowly unraveled.

My head is swimming with stories of our experiences and the lessons we have learned about faith and religion. Here is a sample:

We learned that people, regardless of their religious identity, often compare the ideals of their faith to the realities of another faith; they compare the best of their religion to the worst in another religion. All faiths seem to have at least a few unexplainable concepts that usually only make sense to those raised in the faith. Only believers can defend and justify these concepts. Neither Muslims nor Christians were capable of applying this objectivity to each other's faith, and they ridiculed and criticized any concepts about other faiths that they could not easily understand. The person who truly sought to understand another way to worship God was rare.

We learned that as foreigners living in Egypt, it was easier to be a Christian in a predominantly Muslim country than it is in the United States, where the busyness of daily life and the pursuit of the almighty dollar often interfere with the spiritual life. Egyptians are a religious people and expected us to go to church, to pray, to fast, to have religious pictures hanging in our house, and to dress modestly. Though these things were not necessarily our way of defining a Christian life—what about peacemaking, for instance—had we not done them, we would not have earned people's respect as Christians.

We learned that Coptic Christians see themselves as victims of Muslims, that Muslims see themselves as victims of the west's war on terrorism, and that westerners see themselves as victims of Islamic terrorists. It's a vicious cycle in which all sides get to be victims and passively blame others for their plight, conveniently ignoring their own contribution to the situation.

While certainly discriminated against, Coptic Christians don't have a corner on suffering, for all Egyptians feel suffering. People suffer from crowded, overpopulated living quarters; the dismal educational system; high unemployment and a weak economy that favors the tiny upper class while the masses toil long hours in often dangerous conditions, earning the equivalent of a dollar a day. Egyptians feel worn down by a corrupt and indifferent government that is more concerned with keeping the dominant party in power than with the daily struggles of its citizens. The few brave citizens—male and female—who protest against the repressive regime are arrested. Some languish in prison without charges under special emergency laws that have been in use since 1981; others are tortured into making false confessions.

Living in poverty and insecure about the future, people turn to religion for solace, finding salvation in the unfailing refuge of their faith. For Muslims, increased religiosity is expressed through religious symbols, such as the conservative dress of women and the wearing of beards by men. Similar to fundamentalist Christians in the United States who believe that many of America's problems would be solved if we just "turn back to the Bible," fundamentalist Muslims believe that "Islam is the solution" to their everyday problems, and they call on fellow Muslims to "turn back to the Qur'an."

For Christians, hope lies in preserving their ancient traditions of worship and liturgy, in keeping the community ties of Christians strong within the church walls, and in the dream of emigrating to the United States, Canada, or Australia.

Religion is everywhere experienced through the senses. We saw Muslim men praying in public. We heard Qur'anic tapes playing in every taxi, store, and office. We smelled sweet incense in the Coptic churches. Women constantly adjusted their veils. Fasting was common in both faiths.

But we often asked ourselves: does this exuberant religiosity and piety correlate to an increase in kindness, generosity, and tolerance of those with different ideas and opinions?

We believed more strongly than ever that the prophetic voice of Christianity is to bear witness to Christ as a person of love, mercy, and forgiveness. Violence in Iraq, the Abu Ghraib and Guantanamo prisons, and biased support in favor of Israel at the expense of Palestinians have caused the United States to lose all moral authority in the Middle East. America once stood as a beacon of light for democracy, freedom, and basic human rights, but that light has gradually been snuffed out during the "war on terrorism." I often wonder what conversations we could have had with Egyptians if western Christians and President Bush, instead of invading Afghanistan and Iraq after 9/11, had taken a bold step and acted on Luke 6:27: "This is what I will say to all who will listen to me: Love your enemies and be good to everyone who hates you."

ج

Here is a final story to sum up Christian-Muslim relationships as we experienced them. My friend Amal, the young Muslim woman who decided she would veil when she was spiritually ready and not because cultural conformity demanded it, told this story to me.

She went to a *simsar* (real estate agent) for assistance in finding an apartment for her family. Since she did not veil and her name, Amal, was a common name in both religions, the real estate agent could not identify her religion.

"I told the realtor my name, and he just looked at me strangely so I added, 'I am Muslim.' He said it was good I said that, because otherwise he would not rent an apartment to me. I asked him why, and he said a Christian owned the building next to him, and this Christian refused to rent to Muslims. Because of that, the realtor did not want to rent his building to a Christian. So I asked him, 'Why are you doing the same? Why don't you be better than him?'"

Amal did not defer out of respect to a man in a higher social position. Instead she stepped out of her cultural boundaries and confronted the real estate agent. How many of us have the courage to do as Amal did, even at the risk of losing an available apartment?

I chose this story not because it is unique to Egypt or the Middle East, for neither east nor west holds a monopoly on intolerance, discrimination, and persecution. Such incidents happen in all countries, including "enlightened" democracies. Don't liberal, supposedly open-minded westerners often condemn the wearing of a veil as male oppression instead of accepting it as a woman's right to express her religious beliefs? The "isms" exist on all sides—racism, sexism, classism, and "religionism."

The point of this story is that Amal was actually paraphrasing to the real estate agent the words of the two most revered men in Egypt. The Muslim prophet Muhammad said, "The highest religion one can have is to wish for his brother that what he wants for himself." And Jesus stated, "Treat others as you would have them treat you." Christians and Muslims, rich and poor, black and white—we must all recognize our common God-given humanity. And we must live not only together but also in tolerance and respect of each other.

Amal—that name used by both Muslims and Christians, in Arabic means *hope*.

ξ

"You are crying now, but you will cry even harder when you leave Egypt. You will see all your American friends again, but you may not ever see your Egyptian friends again." Those wise words came from a former MCCer before we left the United States. Three years later, as we were preparing to return home, we discovered she was right. Our last two weeks were filled with lots of packing—how did we accumulate so much?—and lots of goodbyes. And we were crying harder.

Our family did not want to leave, but in a way we knew this was the best time to end our volunteer term in a foreign country. At times, we wanted to continue to serve in Egypt or in another country. But as much as we enjoyed the challenges and daily life, our hearts were back in the United States with our families and with our community, Jubilee Partners. Our last year in Egypt was the most comfortable; we had just gotten the language and culture down pat, and it was time to start packing, though it was difficult to leave.

The kids were all voting to stay and making plans to return again as volunteers when they become adults. Whether those wishes will ever come true remains to be seen, but the fact that they desire it is confirmation enough that our life in Egypt was a profound and positive, life-changing experience for them.

ℰ

One evening I went out for a last stroll through Beni Suef. I stopped by the seamstress to pick up a dress she had made for me. She sat behind her old Singer sewing machine, feeding cloth under the speeding needle, her body fat shaking with the rhythm of the humming machine. Another customer was present, and upon hearing that I was returning to the United States, stood up and declared loudly and animatedly, "Go back and tell the American people that Muslims are good people. We are not terrorists. Every religion has its fundamentalists who do bad things. Islam is a religion of peace." I will tell them, I reassured her.

I walked into the street, which was loaded with its usual chaotic traffic, behind a man on a bicycle who had his young daughter standing precariously on the top bar. She was facing her father, her little arms wrapped around his neck, practically blocking his view. The father had both hands on the handlebars but, testing faith a little further, one hand was clutching a live chicken by the wings. Even the chicken didn't look afraid. Another man bicycled past with a wooden ladder about ten feet long balanced on one shoulder. "Woe to anyone who doesn't see him coming," I thought. Anyone weak in faith who seeks a miracle to believe need only stand at any intersection in Egypt and be convicted of God's presence in keeping us safe.

I stopped in a small grocery store to pick up a few things, inquiring for the last time about butter. The furor over the Danish cartoons had died down, but six months later, the boycott continued. Butter was not available.

After a few more errands, I stopped at my favorite juice bar,

The Fairies of Heaven, named in reference to one of the heavenly delights that await Muslim men in paradise. Because of the name, many of my Christian friends refused to enter. But blissfully ignorant in reading fancy Arabic script, I never knew the name and was a frequent customer. The same young man who was always behind the counter waited on me and was surprised to hear we were leaving.

"But why?" he asked, as if I had personally hurt him. "In Egypt we have Pharaonic history. Islam. And Christians. Is there a better place to live?"

I just smiled and took my juice khalli, on the house.

I sat in one of the green plastic chairs, facing the street, drinking my juice, and watching a slight elderly man dressed in a crisp, white galabaya and white, crocheted prayer cap with strands of white hair poking through the holes. He was preaching to all who passed by: "Oh, you lazy people! You don't pray, and you don't give to charity. You shame yourselves, your people, and your country! Turn to God! Turn to prayer!"

He could have been a lamenting Old Testament prophet warning people to stop their sinful ways. He could have been an American evangelist preaching doom and gloom. Instead he was a self-appointed Islamic sheikh crying out over the current state of the world. All the same, no one paid him any attention.

Evening had come, and I could hear the whirring of the "mosquito truck" before seeing white clouds of pesticide furiously billowing out from the "blowing machine" mounted on the back. A group of boys followed behind it, riding their bicycles in the pesticide clouds. I ducked into a nearby shop to escape the poisons that burned into my lungs as I tried to breathe. The pesticide particles— made to kill mosquitoes—rose to the treetops, drifted through the air, and then settled down on top of fresh bread, fruits, vegetables, and huge slabs of meat that were laid out in the open air for sale. It was a toss-up as to who was more damaged—the mosquitoes or the people.

I took my last stroll over the Nile River bridge, but this time sat down and ordered tea in a bridge-side "café"—a primus stove with a teapot set out on the sidewalk. I no longer cared what it looked like for a woman to sit by herself and drink—tea!—in public.

I thought about our whirlwind week of farewell parties at St. Anthony's Language School, the girls orphanage, the workshop for the disabled, the church, and a party at our house, plus lots of visiting with those who could not leave their homes. The whole week we had been on an emotional rollercoaster—laughing, crying, frustrated, exhausted with little sleep, and running on adrenaline. We made promises to call and e-mail, and promises to visit again, in sha'allah. In my purse, I had a fistful of notes with phone numbers from the sewing lady, milkman, sweet-potato seller, department store clerk, and a host of other characters who had become our acquaintances over the years. What did people do before the age of cell phones?

Some of these farewells were more about our possessions than us leaving. It was mostly lower-class acquaintances who, like vultures, were swarming around me everywhere I went, asking about clothes or cooking pots. Even one of our guards from our first year showed up asking about a bed, and, oh, by the way, could we come to his son's wedding as well? The hustling got so annoying that I avoided visiting with Um Amzat, the fruit and vegetable seller. Yet it was a humbling experience and a good reminder: no matter how much tea I drink with lower-class people, I am not one of them. I am the foreigner, the one with money and the good stuff, and that is how I will always be viewed.

As one can expect, not everything went smoothly in our departure. In our last week, Nicholas was playing with Mumtez, Fatma's son, now nine years old. Mumtez, disobeying his mother because he feared a beating from her, refused to go back in his house and ran off. Nicholas followed him, ambivalent about bringing him back home to get whipped but also not wanting to leave the young boy by himself on the busy streets. In the eyes of Fatma and her mother, Nicholas was encouraging Mumtez to disobey, so when he returned with Mumtez an hour later, Grandmother poured forth her fury on Nicholas. He rudely retaliated with sarcasm. Grandmother fired the final shot by admonishing Nicholas never to return again.

But rarely were there final words. The family, who had just been humiliated and insulted, needed to boldly and loudly reclaim their honor. The girls and I had returned home from a party that same night, at midnight, when the phone rang. After exchanging the standard greetings, Grandmother swiftly and soundly condemned Nicholas. By then, I knew my role: quietly let Grandmother vent her feelings, for she was not interested in getting the full story or in understanding Nicholas's point of view. After she hung up, the doorbell rang. Fatma walked in, took my hand, and escorted me to my bedroom so she could soundly and swiftly condemn Nicholas. It wasn't about us—Fatma called me *ukhti* (my sister) during her tirade—it was about their family's pride and dignity.

The next day, Brad and I swiftly and soundly told Nicholas to stay away from their house. While it was important before departing Egypt to leave in good standing with all our acquaintances, I didn't want to rush it. Their family needed time to feel angry; sometimes an apology and explanation could be premature. Nicholas went to their house anyway. He didn't disobey just because he was fifteen years old, but because, as he explained later, "I had a lump in my throat because I felt so guilty. I just couldn't stand it anymore."

Nicholas prayed on the way to their house. He knocked. The door opened and then closed. Nicholas waited and said another prayer. Five minutes later, the door reopened and he went in. He told us later, "I sat and Grandmother gave me a big lecture how everything I did was 'shame.' I just listened and agreed with everything, even if I didn't really agree with it, and just kept apologizing and telling them how I tried to help Mumtez. After a while she accepted my apology. I gave them a present and a kiss to Mumtez."

Throughout our time in Beni Suef, there was never the question *if* people were talking about us, for that was a given. The question for us was "What are people saying about us?" What they were saying was determined by our behavior, whether or not it was understood. Thanks to Nicholas extending the olive branch of peacemaking, we departed with a good reputation of respecting local tradition.

I thought of Suzanne and our last errand we did together: renewing her passport.

"Are you planning to travel somewhere?" I asked her.

"No," she replied, "but if the opportunity arises, I want to be ready. It's a sign of hope."

I looked out over the Nile River and remembered our last outing, a boat ride with Suzanne, Fatma, and her two boys. We had walked from Fatma's family's house to the Nile, but it wasn't Suzanne and I strolling arm in arm: it was Fatma and Suzanne. I felt I had turned the relationship over to them. They had even exchanged cell phone numbers. Both women, for very different reasons—Fatma because of her failed marriage and rebellious ways and Suzanne because of her blindness—were outside the boundaries of what is socially acceptable in their culture. Fatma saw in Suzanne someone who needed her assistance and Suzanne saw in Fatma someone who needed a friend. May God make a way for them.

I paid for my tea and stopped to watch an elderly man fishing with a thick, strong pole. The man had a scruffy face and a cigarette stub hanging from the corner of his mouth. We had the usual conversation when strangers greet, but this time I added, "We're going back home next week."

"What state?"

"Georgia."

His face drew a complete blank and he shook his head. I tried my family's state.

"Louisiana."

He looked deep in thought. Knitted his eyebrows. Threw his still burning cigarette onto the bridge sidewalk.

"Katrina?"

"Yes."

I was completely surprised. The hurricane had come ten months before!

"Those poor people who lost their homes. Give them my greetings."

ď

Saturday was moving day. It also turned out to be the day I attended my own funeral. Since early morning we had been hauling boxes and furniture, and entertaining drop-by visitors. Suad and her children—with lice-free hair—showed up to clean, play, and add to the general chaos. Later Fatma and her mother dropped by, surprising me because she had recently been in the hospital, and it was with great effort she had walked to our house and climbed the stairs. Um Amzat, the fruit seller, came over. We all sat in the living room, amid wet rags, half-packed boxes, and trash bags stuffed with clothes. The stove was disconnected, so I could not even offer hot tea, serving cold water instead.

Um Amzat began by telling about the time I received spoiled milk from the milkman, how she fussed at him and demanded that he bring fresh milk. She tossed her arms up in the air and called on God to be with us and keep us from harm. Taking the tail of her scarf, she dabbed her teary eyes, wiped the sweat from her face, and cried out to God that she couldn't go on without me. Suad, Fatma, and Fatma's mother all joined in, their despairing voices crying out to the ceiling, wailing their loss of me. Then silence fell on the group. About ten minutes later, Fatma told a story about her troubles and what I did to help, and the whole scenario repeated itself again.

"I am sitting at my own funeral," I thought, as one after another would tell a story recalling some event in which I was involved. Brad walked into the house to see four veiled women—three Muslims and a Christian—lamenting the loss of his wife. He had a bag of grilled chicken in his hands and quickly exited to the bedroom with the kids to eat. It was important for the women and me to say goodbye to each other and to grieve, for who knew if we would ever see each other again? But after two hours passed, I was weary and depressed and realized how good it is that most people are dead at their own funerals.

We had a wonderful final farewell at a church, where Brad gave a sermon to the congregation while Suzanne translated. The text was Matthew 25:35: "When I was hungry and you gave me something to eat. . . . When I was a stranger, you welcomed me."

Brad commented, "I surely was a stranger when I came to Egypt, and so many of you helped me when I did not know the way. And you surely fed me very well! You helped me find a doctor when I was sick and helped me find medicine. You treated me just in the way Jesus instructed us."

Afterward, at ten thirty that night and with the under-construction new sanctuary looming nearby in the darkness, we sat outside amid piles of sand, gravel, and rebar, and had a wonderful fish dinner. The air was cool and breezy; the kids scampered around the new church scaffolding about fifty feet up in the dark, causing me to fear that we would spend our last night in Beni Suef in the hospital.

We left the church at midnight and began our errands. I picked up clothes from the seamstress and ironer. Nicholas and Emily took a taxi to the fish sellers to deliver some promised pictures he had taken of them. Brad went to the camera shop to pick up the last batch of film. Rebecca, the most sensible and organized one, went home and went to bed.

I gave my final gifts to Suzanne—hand sanitizer my mother had left when she visited and her first galabaya. I had the tailor make two so she and I have matching galabayas and can remember each other when we wear them. I left Suzanne's house about two in the morning and walked home alone, unafraid, and amazed by the number of people still out: men at the coffee shops, kids riding bicycles, bakers putting hot bread on the sidewalk to cool off, fruit sellers with carts of cantaloupes or cucumbers, microbus drivers zipping around corners. All men. I was the only woman out, and through it all I heard not one comment. On my final walk through Beni Suef, no one paid me any attention.

"Go and come back in peace! God be with you! God protect you!" Um Amzat was wailing her final goodbyes, dancing a little jig, and throwing her arms up in despair. Meanwhile her husband was quietly picking up the bags of leftover stuff we had just brought down, bringing them over to his fruit stand before we could pile in the taxi. We said our farewells to the guards, having earlier given them some money as appreciation. They had done their jobs well; after all, no harm had come to us during those three years. Brad gave them the last of the photo albums. He had made about thirty, containing pictures of our family's time in Egypt, and distributed them to all our friends and acquaintances. It was a gift well appreciated by all.

We had rushed out of the house, and I regretted not taking the time to stand around, reflect on the memories, and offer prayers and thanksgiving to God. Instead we did it in the taxi on the way to the train station with a loud Qur'anic tape in the background.

"Hurry up and wait" was often our motto, and our final day was no exception. The train was two hours late. A teacher from St. Anthony's came to see us off; Egyptian hospitality is never complete until you are in a vehicle and on your way. The teacher waited with us the whole time. Fatma and her mother once again surprised me by showing up. Yes, they had promised, but I had learned by then that the importance of promises, from friends all the way up to government officials, is in the saying of the words, not the actual doing of them.

"Here, Gigi," Fatma said as she undid the silver chain she always wore around her neck. She slipped off a miniature silver Qur'an and handed me the chain with a small silver heart and a blue bead to ward off the evil eye. I scooped up my hair as Fatma fastened the chain around my neck. It was the symbol I had been looking for: she honestly did think of us as sisters.

We boarded the train and had the usual arguments with people sitting in our reserved seats. Once that was settled, another woman showed up with a ticket for Rebecca's seat, loudly claiming it for herself. But astute Rebecca could read her Arabic train ticket better and pointed out that it was dated for the next day. There was a family with teenagers crammed into the seats in front of us. They kept laughing and jostling among themselves about who would be brave enough to speak to us. Finally the boy turned around and haltingly said, "Welcome in Egypt. What's your name?"

It wasn't long before the boy was in the seat with Nicholas, sharing earplugs so they could listen to Arabic pop music on Nicholas's MP3 player. In this land of hospitality, it's hard to stay strangers.

Appendix

This is the prayer that I had on my wall that gave me encouragement when times were rough. The author is unknown.

***May God bless you** with discomfort at easy answers, half-truths, and superficial relationships so that you will live deep in your heart.

***May God bless you** with anger at oppression, injustice, and exploitation of people and the earth so that you will work for justice, equity, and peace.

***May God bless you** with tears to shed for those who suffer so that you will reach out your hand to comfort them and change their pain into joy.

***May God bless you** with foolishness to think that you can make a difference in the world, so you will do things that others say cannot be done.

Islamic Call to Prayer

God is most great.
I testify that there is no god except God.
I testify that Muhammad is the messenger of God.
Come to prayer.
Come to goodness.
Prayer is better than sleep.
God is most great.
There is no god except God.

MCC Send-off prayer

Go in love.
For love alone endures.
Go in peace.
For it is the gift of God.
Go in safety.
For you cannot go where God is not.

The Author

Jennifer Drago lives and works at Jubilee Partners, an intentional Christian community in Comer, Georgia, that ministers to refugees from war-ravaged countries. In 2003, Jennifer and her family moved to Beni Suef, Egypt, to live among conservative Muslims. They returned to the United States in July 2006. Previously Jennifer worked in psychiatric hospitals in Louisiana, then in a Baton Rouge homeless shelter. She was born in Baton Rouge and holds a master's in social work from Louisiana State University. She and her spouse, Brad, have three children.